The Confluence of Racial Politics in America

Critical Writings

First Edition

Written and edited by Earnest N. Bracey, Ph.D.
College of Southern Nevada

cognella®
SAN DIEGO

Bassim Hamadeh, CEO and Publisher
Kristina Stolte, Senior Field Acquisitions Editor
Alisa Munoz, Project Editor
Abbey Hastings, Associate Production Editor
Emely Villavicencio, Senior Graphic Designer
Greg Isales, Licensing Associate
Natalie Piccotti, Director of Marketing
Kassie Graves, Vice President of Editorial
Jamie Giganti, Director of Academic Publishing

3970 Sorrento Valley Blvd., Ste. 500, San Diego, CA 92121

To my nephew, Prince V. Cole.

Contents

Preface   vii

Introduction   xi

Part I.   Blacks and Higher Education   1

Reading 1.   The State of Black Education: The Politics of Educating African Students at College and Universities   3
Earnest N. Bracey, Ph.D.

Reading 2.   The Significance of Historically Black Colleges and Universities (HBCUs) in the 21st Century: Will Such Institutions of Higher Learning Survive?   13
Earnest N. Bracey, Ph.D.

Reading 3.   ***Brown vs. Board of Education*** and the Unfulfilled Hopes for Racial and Educational Reform: A Political Analysis of Derrick Bell's *Silent Covenants*   37
Earnest N. Bracey, Ph.D.

Reading 4.   What I Have Learned from Conservative Students Teaching American Politics at a Predominantly White Institution (PWIs): Reflections of a Minority College Professor   51
Earnest N. Bracey, Ph.D.

Part II.   Civil Rights and Black Politics   63

Reading 5.   Speaking Truth to the Masses: The Nonviolent Politics of Mahatma Gandhi and Dr. Martin Luther King, Jr.   65
Earnest N. Bracey, Ph.D.

Reading 6.   Ruby Duncan, Operation Life, and Welfare Rights in Nevada   81
Earnest N. Bracey, Ph.D.

Reading 7.   A Political and Credibility Crisis for the Future: Black Democrats and Black Republicans in Conservative America   95
Earnest N. Bracey, Ph.D.

Reading 8.   The Continuing Significance and Relevance of the Congressional Black Caucus
(CBC): A Political Group in Transition   **119**
Earnest N. Bracey, Ph.D.

Part III. Blacks and Social Justice in the United States   137

Reading 9.   The Racist American Eugenics Program: A Crime Against Humanity   **139**
Earnest N. Bracey, Ph.D.

Reading 10.   African Americans and Racial Disparities in the Criminal Justice System   **149**
Earnest N. Bracey, Ph.D.

Reading 11.   Thomas Jefferson, Sally Hemings and the Question of Equality in the United States   **165**
Earnest N. Bracey, Ph.D.

Reading 12.   The Politics and Impact of Environmental Racism   **183**
Earnest N. Bracey, Ph.D.

Preface

For the last several years, I have been thinking and writing about race and politics in America. In profound ways, I firmly believe that writing for professional journals offers an excellent opportunity to become a part of the wider social and political debate. Indeed, exploring the many racial nuances and interracial complexities in our society allows us to understand the sad truth of things, while providing *real* solutions to what ails our divided nation. Thus, this book tries to elucidate and familiarize the reader with some of the broader strokes of African American history and politics in the United States. This book also reveals the darker truths about some of our most serious, intractable racial issues, and our country's failure to give the incontrovertible facts about what has really happened in our past, and over the years in regards to race relations.

Furthermore, this book addresses how African Americans can deal with the systemic racism and structural racial injustices that continue to exist because of white supremacy. Indeed, our national identity is at stake as our race relation problems reverberate throughout our polarized country. Unfortunately, white supremacy in the United States has been the chief driver of racial divisions, inequality, and unfairness toward people of color. To be sure, the historical evidence seems to indicate that our nation has often come up short when it comes to investigating and discussing the serious mistreatment of black people—from slavery, our nation's original sin, until today.

The significance of this book is apparent. This is to say that it explores the racial *zeitgeist* in the United States, without sugarcoating *anything*. This work is also chock-full of updated information, with illuminating insights about the controversial subject of *racism* in this country, and how we can survive as a multiracial democracy, no matter our backgrounds. Also, the racial dynamics explained in this book are palpable and unyielding, but we should ultimately appreciate and respect our differences as humans. Furthermore, we must also demand *justice* and *equality* for all, while sitting down together and seriously discussing complicated racial matters, as well as breaking bread together, while opening up earnest dialogue about the humanity of all mankind.

It has been a lifelong professional journey for me—to make a difference in higher education by my teaching and writings. Of course, writing about specific racial issues and other political truths is something that we should all obsess over. But there will always be new racial challenges. Indeed, how exactly can African Americans *interdict* ingrained prejudices, racial discrimination, and other social injustices while trying to maintain civility? Interestingly, writing about such racial and political matters can translate to my overall profession as a professor of political science and history, especially when explaining how such provocative issues are relatable to my students. To say the least, there is still a political struggle going on across our land; and unfortunately, the hypocrisies of misguided social attitudes and beliefs in some quarters are predominant.

Hence, educating college students about American politics, and the negative influence of white supremacy—as well as the significant societal and economic gaps between whites and blacks—should be of primary concern in higher education. To say the least, disturbing disparities exist between black and white Americans, particularly when it comes to our courts and criminal justice system. Moreover, young people in the United States today must know and understand our *ugly* and sad past, and what is really happening throughout the country today—that is, in regards to race, to ensure that they have a diverse, brighter future, free from the trappings of *racism*.

Although publishing is not a requirement for my current position as a teacher, researching and writing enlightening articles and related projects has enhanced my credibility and *bona fides*, despite some political risks and serious criticisms. No doubt, the axiom "publish or perish" is the norm at most higher levels of academia; however, it is not a requirement at a teaching college. Generally, teaching American politics and African American history has been my *forte* and life for the last twenty-five years, and it is of primary significance to me. Additionally, and for obvious reasons, my research credentials, as evident in this book, are important to me—that is, getting down to the *nitty-gritty*, and writing, without distraction. In the meantime, I have continued my academic career as a college professor and author. By the way, there is nothing particularly wrong with writing for professional journals while working at a teaching college.

And by the same token, interacting with some of my colleagues while providing professional advice to young scholars means relating the good with the bad, especially when talking about race and American politics. Nevertheless, this book has been a solo effort, because the researched information presented in this assemblage of articles was worked out of by me.

More importantly, some of my published articles are *advocacy* related. Indeed, in our contemporary society such writings have become a sort of political strategy and serious stance for doing what is right and decent, because it is important to advocate for the voiceless and powerless. Finally, the following articles attempt to answer two fundamental questions: How can African Americans overcome white supremacy and the unimaginable odds they face, because of race? And, how can black people move forward, while determined to address the mistakes of our past—that is, in terms of some white Americans *atoning* for the cruelties and evils of their ancestors? Needless to say, most poor black people are still suffering or struggling from the ongoing racism that still exists in this country, in almost every endeavor, while trying to find their place in the political sun. In the final analysis, this book tries to deepen our understanding of a destitute black people and their future, while pointing the finger at those who would threaten our multiracial democracy.

—Earnest N. Bracey
Las Vegas, Nevada, 2020

Introduction

THIS COMPILATION OF ARTICLES WAS WRITTEN by me over a period of two decades, and they explore many of the vital and significant issues facing African Americans in regards to politics, past and present. It pieces together a fuller understanding of our past in respect to black people, specifically encapsulating some of the major racial issues that we are confronted with today. More specifically, this collection of articles addresses the negative effect of *racism* and *discrimination* on African Americans currently, and from the inception of our country. Political scientist Amy Kittelstrom writes: "Discrimination on the basis of race or ethnicity or any other involuntary circumstance [corrupts] the instincts essential to democracy."[1] Kittelstrom's perspective is important to understand because black people continue to struggle with issues of race in the United States, as many have been victimized by the dominant culture since the beginning of our republic. Therefore, the *incongruity* of these related topics and articles is a reflection of where we stand in our divided nation, and how black people have been abused and unfairly treated by the dominant group over the years, while living a precarious life.

African Americans have tried to overcome the many obstacles placed before them. Nevertheless, white supremacists and segregationists have gone to great lengths to dehumanize and undermine the very existence of black people, without many repercussions. Indeed, all things seem to matter when *politics* and *race* are presented in conjunction with limited higher education (for blacks), racial inequality, record black incarceration, police brutality, environmental racism, social injustices, and the "longstanding efforts to maintain white supremacy after the Civil War,"[2] no matter the negative consequences. Yet, white supremacists still decry the whole notion of institutional racism in America, which is pervasive and persistent. More importantly, the articles presented in this book "unpack" some of these contentious issues, as many white Americans believe that we live in a less racist society. However, nothing can be further from the absolute truth.

Furthermore, we must keep in mind that the specific racial discrimination in America today "is usually understood to mean negative discrimination—that is, treating [black] people in a way which will disadvantage them relative to other social groups,"[3] or the dominant culture. Indeed, the future of African Americans is still at risk as their earthbound existence is deemed unworthy by those who consider themselves superior. Unfortunately, it is an absolute myth when some Americans argue that we are all equal in the United States today. To paraphrase the late novelist George Orwell, some people in America "are more equal than others."[4] To be sure, African Americans have never really been considered equal to white Americans in this country. This is to say that because of skin color, or *ethnicity*, black people have been enslaved, demeaned, tortured, murdered, segregated, held in contempt, and dismissed as full American citizens throughout generations, because of white, European racialist thinking. This is our reality.

Nevertheless, black people have played a critical role in the founding of our nation, particularly in terms of ensuring that civil rights and civil liberties are provided for all its people, or citizens. To say the least, African Americans have had an outsized influence on American culture and politics. Speaking very broadly, racial hatred, white *racism*, racial politics, as well as other racial issues have always been center stage in our society. And we cannot divorce ourselves from these awful matters. To be sure, *racism* is "an ideology that claims to explain an alleged inferiority of certain racial or ethnic groups in terms of their biological or physical characteristics."[5] But aside from our physical differences, we (human beings) are all the same. Yet, for whatever reason, violent racial confrontations (by domestic white terrorists) continue to plague our country as black people battle the terrible, unmitigated evil of white supremacists. Unfortunately, as columnist Brian Greenspun writes, "Once [racial] hate takes root, it is difficult to snuff it out."[6] Relentless racism has been par for the course in our society, and it is tearing our country apart.

To be clear, "racist beliefs have been used to justify genocide, chronic poverty, and the maintenance of systems of inequality."[7] Therefore, for obvious reasons, the "powers that be" will always try to maintain their power and control over others, no matter the circumstances, or they (the dominant group) will insist on having authority over some humans (like people of color) that they feel are inferior, without having *any* notions of *parity* or racial equality. The political socialization, prejudices, and preconceptions (e.g., racial stereotypes) are enough to carry on *racism* and *discrimination* for generations to come. Indeed, will the children of white supremacists be inculcated with entrenched biases that might never be entirely unlearned? And, perhaps even more important, will white *racialists* in power continue to be a serious problem for our nation? Regardless, African Americans will continue to question, demonstrate, agitate, and defy racist social norms and conventions, no matter the particulars or circumstances.

Furthermore, we must not shut our eyes to the overwhelming evidence of racial bias, or ignore the existence of systemic racism and white supremacy, which are perhaps the most destructive forces in the lives of African Americans, especially for their well-being and future. Indeed, for some black people, there is still an overriding sense of hopelessness. For example, law enforcement officials are still *racially profiling* people of color, without regard to the negative consequences, or the violation of their fourth amendment rights, as with the unconstitutional policy of "stop-and-frisk."[8] Of course, such an unconstitutional policy also threatens to further polarize our nation. Equally important, "we the people" should always be concerned with the human and moral agency of black people, because of what they have been through. Thus, we must work to create a better society while vocalizing the plight of an embattled black people. In so many words, the underbelly of our nation reveals a reality: African Americans don't have a choice but to deal with the hardships of their lives because of *rabid* white supremacists and discrimination. Unfortunately, many Americans today are not even aware of the controversial and political issues and larger racial problems brought out in the following articles.

Needless to say, much of what many Americans have learned about the issues of race has been *sugarcoated*, to use the metaphor. Or are they totally ignorant about such matters, because of the "mutability of the past," to ease the consciousness of the dominant group? Moreover, are we politically *inattentive*? Or are we just culturally insensitive? Or culturally ignorant? And why should we be oblivious to the facts and truth? Perhaps some people living in the United States today don't even care to know about such controversial matters about race. Finally, the following articles are connected and document the critical and disruptive role racial prejudices and discrimination, as well as white supremacy, will continue to negatively play in American life. And what exactly should this mean to the American people? Perhaps this means that all US citizens should take steps to know something about what is really going on in terms of race relations, for the survival of our democracy, as these articles present some of the darkest chapters (or periods) of humanity in the United States.

Notes

1. Amy Kittelstrom. *The Religion of Democracy: Seven Liberals and the American Moral Tradition* (New York: Penguin Books, 2015), 343. We must always think more explicitly about racism and discrimination. To be sure, according to Astead W. Herndon, "an overwhelming majority" of white liberal Americans believe that "racial discrimination [negatively] affects the lives of black people," and this is "why many black people can't get ahead these days" in the United States. See Astead W. Herndon, "How 'White Guilt' in the Age of Trump Shapes the Democratic Primary," *Las Vegas Sun*, October 17, 2019, 1 and 4.

2. Anthony Izaguirre, "Louisiana State Senator Seeks End to Jim Crow-Era Jury Law," *Las Vegas Review-Journal*, April 1, 2018, 15A. All in all, we shouldn't accept the evils of some humans, and the diabolical nature of racialists, or white supremacists, especially when it comes to our various court systems.

3. David Crystal, "Racial Discrimination," in *The Cambridge Encyclopedia*, 2nd ed. (New York: Cambridge University Press, 1994), 915. Black people in the United States have fiercely battled against discrimination and the evils of white racists, and their notion of *racism*.

4. George Orwell. *Animal Farm* (Mumbai, India: Wilco Publishing House, 2018). Unfortunately, in our nation, there are those who have discriminated against others because of their so-called race or ethnic group. Therefore, we cannot ignore the ideals of white supremacists and their false notions of superiority.

5. David Crystal, "Racism," 915. Some African Americans have died violently (for example, by lynching) at the hands of white hate groups, and the unsettling hateful forces that continue to exist and interact in the life of our fragile nation.

6. Brian Greenspun, "It's Time to Eradicate America's Virus of Hate," *Las Vegas Sun*, November 24, 2019, 1. Racial hatred still exists, no matter that some African Americans have succeeded and advanced in many walks of life, and in almost every social and political endeavor. It should also be noted that as human beings, we are more the same than different.

7. David Crystal, "Racism," 915. We must also tell the truth about the racism that exists in law enforcement throughout our country, as well as confront the racial bigotry that still festers in the United States in hateful groups like the vilified KKK, or the neo-Nazis groups of today.

8. See the fourth Amendment to the US Constitution. The Constitution of the United States. *National Center for Constitutional Studies*, 2016, 22.

Part I

Blacks and Higher Education

The State of Black Education
The Politics of Educating African Students at College and Universities

Earnest N. Bracey, Ph.D.

Introduction

From the outset, it should be pointed out that African American citizens should be given the opportunity to attend college or obtain a higher education—that is, in order to have a well-rounded life; and "we the people" should be absolutely supportive and insistent on this educational endeavor. According to Professor Edwin G. West, "it has shown that, at least in the recent past, an American with full college education [will] earned much more than other Americans."[1] Therefore, "research suggests that the best way to address American economic inequality, poverty and crime"[2] is attaining a higher education.

Thus, the goal should be to ensure that current and future generations of African Americans receive the benefits of a college education, especially in terms of earning power over a lifetime. Unfortunately, however, for some young African Americans—receiving a higher education has become a horror story or nightmare, particularly for African American males. Indeed, "the pipeline to America's prisons (from schools) is one littered with black and Latino youth left behind."[3] This is to say that more black males are in American prisons than are attending college. According to former U.S. Senator Jim Webb, statistics "show that a black male without a high school diploma now has a 60 percent chance of going to jail during his young adulthood, and that a black male with a high school diploma has a 30 percent chance"[4] of being incarcerated. These disheartening and dismal statistics are nothing to be proud of. To say the least, this grim, educational reality must change, if we are to become a "more perfect union." If nothing else, the black community with their faith-filled spirit, must get directly involved in the process of educating African American students, especially our vulnerable black, at-risk male students.

Of course, black children "need adults in their lives who care about education and provide support every step of the way."[5] In other words, "we-the-people" should all invest in educating African American students at every educational level, particularly at the university or college level, instead of being harassed into some kind of silence about such an educational matter. Indeed, having some kind of *luck* shouldn't be a factor in determining whether African American students should go to college or not, because education, as mentioned, is the key. Educating young, black people, essentially, has always been the key to a better life and prosperity in the United States. Unfortunately, some self-serving, conservative politicians have scrupulously denied that educating black people, or the general public, is even necessary. After all, some in the dominant group and other existing power structures firmly believe that many African Americans are still (intellectually) inferior—that is, in regards to the *efficacy* of receiving a higher education in the 21st century. For example, Professor David J. Leonard writes:

> Selling the idea of college and its associated world of parties, fancy recreation centers, and posh dormitories, higher education, like Nike [shoes], is too often investing in the bells and whistles—the swag factor—rather than education itself or the production of knowledge, learning, and teaching.[6]

Professor of economics Walter Williams takes this notion a step further by stating, "Many black students are alien and hostile to the education process. [And] they have parents with little interest in their education."[7] But Williams should know that poor black kids "are more likely to have a single teenage mom who is stressed out, who was herself raised in an authoritarian style that she mimics, and who, as a result, doesn't chatter much with the child."[8] Furthermore, it should be understood that poor black students "and those with learning disabilities also tend to be disproportionately disciplined. [Consequently], many end up at low-performing alternative schools, where their educational success" and the possibility of attending college is diminished.[9]

The Prison-Industrial Complex

When it is all said and done, we should rightly dismantle the Prison-Industrial Complex, or the prison system pipeline that often views black males negatively, worthy of imprisonment and humiliation. Michelle Alexander who is the author of *The New Jim Crow: Mass Incarceration in the Age of Colorblindness* has stated that "the school-to-prison pipeline is another *metaphor*—a good one for explaining how [black] children are funneled directly from school into prison. Instead of schools being a pipeline to opportunity, [some] schools are feeding our prisons."[10] To be sure, many young African American males muddle around recklessly (in life), while not really understanding the benefits or very concept of going to college. Alexander put it this way:

> When young black men reach a certain age—whether or not there is incarceration in their families—they themselves are the target of police stops, interrogations, frisks, often for no reason other than their race. And, of course, this level of harassment sends a message to them, often at an early age: No matter who you are or what you do, you're going to find yourself behind bars one way or the other. This reinforces the sense that prison is part of their destiny, rather than a choice one makes.[11]

Indeed, "for those who become ensnared in our criminal justice, prison often become an alternate lifestyle."[12] Clearly, our criminal justice system has failed us in many profound ways, as it concerns African American males. And, as former Senator Jim Webb tells us: "Our failure to address this problem has caused the nation's prisons to burst their seams with massive overcrowding, even as our neighborhoods have become more dangerous. [Hence], we are wasting billions of dollars and diminishing millions of lives."[13] Unfortunately, our criminal justice system has also become part of the problem when it comes to undermining higher educational opportunities for African Americans. Of course, African American students and all citizens should be educated. Therefore, higher education should become fashionable for *everyone,* or all ethnic groups in the United States. But African Americans must assess their own feelings about obtaining a college degree. Not surprisingly, some young black people might argue about the merits of pursuing a higher education, especially if they are convinced that members of the dominant group will continue to marginalize them at every turn, and try to keep them (black people) in their so-called "place."

Moreover, African American students must be realistic about their educational future. It is also crucial that such minority students have a clear understanding or reason for pursuing a college education in the first place. They should also know that:

> Dropouts earn far less than college graduates, rely much more on food stamps and other social services, are more likely to end up in prison and often have children destined to repeat these mistakes in an endless, hopeless cycle.[14]

Additionally, African American students must be willing to finishing their respective degrees, no matter what, or whatever it takes. Education reporter for *The Times,* Richard Perez-Pena points out that "too often [black] students receive little guidance about how to navigate the system and how to choose a combination of classes that will move them closer to graduation."[15] This is where *advisors* or *mentors* should come in to play, and do their part. The whole idea for educators or mentors is to inject themselves in the lives of African American students, by being accountable for improving their achievement.[16] General Colin Powell and Alma Powell tell us that "Students who meet regularly with mentors are 52% less likely to skip a day of school and 37% less likely to skip class than their peers who don't have such guidance."[17]

Therefore, in order for African American students to be highly educated, and to escape the prison-industrial complex, or incarceration, they must have guidance from role models and mentors, as well as being up to the inevitable task—to compete and excel in higher education. Moreover, these African American students need additional help in the face of many social and administrative obstacles placed in from of them, created by the dominant group, or economic impediments that might block their educational path.

The Necessity of Black Education

Meanwhile, historically Black colleges and universities (HCBUs) should also be in the political mix in that such important institutions must demand the same educational goals for all African American students, as other American universities. However, it should be noted that black colleges and universities have the added challenge of being attacked and singled out for consolidation or elimination, with "racial undertones." For example, in 2010, when Republican and former governor of Mississippi, Halely Barbour was in office, he proposed to combine the black universities of Mississippi Valley State and Alcorn State University into Jackson State University, while not touching the historically white institutions in the state.[18] Fortunately, Barbour's proposal didn't go anywhere, or see the light of day, because "in 1992, the U.S. Supreme Court agreed that the State [of Mississippi] still had vestiges of segregation in its university system and sent the case to the lower courts to arrange a settlement,"[19] called the Ayers deal.

But it is possible that such a plan to eliminate the two smaller black universities will be addressed again. Or who's to say that a possible merger of Mississippi's three public historically black universities won't be proposed or introduced again in the future, on "questions over state's funding of those colleges."[20] Equally significant, it should be pointed out that HBCUs "are facing an uphill battle for funding that have left many fighting to survive."[21] But HBCUs are vital to African American students and black communities, generally, throughout the United States. Moreover, financial support for such students at HBCUs is still needed in America today, because of educational inequalities. As a result, according to economist Julianne Malveaux, "We [black educators and HBCUs] are plagued by low endowments but also by our nation's indifference to our service."[22] As further evidence, Executive Director of the White House Initiative on historically Black colleges and universities (HBCUs), John Silvanus Wilson, Jr. once described such daunting financial challenges for HBCUs, as "substantial cracks in the ice under American higher education." He goes on to argue that "many of the cracks stem from atmospheric pressure. In Washington, budgets have rarely been tighter and policies have rarely been coarser."[23] Wilson Summarized:

> In higher education, the competition is stiffer, inequality widens, and it has become much more difficult for institutions with fewer resources to graduate [African American] students who are effectively prepared to enter and thrive in a technologically advanced, information-based, and increasingly competitive workplace. In private philanthropy, many donors are younger and more inclined toward "create tomorrow" investments rather than "save the day" gifts.[24]

Nonetheless, as Malveaux cogently explains: "With its unique mission to prepare and secure the next generation of Black achievers, HBCUs must lobby federal departments just to ensure that their funding stays level or rise."[25] Moreover, such venerable HBCUs should also step up their recruiting efforts, while creating information *networks* and connections at all colleges and universities for African American and minority students everywhere. Additionally, such traditional places of higher learning must make college affordable. As Journalist Frank Bruni has written, "Nothing—nothing is more important than the education of our children, and while various interests will make competing claims about whether it's improving or slipping and how best to measure that, [black] education certainly isn't at the level we want or need it to be."[26] No doubt, professors and teachers at HBCUs must not stand on the sidelines or periphery of educating young African American students, while worrying about their relevance. This is to say that their passion as educators and mentors should translate in to a definitive way for African American students—to engage and learn. According to Malveaux, "Our colleges [HBCUs] are repositories of black knowledge, which some would like to ignore,"[27] but this will be an impossible feat, given the circumstances.

Former educator and actor Tony Danza posits that "we have to convince [black students] that, despite the formidable obstacles that they often face, it's imperative that they do well in school," at all educational levels.[28] Which is to say, African American students must also want to be educated, so that their "academic preparation for college" is "tightly linked to socioeconomic status."[29] So will realistic educational goals for African American students promote *real* equality of educational opportunities? That said, will educators do whatever it takes at selective universities or historically black colleges and universities to educate and nurture minority students, before it is too late to do *anything* to keep them on track? Mentoring, of course, is not simply telling potential African American students what's in erudite books; it also entails letting them know something we, as educators, have learned over the years in a professional career. In a nutshell, moreover, *real* education is being able to nurture students "and that of others."[30] Therefore, it is essential for us to "give back" as teachers and educators—that is, in terms of helping African American students receive a higher education.

Conclusion

On the whole, the job as an educator should be to impart the knowledge we have gained in our educational profession. Indeed, the educator must tell the ambitious African American student how to navigate the stressful educational rigmaroles at the college and university levels, while being truthful and honest about the things to come. According to educator Jennifer Gonzales, "a major stumbling block for [some] college students is remedial education [as well as having the necessary education funds]." Meanwhile, many low-income students who languish in certain "reading, writing or math classes" might "eventually drop out, curtailing their graduation plans."[31] However, some African American students shouldn't be forever propped-up for statistical reasons, or excused for their lack of higher educational knowledge. In an interview, Michelle Alexander tells us that "the reality is we're not going to provide meaningful education opportunities to poor kids, [or] kids of color, until and unless we recognize that we're wasting trillions of dollars on a failed criminal justice system."[32]

Equally important, we must make the case for what African American students should actually be interested in (academically)—or what they really want to do with their lives, because such students can do great things. Indeed, major educational achievements are possible with such students if given the opportunity. We must be especially mindful that colleges and universities can be a stepping-stone (or spring-board) to future financial benefits and educational endeavors for African American students. Indeed, colleges and universities should also be the vanguard and educational battleground for all minority students. But we must try to make it exciting to be educated, if possible. And as mentioned, African American students must make the most of such educational opportunities, despite a *plethora* of obstacles they might face. In essence, a higher education can truly lead to a rewarding and professional life. Therefore, in the end, "colleges and universities [will] continue to play an invaluable role in our society," especially in educating future generations of African American students, and "all the more so as the world changes."[33]

We should also take a hard look at whether African Americans will continue to face financial discrimination in the United States,[34] because this might be something that they cannot overcome, unless there is support from our federal government, or financial contributions from wealthy individuals. Furthermore, as educators, we must improve teaching and learning for all minority students, not only through lecturing and example, but also by a "hands-on" approach to higher education. Ultimately, the education of African American students can be improved immeasurably by all concerned educators, politicians, governors, Congress members and the President of the United States, with the help and assistance from dedicated parents as well. Otherwise, "black youngsters" will be "virtually useless in an increasingly technological economy."[35]

And any significant turn-around from the "school-to-prison pipeline" won't happen, until our entire nation is concerned, and actively involved in this political issue of higher education. In the final analysis, this notion is important to understand, because young black men:

> Who go to prison rather than college face a life time of closed doors, discrimination, and ostracism. Their plight is not what we hear about on the evening news, however. Sadly, like the racial caste systems that preceded it, the system of mass incarceration now seems normal and natural to most, a regrettable necessity.[36]

All this is to say is we need a national debate about this academic matter, to develop the necessary strategy and tools for insuring that all African American students are able to get a higher education, if they so desire, while dismantling the Prison-Industrial Complex as soon as possible. In so many words, the great black educator, W.E.B. DuBois was right when he said that black people and young people in particular, in America, have the mental wherewithal and intellectual capacity to learn, and to compete with anyone in the global community. In this regard, "black leaders should make public education the defining civil-rights issue of our times."[37]

Finally, Dubois, along with other black educators "imagined that black colleges and universities would one day rise to rank among the best in the world."[38] This academic dream, of course, has become reality. Therefore, the educational agenda, as Alexander urge us, should be to expose young African Americans—in classrooms across the United States—to the truth about the dysfunctional American criminal justice system, in terms of black males, in particular, being incarcerated in our many prisons, while not attending college to pursue a higher educational degree. Finally, African American students must develop "their critical capacities" which, no doubt, will "open the door to meaningful engagement and collective, inspired action,"[39] to achieve serious educational goals.

Notes

1. Edwin G. West, *Education and the State: A Study in Political Economy* (Indianapolis: Liberty Fund, 1994), 114.

2. Nicholas D. Kristof, "Do We Invest in Preschools or Prison?" *The New York Times,* October 27, 2013, 11. According to Kristof, education is "the best tool we have to break cycles of [black] poverty."

3. David J. Leonard, "Shoes, Diplomas, and the American Dream," *The Chronicle Review,* September 28, 2012, B2.

4. Jim Webb, *A Time to Fight: Reclaiming a Fair and Just America* (New York: Broadway Books, 2008), 218.

5. Colin Powell and Alma Powell, "One in Three Kids Drops Out of School: What We Can Do," *USA Weekend,* February 26–28, 2010, 6.

6. Leonard, "Shoes, Diploma," B2.

7. Walter Williams, "What to do about the sorry state of black education?" *Las Vegas Review-Journal,* December 23, 2009, 7B.

8. Kristof, "Do We Invest," 11.

9. Chandra Thomas Whitfield, "School Scam: How children of color get stuck in low-performing public alternative schools," *The Crisis Magazine,* volume 119/2, Spring 2012, 23.

10. Jody Sokolower, "Schools and the New Jim Crow: An Interview with Michelle Alexander," *Rethinking Schools,* Winter 2011–2012, 13.

11. Sokolower, "Schools and the New Jim Crow," 14.

12. Webb, "A Time to Fight," 218.

13. Jim Webb, "Why We Must Fix Our Prisons," *Parade,* March 29, 2009, 4. According to Journalist Jody Sokolower, "The United States imprisons a larger percentage of its black population than South Africa did at the height of apartheid. In Washington, D.C., for example, it is estimated that 15 percent of young black men can expect to serve time in prison. See Sokolower, "Schools and New Jim Crow: An Interview with Michelle Alexander."

14. Powell and Powell, "One in Three Kids," 6.

15. Richard Perez-Pena, "The New Community College Try," *Education Life,* July 22, 2012, 18. Perez-Pena writes that "these students do not display the habits or confidence that would have been instilled in a more privileged group."

16. John Cloud, "How to Recruit Better Teachers," *Time,* September 20, 2010, 52.

17. Powell and Powell, "One in Three Kids," 7.

18. Elizabeth Crisp, "Plan to merge black colleges draws outrage," *USA Today,* December 1, 2009, 4A.

19. Ibid., 4A. It should be pointed out that under the Ayers settlement, "the Mississippi Legislature agreed to provide $503 million to the three [black] colleges over 17 hears."

20. Ibid., 4A.

21. Julianne Malveaux, "Is there a War on HBCUs?" *Essence,* volume 44, number 4, August 2013, 120.

22. Ibid., 120.

23. John Silvanus Wilson, Jr., "A Multi-Dimensional Challenge for Black Colleges," *The Chronicle of Higher Education,* September 23, 2011, 76.

24. Ibid., 76.

25. Malveaux, "Is there a War," 123.

26. Frank Bruni, "Teachers on the Defensive," *The New York Times*, August 19, 2012, 1. Professor Jean Twenge posits that some young people feel "entitled: or are over-confident in themselves, much to the chagrin of some academics, where there is "a growing disconnect between self-perception and reality." See Martha Irvine, "Study finds college freshmen over confident," *Las Vegas Review Journal*, June 17, 2011, 10A.

27. Malveaux, "Is there a War," 121.

28. Tony Danza, "What I Learned Teaching Your Kids," *USA Weekend*, August 24–26, 2012, 12.

29. Michele Moody-Adams, "Toward Real Equality in Higher Education," *The Chronicle of Higher Education*, October 5, 2012, A80.

30. Spencer Johnson and Constance Johnson, *The One Minute Teacher: How to Teach Others to Teach Themselves* (New York: William Morrow and Company, Inc., 1986), 107.

31. Jennifer Gonzalez, "3-Year Project on Community-College Practice Seeks to Help Students Graduate," *The Chronicle of Higher Education*, February 10, 2012, A20.

32. Sokolower, "Schools and the New Jim Crow," 16. Alexander goes on to point out rightly that black children are "growing up in communities in which they see their loved ones cycling in and out of prison in which they are sent the message in countless ways that they, too, are going to prison one way or another." Unfortunately, some black teenagers and college age kids also "regard school as the functional equivalent of prison—where they are forced to endure oppressive rules." See Steve Chapman, "Longer incarceration for the young," *Las Vegas Review Journal*, February 2, 2012, 9B.

33. Clayton Christensen and Henry Eyring, "How to Save the Traditional University from the Inside Out," *The Chronicle of Higher Education*, July 20, 2011, 72.

34. Christine Dugas, "Dual system of finance hits minorities," *USA Today*, April 5, 2011, 3B.

35. Williams, "What to do," 7B.

36. Michelle Alexander, *The New Jim Crow: Mass Incarceration in the Age of Colorblindness*, revised edition (New York: The New Press, 2012),190.

37. Michael Meyers, "The NAACP at a Crossroads," *The Wall Street Journal*, September 4, 2007, A17.

38. Wilson, "A Multi-Dimensional Challenge," 76.

39. Sokolower, "Schools and the New Jim Crow," 17.

References

Alexander, M. (2012). *The New Jim Crow: Mass Incarceration in the Age of Colorblindness* (revised ed.). New York: The New Press.

Bruni, F. (2012, August 19). Teachers on the Defensive. *The New York Times*, p. 1.

Chapman, S. (2012, February 2). Longer incarceration for the young. *Las Vegas Review Journal*, p. 9B.

Christensen, C., & Eyring, H. (2011, July 20). How to Save the Traditional University from the Inside Out. *The Chronicle of Higher Education*, p. 72.

Cloud, J. (2010, September 20). How to Recruit Better Teachers. *Time*, p. 52.

Crisp, E. (2009, December 1). Plan to merge black colleges draws outrage. *USA Today*, p. 4A.

Danza, T. (2012, August 24–26). What I Learned Teaching Your Kids. *USA Weekend*, p. 12.

Dugas, C. (2011, April 5). Dual system of finance hits minorities. *USA Today*, p. 3B.

Gonzalez, J. (2012, February 10). 3-Year Project on Community-College Practice Seeks to Help Students Graduate. *The Chronicle of Higher Education*, p. A20.

Johnson, S., & Johnson, C. (1986). *The One Minute Teacher: How to Teach Others to Teach Themselves.* New York: William Morrow and Company, Inc.

Kristof, N. D. (2013, October 27). Do We Invest in Preschools or Prison? *The New York Times*, p. 11.

Leonard, D. J. (2012, September 28). Shoes, Diplomas, and the American Dream. *The Chronicle Review*, p. B2.

Malveaux, J. (2013, August). Is there a War on HBCUs? *Essence*, volume 44, number 4, p. 120.

Meyers, M. (2007, September 4). The NAACP at a Crossroads. *The Wall Street Journal*, p. A17.

Moody-Adams, M. (2012, October 5). Toward Real Equality in Higher Education. *The Chronicle of Higher Education*, p. A80.

Perez-Pena, R. (2012, July 22). The New Community College Try. *Education Life*, p. 18.

Powell, C., &Powell, A. (2010, February 26–28). One in Three Kids Drops Out of School: What We Can Do. *USA Weekend*, p. 6.

Sokolower, J. (2011–2012, Winter). Schools and the New Jim Crow: An Interview with Michelle Alexander. *Rethinking Schools*, p. 13.

Webb, J. (2008). *A Time to Fight: Reclaiming a Fair and Just America.* New York: Broadway Books.

Webb, J. (2009, March 29). Why We Must Fix Our Prisons. *Parade*, p. 4.

West, E. G. (1994). *Education and the State: A Study in Political Economy.* Indianapolis: Liberty Fund.

Whitfield, C. T. (2012, Spring). School Scam: How children of color get stuck in low-performing public alternative schools. *The Crisis Magazine*, volume 119/2, p. 23.

Williams, W. (2009, December 23).What to do about the sorry state of black education? *Las Vegas Review-Journal*, p. 7B.

Wilson, J. S., Jr. (2011, September 23). A Multi-Dimensional Challenge for Black Colleges. *The Chronicle of Higher Education*, p. 76.

Reading 1.2

The Significance of Historically Black Colleges and Universities (HBCUs) in the 21st Century
Will Such Institutions of Higher Learning Survive?

Earnest N. Bracey, Ph.D.

Introduction: An Unbroken Thirst for Knowledge

If the United States were truly a land of equal opportunity, there would never have been a need to create colleges and universities specifically for African Americans. Yet, historically black colleges and universities (HBCUs) still exist today as a legacy of the past. As Roebuck and Murty (1993: 3, 4) describe them:

> Historically black colleges and universities (HBCUs) are black academic institutions established prior to 1964 whose principal mission was, and still is, the education of black Americans. ... They were founded and developed in an environment unlike that [of] surrounding other colleges—that is, in a hostile environment marked by legal segregation and isolation from mainstream U.S. higher education. ... They have maintained a very close identity with the struggle of blacks for survival, advancement, and equality in American society. ... These institutions have championed the cause of equal opportunity, have provided an opportunity for many who would not otherwise have graduated from college, and have served as the custodians of the archives for black Americans and as centers for the study of black culture.

Earnest N. Bracey, "The Significance of Historically Black Colleges and Universities (HBCUs) in the 21st Century: Will Such Institutions of Higher Learning Survive?," *The American Journal of Economics and Sociology*, vol. 76, no. 3, pp. 670–696. Copyright © 2017 by John Wiley & Sons, Inc. Reprinted with permission.

The first HBCUs were established in the late 1800s by ex-slaves (and others) in black churches, or they were affiliated with Christian denominations. They were built because the promise of true freedom at the end of the American Civil War was never fulfilled.

During more than two centuries of slavery, African Americans were generally denied any form of education. Following the Stono Rebellion in 1739 in South Carolina, many states adopted laws that made it illegal to teach a slave to write, and the laws were strengthened after Nat Turner's Revolt of 1831 (Woodson 1915: 193–196). Yet, the laws never broke the spirit of resistance that enabled close to 10 percent of African Americans in the South to achieve literacy by 1865. Despite continued violence against them, black southerners managed to achieve a literacy rate of 55 percent by 1890, a rate of growth that far surpassed the rise of literacy in Spain and Italy during the same period (Blum 2005: 83). Thus, African Americans proved again and again that they were willing to defy oppressive efforts to pursue their education.

The entire history of higher education has been a series of obstacles created for African Americans. Official policies that seemed to the casual observer to have been aimed at overcoming past injustice tended to reinforce those injustices. Powerful interests have sought to keep black Americans from obtaining the tools necessary to gain control of their lives. Restricting the supply of education was one of the easiest ways to maintain a labor force with few avenues for advancement. Despite all of those obstacles, African Americans found ways to prevail by attaining literacy and other forms of knowledge through their own devices.

In the 21st century, black families continue to show their determination to provide their children with the best education possible. As Hamilton et al. (2015) show, black families outspend white families on education as a percentage of household income and net worth:

> Social-science research confirms that black students and their families are doing more with less. Research by economist Patrick Mason and sociologists Dalton Conley and William Mangino demonstrates that blacks attain more years of schooling and credentials than whites from families with comparable resources. Yunju Nam, a professor of social work at the University of Buffalo, has documented that the median net worth of black parents who offer financial support for the higher education of their adult sons and daughters is one-fourth of the median net worth of white parents who do not provide any support for their children's college education.[1]

This evidence demonstrates beyond any doubt that black families value education even more highly than white families do. Unfortunately, this quest for scholarly attainment has not been reciprocated by state governments, which have historically put up roadblocks to black students who wanted to learn.

Limited Support from Federal Assistance

Can the remarkable growth of black literacy be traced to support by the federal government for public colleges and universities? Standard accounts of the land grant universities, first established in the 19th century, might create that impression. But that would be wrong.

Morrill Acts Establish Land Grant Schools

The Morrill Act of 1862 allowed for educational institutions to be established on public lands. Each state was given 30,000 acres of federal land for each senator and representative in Congress, and the land was to be sold in order to finance the creation of a college specializing in the teaching of "agriculture and the mechanic arts" (Committee on the Future 1995: 9; Stevens 2000a: 1102). Some HBCUs later benefited from the provisions that established "traditional academic subjects," especially for black people, or African Americans (Harris and Levey 1975a: 1524).

However, because of racial discrimination, all things considered, African Americans (almost straight out of slavery) were denied access to the land grant colleges, especially in the South. After a few years of partial racial equality during Reconstruction, southern states barred African Americans from entering state colleges and universities. To overcome the overt discrimination that was practiced under the Morrill Act of 1862, Congress adopted the Morrill Act of 1890, which required that states either admit black students to existing land grant colleges and universities or finance schools that would be open to African Americans (Museus, Ledesma, and Parker 2012: 50; Harper, Patton, and Wooden 2009: 395). Southern states, where the majority of African Americans lived, wanted to maintain the flow of federal dollars into the region, so they chose the latter option, creating a system of segregated higher education that was modeled on the segregation of primary and secondary education. Roebuck and Murtry (1993: 27) explain that southern legislatures were willing to allow black colleges and universities to be built

> to get millions of dollars in federal funds for the development of white land-grant universities, to limit African American education to vocational training, and to prevent African Americans from attending white land-grant colleges.

In this way, the Morrill Act of 1890 also had the paradoxical consequence of contributing to the segregation of educational facilities.

Since white-controlled state legislatures controlled the flow of money for education, they were able to restrict the financing of higher education for African Americans. As Harper, Patton, and Wooden (2009: 396) describe the situation in the 1890s and beyond:

Public HBCUs remained disproportionately underfunded. ... White land-grant institutions were still receiving state appropriations at a rate of 26 times more than Black colleges. ... The per-pupil state expenditure rate for African Americans equaled about one-fourth the rate for whites.

Although the law ostensibly required "separate but equal" forms of higher education, the reality was that HBCUs in the public sector were restricted by segregationist policies to prevent them from offering truly equal opportunities to African Americans.

The Adverse Racial Consequences of the G.I. Bill

Another case in which federal money for higher education was redirected from black institutions into predominantly white institutions (PWIs) was the Servicemen's Readjustment Act (1944: Pt. VIII: 288–290), which is popularly known as the G.I. Bill of Rights. Although the federal legislation was racially neutral, its implementation in the segregated South was not. Herbold (1994–1995: 108) reports that approximately 95 percent of black veterans who took advantage of educational benefits under the G.I. Bill were educated in the South. That helps explain why, as Mettler (2005: 56) notes, only 12 percent of African Americans used the G.I. Bill to enroll in colleges and universities, compared to 26 percent for veterans as a whole. The lower rate among African Americans did not mean they were not interested in furthering their education. In fact, blacks made use of the educational benefits of the G.I. Bill more often than whites did, but their enrollment options were limited because of segregation. Herbold (1994–1995: 107) points out:

> Overcrowding at the historically black institutions of the South, and discriminatory admissions policies at other colleges and universities, meant that for many veterans in search of a college degree, vocational training programs and trade schools were the only available options.

As a result, black applicants most often participated in nonacademic programs that were supposed to provide skills needed for higher-paying jobs. However, southern offices of the Veterans Administration provided little assistance to black veterans in learning about such programs, instead directing them to "on-the-job training" programs that put black veterans to work at menial jobs (Onkst 1998: 519–520, 523–524). Those who enrolled in vocational schools discovered that a large number of them were either substandard or fraudulent operations with no curriculum (Onkst 1998: 528–529, Katznelson 2005: 129–130). Turner and Bound (2003: 172) conclude that the relative status of southern blacks was actually harmed: "For those ... limited to the South in their collegiate choices, the G.I. Bill exacerbated rather than narrowed the economic and educational differences between blacks and whites." Thus, despite the almost entirely favorable reputation of the G.I. Bill among historians and the public, this was just one more case of a system designed to prevent the advancement of African Americans.[2]

The Imposed Need for HBCUs

From the 1860s onward, black Americans had no alternative but to establish their own higher educational institutions, often with the assistance of northern white churches and the Freedmen's Bureau, to escape unequal treatment by white Americans in colleges, universities, and professional schools. Indeed, many historically black colleges and universities (HBCUs) were established solely to educate newly emancipated black African slaves because they were mostly banned at white colleges and universities, a practice that continued well into the 1960s.

Although a number of co-educational public institutions were founded primarily for educating African-American students, it is simply wrong to think that HBCUs were created because black people wanted their own separate, higher educational institutions. Nothing could have been further from the truth. Given that African Americans could not attend the many predominantly white institutions of higher education (PWIs), enforced segregation denied black students a choice. Their only option was to attend a separate institution, one of the HBCUs. Table 1.2.1 is a list of private HBCUs that were founded in the 19th century. Table 1.2.2 is a list of HBCUs that were founded as land grant colleges.

TABLE 1.2.1 Private HBCUs Founded in the 19th Century

Name	Location	Year Founded
Cheyney University	Cheyney, PA	1837
Lincoln University	Lincoln, PA	1854
Wilberforce University	Wilberforce, OH	1856
Atlanta University	Atlanta, GA	1865
Clark College	Atlanta, GA	1869
Shaw University	Raleigh, NC	1865
Fisk University	Nashville, TN	1866
Lincoln Institute	Jefferson City, MO	1866
Shaw University	Holly Springs, MS	1866
Alabama State University	Montgomery, AL	1867
Barber Memorial College	Concord, NC	1867

(Continued)

Name	Location	Year Founded
Fayetteville State University	Fayetteville, NC	1867
Howard University	Washington, DC	1867
Johnson C. Smith University	Charlotte, NC	1867
Morehouse College	Atlanta, GA	1867
St. Augustine's University	Raleigh, NC	1867
Talladega College	Talladega, AL	1867
Hampton University	Hampton, VA	1868
Claflin University	Orangeburg, SC	1869
Dillard University	New Orleans, LA	1869
Tougaloo University	Hinds, MS	1869
Allen University	Columbia, SC	1870
Benedict College	Columbia, SC	1870
Wiley College	Marshall, TX	1873
Bennett College	Greensboro, NC	1873
Knoxville College	Knoxville, TN	1875
Tuskeegee University	Tuskegee, AL	1881

TABLE 1.2.2   HBCUs Founded as Land Grant Colleges

Name	Location	Year Founded
Alabama A&M University	Normal, AL	1875
Alcorn State University	Lorman, MS	1871
Delaware State College	Dover, DE	1891
Florida A&M University	Tallahassee, FL	1887
Fort Valley State College	Fort Valley, GA	1895
Kentucky State University	Frankfort, KY	1886
Langston University	Langston, OK	1897
Lincoln University	Jefferson City, MO	1866
North Carolina A&T State University	Greensboro, NC	1891
Prairie View A&M University	Prairie View, TX	1876
South Carolina State College	Orangeburg, SC	1896
Southern University and A&M College	Baton Rouge, LA	1880
Tennessee State University	Nashville, TN	1912
University of Arkansas at Pine Bluff	Pine Bluff, AR	1873
University of Maryland—Eastern Shore	Princess Anne, MD	1886
Virginia State University	Petersburg, VA	1882
West Virginia State College	Institute, WV	1891

Some exceptions were made to segregation policies, at least in northern state schools. For example, the famous botanist and scientist George Washington Carver, a former black slave, was able to attend Iowa State Agricultural College, a PWI of higher learning. Nevertheless, many white colleges and universities were simply not open to black students, even if they were qualified. Of course, some white Americans, particularly in the South, after the Civil War, believed in the complete separation of the so-called races.

From their beginning, historically black colleges and universities were not separatist. Unlike white institutions of higher learning, HBCUs always allowed all qualified students to attend their schools because they have, for the most part, been nonjudgmental in terms of who should be educated. Additionally, these black, higher educational institutions have especially hired white faculty and administrators. Bluefield State College, in West Virginia, which is no longer a majority black college, is an example of the openness practiced by HBCUs. Indeed, the population of Bluefield State College today is approximately 90 percent white, with a white, female president, Marsha Krotseng. Therefore, the demographics and the historical mission, as well as the student landscape, has changed. Such changes or a similar racial transformation was never voluntarily reciprocated by PWIs.

The Distinctive Character of HBCUs

There are still 101 historically black colleges and universities across the United States today—in 19 states, the District of Columbia, and the U.S. Virgin Islands. This is important to note because HBCUs are known for nurturing black, underserved students, while offering specialized instruction, such as exploring the deepest questions about what it means to be a black college student. In addition, the political and social issues facing the respective black communities are also addressed at these HBCUs. Since the late 1800s, these schools have been teaching the history of a formerly enslaved people, forcibly taken from mostly the west coast of Africa and brought to the Americas in bondage.

An important feature of HBCUs has been their provision of a welcoming environment for black students, who are able to thrive in a context of acceptance and mutual support. As Roebuck and Murty (1993: 16–17) explain this phenomenon:

> Those enrolled at HBCUs escape the campus conflict between black and white students that is frequently found on white campuses. ... HBCUs emphasize the development of black consciousness and identity, black history, racial pride, and ethnic traditions. They provide an African-American culture and ambiance that many students find essential to their social functioning and mental health. ... As a result of racial segregation in the United States ... establishing a

meaningful personal identity, cultivating personal relationships, and gaining social acceptance are difficult for black students on white campuses.

The presence of social support networks for black students at HBCUs may help to account for the fact that the graduation rate for black undergraduates was more than 50 percent higher at HBCUs than at predominantly white institutions (PWIs) in the 1980s (Roebuck and Murty 1993: 4).

Some HBCUs have also become principal educational centers for the continuing study of black culture. Furthermore, black higher educational institutions have advocated for "economic parity" and civil and political equality with white institutions. Many of the leaders of the civil rights movement in the 1950s and 1960s were graduates of HBCUs. The following is a partial list of those leaders and the HBCUs they attended:

- A. Philip Randolph (Bethune-Cookman University)
- Zora Neal Hurston (Morgan State University, Howard University)
- Ella Josephine Baker (Shaw University)
- Thurgood Marshall (Lincoln University, in PA)
- Bayard Rustin (Wilberforce University)
- Rosa Parks (Montgomery Industrial School for Girls)
- Claude Black (Morehouse College)
- James L. Farmer (Wiley College)
- Whitney Young (Kentucky State University)
- Joseph Lowery (Knoxville College, Alabama A&M University)
- Medgar Evers (Alcorn State University)
- Ralph Abernathy (Alabama State University)
- Martin Luther King, Jr. (Morehouse College)
- Andrew Young (Dillard University, Howard University)
- Diane Nash (Howard University, Fisk University)
- Julian Bond (Morehouse College)
- John Lewis (American Baptist College, Fisk University)
- Kwame Ture (b. Stokely Carmichael) (Howard University)
- Jesse Jackson (North Carolina A&T State University)
- Benjamin Chavis (St. Augustine's University, Howard University)

Some HBCUs were themselves the locus of events that were at the forefront of the modern-day civil rights movement. Jackson State University, in Jackson, Mississippi, is an important example. On May 15, 1970, the main campus was attacked by white law enforcement officials. Two students were killed and 12 were wounded in an unprovoked, 28-second barrage of continuous gunfire by the police, at least one of whom was armed with a machine gun (Spofford 1988). The rationale for the police attack was supposedly because of rioting by black students. But it was really about black students protesting the Vietnam War, and "the racism they, their community and their school was subjected to by the surrounding white community and the white establishment that ignored the concerns of the students and [Jackson State University]" (Ann 2008; Spofford 1988). Ten days earlier, four white students were killed at Kent State in Ohio. That was national news. The deaths of two black students in Mississippi went almost unreported.

Equally important, HBCUs have emphasized such academic programs that cater to the individual talents and educational needs of African-American students, some of whom are first-time college students from long-suffering black families. Further, HBCUs have long been important institutions for training African Americans in the teaching professions. These unique schools have subsequently become the dominant voice of the black community, while promulgating the view that black people are the equal to white Americans and their predominantly white institutions (PWIs). These HBCUs are usually comprised of liberal arts and the sciences, and selective graduate schools, offering a limited number of professional degrees. However, historically black colleges and universities have had stronger programs in the arts and sciences. Many of these one-of-a-kind schools also explore—but not exclusively—U.S. race relations.

Furthermore, many HBCUs offer broad curricula and advanced degrees in addition to significant undergraduate degrees. In fact, some of these private and public schools of higher learning have achieved international acclaim. Moreover, HBCUs allow for African-American students to be introspective and play catch-up educationally as they are being nurtured by concerned and conscientious professors and administrators. Indeed, some black students "have to ingest entire bodies of knowledge in only a few years—to say nothing of overcoming a plethora of inheritances ... [like] racism, systemic oppression, poverty, [and] failing [public] schools" (Liontas 2016: 5). However, black students feel validated by attending HBCUs, as these places of higher education may represent a response to the social and economic oppression that motivates students to attend these schools in the first place. Indeed, black students are exposed to both an Afrocentric and Eurocentric education, at the highest levels. No doubt, some black or African-American students anticipate and actually prefer going to these HBCUs because they are excited by the collective and diverse college experience, or the prospect of interacting with different people.

Nevertheless, many of these HBCUs have been underrated, and ignored by the larger society. Furthermore, some of these reputable schools, like Howard University and Hampton University, have won national and international recognition. Hampton University, founded in 1868 by Samuel Chapman Armstrong, was the first predominantly black college that also pioneered Native-American education (Harris and Levey 1975b: 1186). It has been argued, however, that Carlisle Indian School, which was founded in 1879 and closed in 1918, was "the first federally supported school for [Native Americans] to be established off a reservation" (Harris and Levey 1975c: 458). But Native Americans were educated at Hampton University long before the establishment of Carlisle Indian School.

Howard University, in Washington, DC, is another prestigious HBCU, which was "founded with a special obligation to educate African American students" in *all* the professional degrees (Stevens 2000b: 771). Finally, Tuskegee University has the distinction of being the first predominantly black institution "to provide adequate education for [African Americans]" (Harris and Levey 1975d: 2809). Tuskegee "has since its beginning, stressed the practical application of learning," especially as black pilots (known as the Tuskegee Airmen) were trained at Tuskegee—to fight Nazi Germany. Indeed, many HBCUs have become preeminent intellectual centers for black, scholarly endeavors and life studies. Consequently, black students thrive at these great places of higher learning, even though "polarization has created a postsecondary system that is both separate and unequal" (Carnevale and Strohl 2011: B2). These forms of social, higher educational, and economic polarization still exist in the 21st century.

Separate and Unequal in Higher Education

The history of the conflict over equal access to education since the late 19th century has been a defining feature of American political life. It shows clearly the extent to which racism in the United States has always been a matter of law and institutions, not just a matter of personal prejudice.

Locking Segregation in Place with Plessy

The Supreme Court ruled in the infamous *Plessy v. Ferguson* (1896: 163 U.S. 537) case that states could legally "provide equal, but separate, accommodations for the white and colored races, by providing two or more passenger coaches for each passenger train." This ruling was extended to all public and regulated services, and thus allowed states to provide separate institutions or accommodations to black and white citizens. "States had the right to segregate blacks and whites, so long as the accommodations were equal" (Harris and Levey 1975e: 1903). Essentially, the highest court in the land condoned legal segregation, which controlled almost every aspect of African-American life, including their schools of higher education. This was unfortunate for HBCUs, as things were certainly segregated, but not equal. To put it bluntly, separation of higher educational institutions was not equal by any stretch of the imagination, nor were African Americans at HBCUs better off, as their educational justice was often denied. Therefore, the low level of black higher education was still the norm, even with some important strides made at HBCUs.

Debate Over "The Atlanta Compromise"

In the early 20th century, a debate took place between two groups of African-American leaders about the type of higher education that should be made available to African Americans. On one side of the debate were accommodationists. The leading figure was Booker T. Washington, a former black slave, and the founder of Tuskegee Institute (now Tuskegee University). Washington's (1895: 584, 586) address at an international exposition in the South soothed the fears of his white audience by assuring them that former slaves sought no higher position in life than to continue to serve their former masters with a bit of technical education:

> Our greatest danger is that in the great leap from slavery to freedom we may overlook the fact that the masses of us are to live by the productions of our hands, and fail to keep in mind that we shall prosper in proportion as we learn to dignify and glorify common labor, and put brains and skill into the common occupations of life; shall prosper in proportion as we learn to draw the line between the superficial and the substantial, the ornamental gewgaws of life and the useful. No race can prosper till it learns that there is as much dignity in tilling a field as in writing a poem. It is at the bottom of life we must begin, and not at the top. Nor should we permit our grievances to overshadow our opportunities. ... The wisest among my race understand that the agitation of questions of social equality is the extremest folly, and that progress in the enjoyment of all the privileges that will come to us must be the result of severe and constant struggle rather than of artificial forcing.

In short, Washington argued that "it was foolish for blacks to agitate for social [justice] and equality before they had attained economic equality" (Harris and Levey 1975f: 2933). He did not approve of educational parity of black and white colleges and universities. He accepted the second-class status to which African Americans were consigned. In return for this deference to whites, Washington asked only for crumbs: the right to vocational education that southern states and northern philanthropists were providing and the right to limited protection under the law.

On the other side of the debate were educated black men, primarily in northern states, who favored agitation for the full rights of African Americans, including an education that was not restricted to skills associated with manual labor. Specifically, they argued that a liberal arts education of the sort that could lead to advanced professional degrees in law or medicine should be available to any African American on the same basis as whites. W. E. B. Dubois was the leading intellectual among those who regarded Washington's simplistic goal or attitude as so much nonsense. Calling Washington's speech "The Atlanta Compromise," Dubois argued that it demeaned black people for their capacity to learn and think as academic scholars and philosophers. In his response to Washington's moral resignation, Dubois (1903: 50–51) wrote:

> Mr. Washington represents in Negro thought the old attitude of adjustment and submission. ... In other periods of intensified prejudice all the Negro's tendency to self-assertion has been called forth; at this period a policy of submission is advocated. In the history of nearly all other races and peoples the doctrine preached at such crises has been that manly self-respect is worth more than lands and houses, and that a people who voluntarily surrender such respect, or cease striving for it, are not worth civilizing.

Dubois (1903: 51–52) wanted to know why African Americans should give up the claim to full humanity by demanding full political, civil, and educational rights, when Washington's advice was based on an unacknowledged paradox:

Is it possible, and probable, that nine millions of men can make effective progress in economic lines if they are deprived of political rights, made a servile caste, and allowed only the most meagre chance for developing their exceptional men? If history and reason give any distinct answer to these questions, it is an emphatic No. And Mr. Washington thus faces the triple paradox of his career:

1. He is striving nobly to make Negro artisans business men and property-owners; but it is utterly impossible, under modern competitive methods, for workingmen and property-owners to defend their rights and exist without the right of suffrage.
2. He insists on thrift and self-respect, but at the same time counsels a silent submission to civic inferiority such as is bound to sap the manhood of any race in the long run.
3. He advocates common-school and industrial training, and depreciates institutions of higher learning; but neither the Negro common-schools, nor Tuskegee itself, could remain open a day were it not for teachers trained in Negro colleges, or trained by their graduates.

The final element in the paradox brings us to the question at the center of this article: How are African Americans expected to achieve full equality in the United States if they are barred from equal educational opportunity?

The 1954 *Brown* Decision to Desegregate Schools

Fortunately, the U.S. Supreme Court declared, "in *Brown v. Board of Education of Topeka, Kansas* (1954: 347 U.S. 494, 495), that "separate educational facilities are inherently unequal" and ordered the desegregation of the nation's school systems on the following grounds:

> Segregation of white and colored children in public schools has a detrimental effect upon the colored children. The impact is greater when it has the sanction of the law, for the policy of separating the races is usually interpreted as denoting the inferiority of the negro group. A sense of inferiority affects the motivation of a child to learn. Segregation with the sanction of law, therefore, has a tendency to [retard] the educational and mental development of negro children and to deprive them of some of the benefits they would receive in a racial[ly] integrated school system.

Therefore, "racial segregation in public school education was declared unconstitutional" (Barker, Jones, and Tate 1999: 125–126). The landmark case of *Brown* was argued successfully by Thurgood Marshall, the great liberal jurist and African American, who was later selected as an associate justice of the U.S. Supreme Court. The 1954 ruling extended to all domains of public life and "established equal protection for blacks in housing, voting, employment and graduate study" (Stevens 2000c: 1021). Nevertheless, *Brown* did not stop some white Americans, particularly in the South, from thumbing their noses at this famous ruling, as racial discrimination continued to occur at all educational levels in our country. Advocates of white supremacy and white segregationists, like the late George Wallace, once the governor of Alabama, pledged "to stand in the schoolhouse door to prevent enrollment of black students at the University of Alabama" (Stevens 2000d: 1717). That was a sad state of affairs.

Similarly, this racist attitude happened in many southern states, like what occurred in Mississippi in 1961, where James Meredith, a black man and smart college student, who applied for admission to the University of Mississippi or Ole Miss (a PWI), was initially denied because of his race. Even the governor at that time, Ross Barnett, a white segregationist, "became involved and launched an all-out legal battle to ensure that the state's flagship university [Ole Miss] remained segregated." It finally took President John F. Kennedy's intervention— that is, when he sent in "federal troops to Mississippi to execute the court order" to integrate Ole Miss, and to "ensure Meredith's safety, and prevent bloodshed" (Lambert 2010: 3, 115).

Political Contradictions and Controversies

Today, our nation is still struggling with racial segregation and injustices in higher education. This is to say that white supremacists still show intransigence toward racial integration in higher education—that is, unless supremely talented "black" athletes are somehow involved, or recruited to play sports. Moreover, according to the U.S. Government Accountability Office (US-GAO 2016):

> More than 60 years after the Brown decision, our work shows that disparities in education persist and are particularly acute among schools with the highest concentrations of minority and poor students. Further, Black and Hispanic students are increasingly attending high-poverty schools where they face multiple disparities, including less access to academic offerings. Research has shown a clear link between a school's poverty level and student academic outcomes, with higher poverty associated with worse educational outcomes.

As one commentator put it: "America's public schools [and public universities]—62 years after the Supreme Court's historic *Brown vs. Board of Education* decision—are increasingly segregated by race and class" (Toppo 2016: 3). So, despite words to the contrary, and without any question, "education apartheid" still exists in our country in the 21st century. Is this because of the institutional racism that continues to plague our country, which will be hard to eliminate?

Ongoing Denigration of HBCUs

According to former Vice President Joe Biden: "Racism remains an economic anchor that holds back African-Americans and other minority groups" (Bennett 2016: A9). Of course, Biden is absolutely correct. But the issue is really all about the further denigration of black people and the delegitimizing of HBCUs. Consider the fact that historically black colleges and universities only "gained credibility and respect when the Southern Association of Colleges and Schools began formally surveying and accrediting them in 1928" (Purnell 2012). Why did it take so long for this esteemed higher education association to do the right thing? Was it all about race or racism? Fortunately, most HBCUs have been awarded full college or university status today, which is an important factor when state legislatures have to determine if these schools receive state funds.

Of course, a historically black college and university "may be an independent private institution or an undergraduate division of a university" (Stevens 2000e: 368). These institutions do exist, even if many Americans are unaware of them, or are ignorant of the historical significance of these black schools. Unfortunately, some HBCUs have had to close their doors or have declined somewhat in numbers because black students are finally able to attend some white, public universities (PWIs) in greater numbers.

Continuing Efforts to Deny Educational Opportunity

The decline of HBCUs is not necessarily a sign of increased access by African Americans to PWIs. White supremacists are still upset and bitterly opposed to the very idea of integration at *any* white higher educational school level. Long after the *Brown* decision, they continue to throw up as many roadblocks as possible to overcoming the long history of educational apartheid. In this regard, there is still "the highly charged question of race in admissions to public [white] universities" (Biskupic 2015: A9). For example, in *Regents of the University of California v. Bakke* (438 U.S. 267), the U.S. Supreme Court ruled in 1978 that quotas are not permitted, "but the goal of achieving a diverse student body is sufficiently compelling to justify consideration of race in admissions decisions under some circumstances." Thus, it is permitted to have a policy designed so that black students can attend predominantly white colleges and universities, but, in practice, African Americans are still being denied attendance at these prestigious places of higher learning. So is this educational discrimination—by way of non-admission of black students at PWIs—a defense mechanism against the total integration of different ethnic groups? Do PWIs truly want racial diversity?

According to journalists Maria Abascal and Delia Baldassarri (2016: 10): "The real problem is unequal opportunity." Minorities at the PWIs face greater obstacles than white students. Many naysayers and higher education critics believe that African-American and Hispanic students are less qualified to attend these PWIs, especially if they graduate from a segregated, minority high school, because, as Kerr (2016: 2A) points out:

> These [high] schools [tend] to provide fewer math courses, with calculus and seventh and eighth-grade algebra seen as particularly lacking. In science [these segregated schools have fewer] biology, chemistry and physics courses than their more affluent counterparts with fewer minority students.

When it is all said and done, we have only ourselves, as a nation, to blame if African Americans and other minority students are unprepared for college, mostly because of the continued existence of inadequate, segregated minority schools.

The Voucher Menace

In recent years, white Americans have devised another method of circumventing laws requiring desegregation in schools. Private schools, charter schools, white academies, and voucher schools have been established, especially in the southern states. We have wrongly allowed these new methods of undermining our public school system and secondary education.

Proponents of voucher schools have unjustly complained that some state governments "are stifling their liberty by thwarting their attempts to recoup the money they sent to the state to pay for educating their children, but this is a false narrative" (Story 2015: E3). These misguided proponents, mostly white parents, also think that by allowing their children to go to voucher schools or charter schools, they might have a better chance to get into a great college or university. Those parents are particularly supportive when it comes to the creation of all-white voucher schools, private academies, or religious schools. Therefore, this social and political issue is really about white parents not wanting their children to go to primary and secondary schools with supposedly inferior black students and other minority children. Could that perhaps be the result of some notion of racial superiority?

An Unwelcoming Atmosphere

African-American students and other "unprivileged children certainly need a boost because the admission process [to PWIs] typically has discriminated against them" (Bruni 2016: 3). But merely opening the admissions process to predominantly white institutions is not enough. If an African American is admitted to a university and then repeatedly insulted and snubbed socially on campus, that can hardly be categorized as a case of equal educational opportunity. The context in which education occurs is just as important as the content of the curriculum.

Thus, when African-American students are admitted to predominantly white institutions of higher education, white administrators often lack sensitivity to the educational needs of their black students. Sometimes that means taking them for granted, even as they pay lip-service to the challenges faced by low-income black parents and first-generation African-American college students. The former and late President of Virginia Tech, Dr. T. Marshall Hahn, Jr., a white man, even admitted that "*token* integration is still the rule at many Southern institutions that must look to the state for [financial] support" (Fox 2016: 22).

Peer-group support is an important part of success in higher education. Where an emotionally and financially supportive environment fails to materialize, college graduation rates of blacks are generally about 20 percentage points lower than for whites (JBHE 2009: 65). That situation is not inevitable, and one of the most important characteristics of the colleges and universities that have resolved the problem is that they have overcome tokenism. One of the single biggest factors at many of the postsecondary schools with high graduation rates among blacks is the fact that they make up a significant portion of the student body. In those schools, blacks are not isolated:

At Pine Manor College in Chestnut Hill, Massachusetts, the black student graduation rate is 56 percent. This is 16 percentage points higher than the rate for whites. [A high enrollment rate of blacks may explain this situation.] Blacks make up 41 percent of the undergraduate enrollments at Pine Manor College. Clearly, the large percentage of black students on campus makes Pine Manor a welcome place for African Americans. This undoubtedly is a factor in the high retention and graduation rates. (JBHE 2009: 66)

At the other extreme are colleges and universities where the graduation rate of blacks is far below the rate of whites. Some of this is due to the financial strains of high tuition and fees that fall harder on families with lower incomes. But the racial climate on a campus also makes a big difference:

A large graduation rate gap may also mean that blacks simply do not feel comfortable on the particular campus. This can be caused by poor race relations among students, a lack of cultural and social activities geared toward African Americans, or a surrounding community that is inhospitable to blacks or that offers no cultural amenities to the African-American community. Blacks on these campuses with large racial gaps in graduation rates may simply decide to complete their college education elsewhere. (JBHE 2009: 68)

In addition, many predominantly white colleges and universities have a serious problem with hiring and retaining African-American faculty. Dickey (2016: 16) reports on the scope of this problem:

Less than 6% of full-time faculty at four-year [white] institutions are African American. ... Faculty diversity has proved harder to pull off than student body diversity; the problem comprises not only universities' struggle to keep [black] professors from leaving but also the difficulty in diversifying doctoral programs.

The fact that the "black professoriate" is limited or almost nonexistent at some PWIs is an old, sad story in higher education. Even the great Dr. W. E. B. DuBois, who was the first black graduate student to earn his Ph. D. from Harvard University in 1895, could not teach at prestigious Harvard at that time when he applied for employment as a professor, because of his race.

Continuing Need for HBCUs

For all the aforementioned reasons, and until full educational equality for African Americans at white colleges and universities is truly achieved, the need for HBCUs is still necessary—to educate the descendants of black African slaves. This includes the hiring of black faculty—to serve as role models, educational coaches, and mentors. About HBCUs, and toward this end, black scholar Robin White Goode (2016: 1) writes:

> Critics have called them a race-based *anachronism*. Others have said worse: They're inferior, they're in need of a new mission, or they should be managed by for-profit entities. Yet, the data show that historically Black colleges and universities [HBCUs] contribute significantly to the Black middle class and the nation's economy, and in spite of fewer resources, graduate impressive numbers of majors in education and in science, technology, engineering, and mathematics. Although most have a majority Black student body, the faculty at many HBCUs is strikingly diverse, some more than 50% non-Black. [Finally], these institutions have never discriminated on the basis of race.

As far as white colleges and universities (PWIs) are concerned, they must proactively remake their higher educational systems—to benefit all Americans, no matter a person's race or skin color, culture, political beliefs, or religious faith. But "making black students and professors feel truly welcome at predominantly white U.S. colleges will [also] require heavy lifting" (Dickey 2016: 16). More importantly, these white, higher educational institutions, or PWIs, can only change for the good if they open up their universities—to all American citizens and students.

Conclusions

Despite long-standing efforts to undermine their legitimacy, historically black colleges and universities have survived. This is a testament to the strength of will that underlies them. Many HBCUs were established by Christian churches and denominations. Indeed, some of the HBCUs, like Spelman College, began in a church basement in Atlanta, Georgia. In this respect, HBCUs built "their own metrics for success within the realm of their resources, talents, missions, and based on their unique positions as minority serving institutions" (Harris and Gaston 2015: 4). These higher educational schools are rightly devoted exclusively to enabling African-American students to graduate, to better their positions in life, and to take their place as leaders in the larger society. Additionally, as mentioned, these educational objectives are still being met successfully today. More importantly, predominantly black universities are open to students of *any* race or ethnicity, which is a goal predominantly white institutions (PWIs) should strive for, too.

Unfortunately, there is "an ongoing debate at the collegiate and legislative levels across the U.S. ... about the relevance of historically black colleges and universities (HBCUs)" (Harris and Gaston 2015: 1). In contrast to HBCUs, which have never practiced racial segregation or exclusion, predominantly white institutions have practiced separation at the higher education level as a form of "education apartheid." As African Americans have turned their attention to perfecting higher education and other economic issues, southern racists have favored the revival of discriminatory measures. Racists and white segregationists want to maintain the unequal status of African-American students forever, even in higher education. Or so it seems. To be sure, we should be reminded that the goal of white segregationists has always been to keep America divided along racial lines, where "educational apartheid" exists in *perpetuity*. No matter how much progress in education has been made in this country, some white Americans and educators will never be ready for racial equality when it comes to higher education; nor will some be ready for other societal endeavors, particularly when it comes to educational equality. Therein lies the continuing problem.

Therefore, we must ask if there will ever be educational *parity* between HBCUs and PWIs—assuming the former are allowed to continue to exist. Probably not. Behind the scenes, there is a silent war of attrition against all public institutions of higher education, but the HBCUs are hardest hit because they have been underfunded through their entire history. As a result, Harris and Gaston (2015: 2) ask: "Can HBCUs fiscally manage in these turbulent and uncertain times and still remain relevant, as many state legislatures have continued to decrease funding to [all] institutions of higher education?" Of course, dividing a diverse nation or multiracial democracy across racial or ethnic lines has never been a good thing, particularly when there has been so much focus on nationality, citizenship, and higher educational preparedness.

Nevertheless, African Americans will continue to actively protest their dissatisfaction with the *unfair* educational systems across our country. Rightly so, given that higher education is the key to a better life in the United States. Finally, it should be an obligation for our entire society to educate, in a fully integrated way, the descendants of former black African slaves, and everyone else for that matter. In this way, there will not be some kind of fixed quota system for African-American students at professional and higher educational institutions. Unless predominantly white institutions abandon the practice of considering race, religion, gender, or the wealth of a particular student in admission decisions, this education issue will always be with us, and never solved.

It should be noted, nonetheless, that providing educational equality and diversity at *all* higher educational institutions is still more complicated than we can imagine. Of course, it is going to be a colossal educational challenge—to fully integrate all of our HBCUs and PWIs. Yet, it is not an impossible thing to achieve. Finally, it is astonishing that some American citizens cannot realize the necessity of these higher education goals. Indeed, if our nation cannot integrate our higher educational institutions as a cohesive whole, the government and our country will never solve our considerable and intractable racial and education problems at all levels of higher education. In that case, the need for separate colleges and universities will always be with us.

Notes

1. The research referenced in this quotation can be found at: Mason (1997), Conley (1999), and Mangino (2010).

2. Lest one imagine that the discrimination encountered by black veterans in education was compensated by other features of the G.I. Bill in housing and business loans or unemployment benefits, those aspects of the program were even more tightly restricted to whites by the Veterans Administration (Murray 2008: 980–981): "Both the loan program and the unemployment assistance program operated at the local level and were prone to parochialism and racism in the distribution of benefits."

References

Abascal, Maria, and Delia Baldassarri. (2016). "Don't Blame Diversity for Distrust." *New York Times* May 22: 10.

Ann. (2008). "Jackson State and Kent State—1970." *Beautiful, Also, Are the Souls of My Black Sisters.* Blog. https://kathmanduk2.wordpress.com/2008/04/jackson-state-and-kent-state-1970

Barker, Lucius J., Mack H. Jones, and Katherine Tate. (1999). *African Americans and the American Political System,* 4th ed., pp. 125–126, Upper Saddle River, NJ: Prentice Hall.

Bennett, John T. (2016). "Institutional Racism Plagues Minorities, Biden Says." *Las Vegas Review Journal.* May 20.

Biskupic, Joan. (2015). "Affirmative Action in Admissions to be Revisited." *Las Vegas Review Journal* December 7: A9.

Blum, Edward J. (2005). *Reforging the White Republic: Race, Religion, and American Nationalism, 1865–1898.* Baton Rouge: Louisana State Press.

Bruni, Frank. (2016). "More Low-Income College Students a Boon to All." *Las Vegas Sun* June 2: 3.

Carnevale, Anthony P., and Jeff Strohl. (2011). "Our Economically Polarized College System: Separate and Unequal." *Chronicle of Higher Education* September 30: B32.

Committee on the Future of the Colleges of Agriculture in the Land Grant University System. (1995). *Colleges of Agriculture at the Land Grant Universities: A Profile.* Washington, DC: National Academy Press.

Conley, Dalton. (1999). *Being Black, Living in the Red: Race, Wealth, and Social Policy in America.* Berkeley, CA: University of California Press.

Dickey, Jack. (2016). "What Schools Should Learn from Student Protests." *Time* May 23: 16.

Dubois, W. E. Burghardt. (1903). *The Souls of Black Folk: Essays and Sketches,* 2nd ed. Chicago: A. C. McClurg and Co. https://archive.org/details/cu31924024920492

Fox, Margalit. (2016). "Obituary, T. M. Hahn, 89, President Who Remade Virginia Tech." *New York Times* June 5: 22.

Goode, Robin White. (2016). "The HBCU Debate: Are Black Colleges & Universities Still Needed?" *Black Enterprise:* 1–2. http://www.blackenter-prise.com/lifestyle/are-hbcus-still-relevant

Hamilton, Darrick, Tressie McMillan Cottom, Alan A. Aja, Carolyn Ash, and William Darity Jr. (2015). "Still We Rise: The Continuing Case for America's Historically Black Colleges and Universities." *American Prospect* November 9. http://prospect.org/article/why-black-colleges-and-universities-still-matter

Harper, Shaun R., Lori D. Patton, and Ontario S Wooden. (2009). "Access and Equity for African American Students in Higher Education: A Critical Race Historical Analysis of Policy Efforts."*Journal of Higher Education* 80 (4): 389–414.

Harris, Gregory J., and Herron Gaston. (2015). "The Enduring Relevance of HBCUs in America." *Huffpost College* March 23: 1–5. http://www.huffingtonpost.com/herron-keyon-gaston.

Harris, William H., and Judith S. Levey, eds. (1975a). "The Morrill Act (1862)." *The New Columbia Encyclopedia.* New York: Columbia University Press.

———. (1975b). "Hampton University." *The New Columbia Encyclopedia.* New York: Columbia University Press.

———. (1975c). "Carlisle Indian School." *The New Columbia Encyclopedia.* New York: Columbia University Press.

———. (1975d). "Tuskegee Institute." *The New Columbia Encyclopedia.* New York: Columbia University Press.

———. (1975e). "Plessey vs. Ferguson." *The New Columbia Encyclopedia.* New York: Columbia University Press.

——— (1975f). "Washington, Booker Taliaferro." *The New Columbia Encyclopedia.* New York: Columbia University Press.

———. (1975g). "Thurgood Marshall." *The New Columbia Encyclopedia.* New York: Columbia University Press.

Herbold, Hilary. (1994–1995). "Never a Level Playing Field: Blacks and the GI Bill."*Journal of Blacks in Higher Education* 6: 104–108.

JBHE. (2009). "College Graduation Rates: Where Black Students Do the Best and Where They Fare Poorly Compared to Their White Peers." *Journal of Blacks in Higher Education* 65 (Autumn): 65–69.

Katznelson, Ira. (2005). *When Affirmative Action was White: An Untold History of Racial Inequality in Twentieth-Century America*. New York: W.W. Norton.

Kerr, Jennifer C. (2016). "Segregation in Public Schools Deepening." *Las Vegas Review Journal* May 18: 2A.

Lambert, Frank. (2010). *The Battle of Ole Miss: Civil Rights vs. States' Rights*. New York: Oxford University Press.

Liontas, Annie. (2016. "Inherit the Word." *New York Times Book Review* June 5.

Mangino, William. (2010). "Race to College: The 'Reverse Gap.'" *Race and Social Problems* 2(3):164–178.

Mason, Patrick L. (1997). "Race, Culture, and Skill: Interracial Wage Differences Among African Americans, Latinos, and Whites." *Review of Black Political Economy* 25 (3): 5–39.

Mettler, Suzanne. (2005). *Soldiers & Citizens: The G.I. Bill and the Making of the Greatest Generation*. New York: Oxford University Press.

Murray, Melissa. (2008). "When War Is Work: The G.I. Bill, Citizenship, and the Civic Generation." *California Law Review* 96 (4): 967–998.

Museus, Samuel D., Maria C. Ledesma, and Tara L. Parker. (2015). *Racism and Racial Equity in Higher Education*. ASHE Higher Education Report 42(1). Hoboken, NJ: Wiley Periodicals. https://books.google.com/books?id=w2pcCwAAQBAJ

Onkst, David H. (1998). "'First a Negro … Incidentally a Veteran': Black World War Two Veterans and the G. I. Bill of Rights in the Deep South, 1944–1948." *Journal of Social History* 31(3): 517–543.

Purnell, Hannah. (2012). "The History of Historically Black Colleges and Universities: A Tradition Rich in History." *College View* 1–5. http://www.collegeview.com/articles/article/the-history-of-historically-black-colleges-and-universities

Roebuck, Julian B., and Komanduri Murty. (1993). *Historically Black Colleges and Universities: Their Place in American Higher Education*. Westport, CT: Praeger.

Servicemen's Readjustment Act. (1944). *United States Statutes at Large* 58: 284–291. http://www.loc.gov/law/help/statutes-at-large/78th-congress/c78s2.pdf

Spofford, Tom. (1988). *Lynch Street: The May, 1970 Slayings at Jackson State College*. Kent, OH: Kent State University Press.

Stevens, Mark A., ed. (2000a). "Morrill (Land Grant College) Act of 1862." *Merriam Webster's Collegiate Encyclopedia*. Springfield, MA: Merriam-Webster, Inc.

——. (2000b). "Howard University." *Merriam Webster's Collegiate Encyclopedia*. Springfield, MA: Merriam-Webster, Inc.

——. (2000c). "Marshall, Thurgood." *Merriam Webster's Collegiate Encyclopedia*. Springfield, MA: Merriam-Webster, Inc.

——. (2000d). "Wallace, George Corley." *Merriam Webster's Collegiate Encyclopedia*. Springfield, MA: Merriam-Webster, Inc.

———. (2000e). "College." *Merriam Webster's Collegiate Encyclopedia.* Springfield, MA: Merriam-Webster, Inc.

Story, Tod. (2015). "Vouchers Violate State's Constitution." *Las Vegas Review Journal* September 27: E3.

Toppo, Greg. (2016). "Segregation Worsening in U.S. Schools, Study Finds." *USA Today* May 18.

Turner, Sarah and John Bound. (2003). "Closing the Gap or Widening the Divide: The Effects of the GI Bill and World War II on the Educational Outcomes of Black Americans." *Journal of Economic History* 63 (1): 145–177.

U.S. General Accounting Office (US-GAO). (2016). *K–12 EDUCATION Better Use of Information Could Help Agencies Identify Disparities and Address Racial Discrimination.* April. GAO-16-345. Washington, DC: U.S. General Accounting Office. http://www.gao.gov/assets/680/676745.pdf

Washington, Booker T. ([18951 1974). *Atlanta Exposition Address.* Speech delivered in Atlanta at the Cotton States and International Exposition. In *The Booker T. Washington Papers, Vol. 3.* Ed. Louis R. Harlan, pp. 583–587. Urbana: University of Illinois Press. Speech available at http://history-matters.gmu.edu/d/39/

Woodson, Carter G. (1915). *The Education of the Negro Prior to 1861: A History of the Education of the Colored People of the United States from the Beginning of Slavery to the Civil War.* New York: G. P. Putnam's Sons. https://archive.org/details/educationofnegrooowooduoft

Brown vs. Board of Education and the Unfulfilled Hopes for Racial and Educational Reform

A Political Analysis of Derrick Bell's *Silent Covenants*

Earnest N. Bracey, Ph.D.

Introduction

The late professor Derrick Bell's book, *Silent Covenants* succinctly explores the political consequences of the *Brown vs. Board of Education (of Topeka)* decision in terms of racial justice and equality for African Americans. In this regard, "the U.S. Supreme Court ruled unanimously that racial segregation in public schools violated the 14th Amendment to the U.S. Constitution, which says that no state may deny equal protection of the laws to any person within its jurisdiction."[1] Bell also examines the various compromises of the 1954 case, which has been unfortunately undermined in recent years, especially in regards to school integration in public schools throughout the United States. Although the *Brown* decision was "restricted in application to *de jure* [or legal] segregation, the decision was applied mainly to Southern [school] systems."[2]

Additionally, Bell weaves a compelling and controversial argument that tries to get Americans to think critically about the necessity and importance of racial cooperation. When the famous *Brown* case was finally decided upon, it was "hailed by many Americans as a firm judicial statement of the nation's commitment to racial equality."[3] Not surprisingly, the *Brown* decision has not been embraced or accepted by everyone, especially some staunch conservatives throughout the years. Indeed, the late Supreme Court Justice Thurgood Marshall "completely misread the fierce determination of *white crackers* in the Deep South to maintain the Jim Crow system of segregated schools."[4] Moreover, in a sense, the famous ruling has been almost rendered moot by many Americans, as they see it, perhaps, as unnecessary. However, we must be cognizant

Earnest N. Bracey, "Brown vs. Board of Education and the Unfulfilled Hopes for Racial and Educational Reform: A Political Analysis of Derrick Bell's Silent Covenants," *International Journal of Business and Social Research*, vol 3, no. 10, pp. 13–20. Copyright © LAR Center Press (CC BY 4.0).

that the *Brown* decision "rested on the principle that intentionally public action to support segregation was a violation of the U.S. Constitution."[5]

Equally important, Bell makes it clear that some Americans would like to relegate this historical and ground-breaking case to our collective memories, or perhaps *consign* it to the annals of history, instead of prominently reminding our school children and their parents of its significance. Moreover, the *Brown* decision "provided a tremendous impetus to the civil rights movement of the 1950s and 1960s and immeasurably hastened the end of segregation in all public facilities and accommodations."[6] However, in some quarters, the *Brown* decision is being ignored in the curriculums of high schools and some major colleges and universities. Or so it seems. Some might even say that the *Brown* decision has all but been forgotten, at least for some people. Is it simply because Americans today could care less about this righteous decision made by the Supreme Court to legislate equality in this country, especially as it concerns the broken public education system in the United States?

And as more and more young Americans spend less time reading, contemplating and especially thinking critically about this important case—or even considering such matters as racial justice and equality—the more insignificant the *Brown* decision has become for them. However, it should be remembered that this case also led to "the landmark Civil Rights Act of 1964," which fortunately "ended not only segregation's rank injustice but also a paralyzing stigma on the white South, leading to Sunbelt prosperity."[7] Therefore, in our current political environment, Bell's controversial book, *Silent Covenants,* should be a welcomed and needed kick to our collective *psyches* or ill-fitting pants, figuratively speaking, in that we should be required to remember the importance and percepts of the Supreme Court's *Brown* decision, to truly understand what is happening in our high-schools, as well as college and university classrooms across the United States. Furthermore, according to Bell, we are now fighting a losing battle, so to speak, in terms of realizing the promise of the *Brown* decision. Indeed, there has been a serious disconnect with our young people being cognizant of *Brown vs. Board of Education of Topeka,* and the civil rights movement of the 1960s. As Bell suggests, moreover, there hasn't been any significant progress toward dismantling racial prejudice and discrimination in some American schools, particularly in the Southern states,[8] because of the landmark decision. Furthermore, the decision has often been misinterpreted, misrepresented and undermined, as will be explained later. There are those that even think that the famous *Brown* decision was ill-conceived, and executed. For example, many southern politicians "denounced the Court's decision."[9]

And even under Federal Court orders and the threat of loss of Federal funds, some Southern states, like Mississippi, Louisiana, South Carolina and others are still resisting (indirectly) the integration of public schools after the *Brown* decision. Is this because white Southerners are still not ready for total racial equality and desegregation? Probably not. In this respect, Bell's *Silent Covenants* is a profound effort to describe some of the major difficulties, as mentioned, in fully implementing all aspects of the *Brown* decision, even in the twenty-first century. Hence, the ignorance (by many Americans) of the *Brown* decision is more of an indictment on America's reluctance to do the right thing toward its minority groups. Of course, a more enlightened citizenry should be able to clearly see that there is still the need for racial integration in our various schools and society at large. Unfortunately, according to Bell, the *Brown* decision has not advanced beyond some American citizen's dark imaginings about the fairness of education in the twenty-first century.

No doubt, there was something deeply disingenuous about the 1896 Supreme Court's condoning of unfair segregation laws, essentially making them legal, like sanctioning the racist "separate-but-equal doctrine." Put another way, the 1896 U.S. Supreme Court ruling "established the legality of racial segregation so long as facilities were "separate but equal.""[10] But this was a decision that was on the wrong side of history. Indeed, this discriminatory edict by the highest court "was used to justify segregation in many areas of American life for nearly sixty years."[11] Moreover, the insensitive decision by the U.S. Supreme Court at that time upheld the misguided Louisiana law, "requiring separate rail cars for blacks and whites."[12] Ultimately, the racial decision "led to the adoption throughout the South of a comprehensive series of Jim Crow Laws,"[13] which controlled almost every aspect of a black person's life. Political historian Michael Meyerson writes:

> In upholding a Louisiana law requiring railroad companies to provide separate coaches for whites and African Americans, the Supreme court declared that any perception that the law inflicted a "badge of inferiority" was only in the minds of those challenging the law: if this be so, it is not by reason of anything found in the act [Plessy vs. Ferguson], but solely because the colored race chooses to put that construction upon it.[14]

What nonsense. Or was this so much misguided, illogical thinking? The idea of denying one particular ethnic group or poor people their rights of social justice, and educational equality and opportunity, because of race or skin-color, is clearly a manifestation of evil, and plain ignorance. Eventually (and unsurprisingly), the Supreme Court in the *Brown* decision "stressed that the badge of inferiority stamped on minority children by segregation hindered their full development no matter how equal the physical facilities."[15] Furthermore, some might say that the *Brown* decision was a bold, decisive and courageous act on the part of the Supreme Court. However, changing the racist "separate-but-equal" policy was an amazing leap of faith, especially for progressively-minded Supreme Court Justice Earl Warren, a white man, who led "the 1954 unanimous decision of the court ... ending segregation in the nation's schools."[16] To say the least, the *Brown* decision was never a mistake or misguided idea in that it was a recognition of African Americans' humanity and citizenship. Indeed, "the unequal treatment of [black] children violated the equal protection clause of the Fourteenth Amendment to the U.S. Constitution."[17]

Fortunately, for all American citizens, the *Plessy vs. Ferguson* ruling was rightly overturned in 1954 by the *Brown* decision, but it was not without a fight and other difficulties. This is to say that the *Brown* decision was far from inevitable, especially for white conservatives in the segregated South. Many white Southerners, as well as some prejudiced, cowardly federal district judges, like John Parker of South Carolina, found themselves totally opposed to total desegregation and integration in American schools.[18] And according to professor Peter Irons:

> Even those [federal judges] who felt themselves bound by their judicial oath to uphold the Supreme Court's rulings had little enthusiasm for ordering any "forth with" integration in districts where local officials had vowed to close schools rather than allow white and black students to sit in the same classroom.[19]

More importantly, the hostile reaction, as mentioned, by some in the white community was actually common place throughout most of the United States at that time. The *Brown* decision certainly wasn't a fool proof method of eliminating racial inequality in our public school systems, and other segregated places; but it was, nonetheless, a serious attempt by the Court to correct things for African Americans in terms of education. It was also hoped, particularly by the 1954 Supreme Court, that many racist people would possibly adjust their narrow-minded ideas and thinking, as well as their prejudice attitudes or mind-sets, rather than continuing to embrace White Supremacy, and the racist philosophy of the dominant group. Nevertheless, this matter came to a head "on May 17, 1954," where "the Supreme court of the United States" completely "outlawed racial segregation in public schools," finally setting aside the "separate but equal" doctrine that the court had upheld in 1896."[20] In essence, the Supreme Court rejected and overturned the "separate but equal" doctrine, disavowing the infamous *Plessy vs. Ferguson* decision.[21]

For members of the civil rights community, the *Brown* decision was an incredible, humane accomplishment, as well as an amazing breakthrough in terms of race relations and racial equality. Consequently, we must ask the question: Were *all* Americans at the time of its implementation even capable of meeting the objectives and specifics of the historic Supreme Court ruling? Apparently not. White Southerners, of course, frowned upon any principles of freedom and justice for African Americans. Or so it seemed. Perhaps most important, according to Bell, a due diligent assessment of the *Brown* decision should have been made, as it is an illusion (then and now) to think that people don't draw the line when it comes to race. For example, the *Brown* decision was devastating to white racists, who believed that black people shouldn't have any rights whatsoever. In retrospect, these Americans were/are without conscience. Even more important, it should be uppermost in our minds that the *Brown* decision "was actually four cases brought from different areas of the South and the border states, involving public elementary or high-school systems that mandated separate schools for blacks and whites."[22]

In this respect, and presumably, the argument and confrontation over segregation in America's public schools also renewed long-standing allegations of institutional racism. Which is to say that racial segregation was never an *aberration,* but it was a reality, a deliberate act to maintain power and control over the destiny of a group of American minorities, or different ethnic groups, and educational policies in the United States. So was racial discrimination, regarding the segregation of public schools, a "broadly shared cultural phenomenon or condition" inculcated in only white Americans? Perhaps. It is interesting to note here that Bell tells us in *Silent Covenants* that some dominant group members have an obsessive need to dominate and discriminate against people of color. Indeed, denying minorities their Constitutional rights has been more than a past time by some racists, especially on top of the American political, social, and economic pyramid. But why should we try to fully understand or comprehend the state of mind of racists? And why should it matter? As mentioned, the 1954 Supreme Court took extraordinary measures to prepare white Americans for the new, education policy changes—that is, in regards to the *Brown* decision, particularly in the South. But the court failed in that regard.

Maybe it wasn't enough. In view of all this: How exactly could the Supreme Court positively stress that the *Brown* decision was more of a collective challenge, and not a threat? Or did the court really think about the political ramifications? As discussed earlier, the *Brown* decision has never been fully accepted by some conservatives and White Southerners. Perhaps this is why some have all but abandoned public schools and established their own private, voucher and religious academies. Sidlow and Henschen explain it this way:

> The Supreme court ruling [or the *Brown* decision] did not go unchallenged. Bureaucratic loopholes were used to delay desegregation. Another reaction was "white flight." As white parents sent their children to newly established private schools, some formerly white-only public schools became 100 percent black.[23]

Perhaps a certain note of fragility should have been noted initially about the *Brown* decision, as it appears that things have not necessarily worked out for the best, in terms of school desegregation. What is very surprising about this notion is the fact that "the *Brown* decision was limited to the public schools, but it was [also] believed to imply that segregation [was] not permissible in other public facilities."[24] Notwithstanding, the problems of the *Brown* decision could not have been clearly foreseen. And after the Supreme Court ordered that schools integrate, resistance and ill-feelings followed immediately in most Southern states. Indeed, the ubiquitous efforts to *interdict* and circumvent the *Brown* decision has been in full swing, for many years; and continuously undermined behind the scenes in some quarters in the United States. Although "guidelines for ending segregation were presented and school boards were advised to proceed "with all deliberate speed,"[25] there has always been those who have stood in the way of full implementation. And it would be fair to conclude that the ruling is precariously balanced. Moreover, it is perhaps unfortunate that the desegregation of public schools in America had to be adjudicated rather than legislated.

Nevertheless, the Supreme Court still ruled that all public schools should integrate with "all deliberate speed," based on equitable principles and a "practical flexibility," which are quite mysterious, non-committal words, as suggested previously. But needless to say, the Supreme Court *never* actually ordered the immediate end to racial segregation in the United States. Why not? And what exactly did the Court mean by ending segregation in schools "with all deliberate speed?" Indeed, this is a very elusive statement or *phrase*. According to Bresler and others, "deliberate speed proved to be a turtle's pace."[26] In fact, "a decade after the Court's pronouncement, less than one percent of the [African] American children in the states of the old Confederacy were attending public school with white children. [And] in six border states and the District of Columbia the figure [is] much higher: 52 percent."[27] Put another way, the *Brown* decision:

> Made the cautious and ultimately disastrous, declaration that the Southern schools districts must undertake desegregation measures "with all deliber-ate speed," a phrase which many southern school districts chose to interpret as sometime in the *afterlife*.[28]

Unfortunately, because of the under-belly of racial animus that still exist in this nation, we still have people who reject the idea of integration and progressive educational changes. But the clock will never be turned back because of such racial misgivings.

Ostensibly, the nine Supreme Court justices involved in the *Brown* decision were also saying that White Supremacy *anywhere* must be challenged *everywhere*, while dismissing the racist notion that black people are somehow inferior. Far more significant, how exactly can we mea-sure the untold psychic damage done to many African Americans? Or should we ignore this specific racial point completely? These questions posed by Bell in *Silent Covenants* inform us that we should *never* dismiss such important and overriding notions. Additionally, American citizens must *never* forget the sacrifices made by African Americans and white Americans, so that the *Brown* decision could actually become reality. Thurgood Marshall, who became the first African American Supreme Court Justice in 1967, should be praised, and *never* forgotten, for his part in the desegregation effort. After all, Marshall was the great black legal scholar and attorney who successfully argued the controversial *Brown vs. Board of Education* case before the Supreme Court as the chief legal counsel of the NAACP. Marshall later became the calm, pragmatic liberal voice of the Supreme Court when he became a member himself after serving as the U.S. Solicitor General for two years previously. In addition, Thurgood Marshall "was a steadfast liberal during his tenure on the Court, championing the rights of the individual, 1st Amendment freedoms, and affirmative action."[29]

Consequently, Thurgood Marshall was uniquely positioned to fight for the rights of African Americans, persuading the Supreme Court to do the right thing for all Americans in their controversial rulings, which was certainly advantageous to black people and other minorities in the United States. And as many might know, Marshall was *both* hated and feared because of his oratory and brilliant lawyering skills, as well as his audaciousness. For example, Marshall "won 29 of 32 cases he argued before the U.S. Supreme Court … and others that established equal protection for blacks in housing, voting, employment, and graduate study."[30] And before his death in 1997, Marshall became the most eloquent and unique voice of social consciousness, and the champion on the court for progressive liberal causes and the rights and liberties of every American citizen. Evidently, without the *Brown* decision, school desegregation probably would have been unthinkable, and never realized in any fashion. Hence, we must all keep in mind this monumental case as we consider dealing with the ugliness of our American society in terms of minority education and academics.

The Reintroduction of School Segregation

Many Americans, moreover, remain in denial about the necessity for racial integration in all of our schools and society, as they are perhaps intellectually *bankrupt* by not being taught the truth about the intrepid *Brown* decision, and the real good it provides in regards to race-relations. In this sense, American citizens should be seized with concern about the re-segregation of K–12 schools, especially in Southern States. In other words, it is essential to recognize that *education inequality* continues to exist in the United States, no matter what the respective states have tried to do to equalize and integrate things. Furthermore, racial discrimination and other educational problems have increased, as fairness and the objectives of educational laws are routinely ignored by government leaders in mostly Southern States. Additionally, residential segregation continues in many wealthy housing and suburban neighborhoods, unabated, today, especially because of the elimination of massive school busing to achieve more integrated school settings. Equally important, "America funds its schools through property taxes, ensuring the most disadvantaged students are warehoused together in the worst schools."[31]

Moreover, in the 1980s and 1990s, the Supreme Court allowed cities and respective states to discontinue its school integration efforts, which were set down or established by the *Brown* decision. As professor Meyerson has written: "There should be no disagreement years after the 1954 ruling of *Brown* vs. Board of Education and the Civil Rights Act of 1964, as school systems and employers [continue] to be found guilty of deliberate racial discrimination, [and] the paths for success ... of greatly disproportionate length. One also needs not be a Pollyanna to assert that the situation has since improved."[32] Or this assumption is what some opponents of *Brown* want us to believe. Truth be told, things really haven't changed significantly in terms of educating our young people today, in a fully integrated way. Which is to say, the United States hasn't shown real maturity in embracing the *Brown* decision. And perhaps even worse, we are repeating the history of our past by re-segregating our various schools again, which is basically segregated at the same level as they were during the 1970s, in the South. Orfield puts it this way:

> Public decisions that re-create segregation, sometimes even more severe than before desegregation orders, are now deemed acceptable. These new re-segregation decisions legitimate a deliberate return to segregation. As long as school districts temporarily maintain some aspects of desegregation for several years and do not express an intent to discriminate, the Court approves plans to send minority students back to segregation.[33]

In this regard, and for some, as mentioned, *Brown vs. Board of Education* is just a temporary ruling or outdated decision; and will be eventually overturned, in time. But needless to say, there is still the necessity to be true to the spirit of the law. To deny that the *Brown* decision is not necessary today is to be naïve and foolhardy, as interracial schooling is vital to the well-being of our nation and multiracial democracy. In so many words, we have a moral obligation to live together as humans, no matter what racists say to the contrary. Paradoxically, Bell believed that the success of the *Brown* decision is an illusion. No doubt, his position has confounded almost *everyone*, especially in the predominantly white academia. Obviously, Bell's focus was not to praise the *Brown* decision as some crowning achievement, because he firmly believed—before his death—that the opposite was true; nor has the ground-breaking Court ruling proved to be as influential as it should. Indeed, Bell argues that the principle ideas of the *Brown* decision have not been fully realized. Therefore, the consequences have been somewhat mystifying and ineffective. Thus, to praise the *Brown* decision now, as evidence of the progress the United States has made, in terms of education and race-relations, is disingenuous at best. It has obviously been difficult carrying out the important things spelled out in the *Brown* decision.

Equality of Education in The United States

Undoubtedly, *Brown vs. Board of Education* is a powerful expression of how things ought to be in educating the American people. The facts, however, tell a more damning story. Or the truth is that African Americans continue to be deeply and profoundly harmed by the racism that still exist in our education systems. Perhaps some in the dominant group cannot get used to the fact that African Americans and other minorities are not inferior human beings, or some sub-human species. More than fifty years ago, the Supreme Court boldly proclaimed that:

> Separate educational facilities are inherently unequal. ... Liberty under law extends to the full range of conduct which an individual is free to pursue, and it *cannot* be restricted except for a proper governmental objective. [And] segregation in public education is not reasonably related to any proper governmental objective.[34]

Although the education system in the United States will continue to change from time to time, or in the near future, there solution of school desegregation or integration must be faced "head-on," not ignored, or summarily dismissed by our educators. Indeed, separating people or students on the basis of race or different ethnic groups—by devising discriminatory policies, as well as certain outrageous schemes of law—should never be condoned or tolerated. Unfortunately, Americans remain somehow uncertain about how to achieve or insure equality of education for all of its citizens. Hence, there is no doubt that while minimal changes have been made in our public school systems, it is not possible to put on a false or misleading front anymore about the reality of the *Brown* decision. Bell wrote:

> Over the decades, the *Brown* decision, like other landmark cases, has gained a life quite apart from the legal questions it was intended to settle. The passage of time has calmed both the ardor of its admirers and the ire of its detractors. Today, of little use as legal precedent, it has gained in reputation as a measure of what law and society might be. That noble image, dulled by resistance to any but minimal steps toward compliance, has transformed *Brown* into a magnificent mirage, the legal equivalent of that city on a hill to which all aspire without any serious thought that it will ever be attained.[35]

Should we object to Bell's terse reasoning and harsh pronouncements? Or is his main premise simply the truth? Of course, Bell is equally dismissive of *any* talk about not needing to adhere to the *Brown* decision anymore, because we live in a post-racial America, which is a myth. Furthermore, the *Brown* decision, as mentioned, should not be considered irrelevant today as some legal, conservative scholars have suggested. In this regard, Bell makes a lot of sense, and was most convincing when he got on his proverbial soapbox, rhetorically speaking, like an influential televangelist, who told us that we should supplant *White Supremacy* in the United States with total integration, and equality—that is, for the *Brown* decision to work properly, or at all in the future. Or will the famous ruling fail because of white American resistance? More importantly, should we view the *Brown* decision as a bothersome complexity of judicial activism?

Bell, of course, provides, in *Silent Covenants,* the intellectual wherewithal and reasoning to ultimately explore the future necessity of the *Brown* decision. Bell also provides us with his revelation about the continuing inequality that exist in America today, not only in our educational schools systems, but also in our national psyche as well. It seems that we cannot ignore the politics of this important issue. But those who are intimately acquainted with the famous *Brown* ruling see it as more of only an educational issue, not a political matter. Nonetheless, some conservative Americans are determined and dedicated to overturning or repealing the *Brown* decision, eventually, which might send an ominous message to all Americans: that it is okay to separate our people in educational pursuits and endeavors along racial lines; and to unjustly discriminate based on skin-color. The "mutability of the past," in regards to the *Brown* decision tells us that minority citizens should not have to face terrible racial indignities again, such as educational segregation, and societal disenfranchisement.

Conclusion

When it is all said and done, it might be very difficult, perhaps, to keep concerns about school equality in perspective, or in the political limelight, if not for the *Brown* decision. Toward this end, it should be noted that the public schools in our nation today are facing a crisis in terms of *re-segregation* and their total elimination. In addition, there is no general or infallible agreement on the matter of integration in our schools nationwide, despite the *Brown* decision. Unfortunately, some opponents of the *Brown* decision see the public school system/ educational institutions as monolithic, government-sanctioned entities, which are no longer needed. But this is a misperception. Furthermore, it should be noted that the *Brown* ruling wasn't easy for the Supreme Court to make, nor was it a desperate measure. Indeed, it was the right thing to do, even though it has been considerably more troublesome than first envisioned, particularly in the Southern states. But despite the failure of full implementation, the *Brown* decision is still necessary, because of the nation's long history of racial pluralism and discrimination against African Americans and other minorities.

Perhaps America will lose its way, as Bell predicts, if we forget why the *Brown* decision was established in the first place. Some educators, moreover, see the education of all Americans in an integrated way as trivial. In the end, it would be a disservice to all of us if we ignore the lessons of the *Brown* decision. Finally, on a broader level, we must find a means to communicate and remind Americans about the significance of the *Brown* decision, without fear of some repercussion. Additionally, this famous Supreme Court ruling should resonate and matter to all Americans. Ultimately, understanding the positive aspects or intricacies, and meaning of the *Brown* decision should be an essential part of our primary and formal education. Nor should we forget that "we-the-people" were once on the verge of doing great things in terms of education because of the *Brown* decision. But without a commitment from the Court today, it seems like we are regressing when it comes to public school integration, and educational equality. Is this because our federal government is indifferent? Or more conservative? Or is it because of the apathy of the American people?

According to professor Meyerson, "there is no common unit agreed on for measuring the amount of equality in a society."[36] However, there should be some way to check the tyranny of the dominant group and an activist Supreme Court. Journalist Adam Liptak tells us that the current Court is "one of the most activist courts in history," with a "readiness to over-turn legislation" like the *Brown* decision.[37] To be sure, this controversial Court ruling tries to resolve some of the inequalities in our many public school systems. But the decision has had, over the years, varying levels or degrees of success and failures. In this respect, the *Brown* decision will not be viewed by all Americans as the defining document (in terms of racial integration) it was meant to be, particularly in our educational systems. The prob-lem still lies in trying to correctly discern and apply this important Supreme Court ruling, especially for the future.

Bell's *Silent Covenants* also provides an interesting back story about the history and future of the *Brown* decision. Finally, Bell advises us to pay attention to what matters most in educating the American public. Hence, the dominant group must *never* undermine the core essence of the *Brown* decision, which might possibly disrupt our country and educa-tional institutions, as in the past, along racial lines, tearing our nation apart from within. Unfortunately, some opponents believe that their lives would be secured by eliminating such a monumental ruling as the *Brown* decision, which has tried to equalize education for all its people; but such a move just might spell the end of our democracy, and sabotage the idea of creating a more perfect Union.

Notes

1. Mark A. Stevens, ed., *Merriam-Webster's Collegiate Encyclopedia* (Springfield, MA: Merriam Inc., 2000), 240.

2. William H. Harris and Judith S. Levey, "Brown vs. Board of Education of Topeka, Kansas," *The New Columbia Encyclopedia* (New York: Columbia University Press, 1975), 380. It should be pointed out that school segregation in southern states had been "achieved through the Gerrymandering of school districts."

3. Peter Irons, *Jim Crow's Children: The Broken Promise of the Brown Decision* (New York: Penguin Books, 2002), x.

4. Ibid., 172.

5. Gary Orfield, "Dismantling Desegregation: The Quiet Reversal of Brown vs. Board of Education," in *Civil Rights and Civil Liberties*, ed., M. O'Brien, 2nd ed., (Baltimore MD: Lanahan Publishers, Inc., 2003), 252.

6. Harris and Levey, "Brown vs. Board of Education," 380.

7. Taylor Branch, "Remembering the March," *USA Weekend*, August 16–18, 2013, 8.

8. Derrick Bell, *Silent Covenants: Brown vs. Board of Education and the Unfulfilled Hopes for Racial Reform* (New York: Oxford University Press, 2004), 4.

9. Irons, *Jim Crow's Children*, 172–173. It should be noted that the federal district courts have "jurisdiction over lawsuits to enforce the desegregation decision. ..." See Harris and Levey, "Integration," *The New Columbia Encyclopedia* (New York: Columbia University Press, 1975), 1347.

10. Stevens, *Merriam Webster's Collegiate Encyclopedia*, 1279.

11. Edward Sidlow and Beth Henschen, *America at Odds*, 4th ed. (Belmont, CA: Wadsworth/Thomson Learning, 2004), 103.

12. Stevens, *Merriam-Webster's Collegiate Encyclopedia*, 1279.

13. Harris and Levey, "Plessy vs. Ferguson," *The New Columbia Encyclopedia* (New York: Columbia University Press, 1975), 2168.

14. Michael Meyerson, *Political Numeracy: Mathematical Perspectives on Our Chaotic Constitution* (New York and London: W. W. Norton & Company, 2002), 142.

15. Harris and Levey, "Brown vs. Board of Education, 380.

16. Harris and Levey, "Earl Warren," *The New Columbia Encyclopedia* (New York: Columbia University Press, 1975), 2930.

17. Harris and Levey, "Brown vs. Board of Education," 380.

18. Irons, *Jim Crow's Children*, 174.

19. Ibid., 174. It must be pointed out that you cannot legislate a racist person's feelings or ideological direction.

20. Langston Hughes, Milton Meltzer, C. Eric Lincoln, and Jon Michael Spencer, *A Pictorial History of African Americans* (New York: Crown Publisher, Inc., 1995), 301.

21. Ibid., 301.

22. Karen O'Connor and Larry J. Sabato, *Essentials of American Government Continuity and Change*, 2004 ed. (New York: Pearson/Longman, 2005), 149.

23. Sidlow and Henschen, *America at Odds,* 103–104. For some white Americans, the *Brown* decision has always been controversial and despised. Indeed, many white conservatives thought that it was a terrible idea. Those who also objected to theruling saw it as absolutely dictatorial.

24. Stevens, *Merriam-Webster's Collegiate Encyclopedia,* 240.

25. Ibid., 240.

26. Robert J. Bresler, Robert J. Friedrich, Joseph J. Karlesky, D. Grier Stephenson, Jr., and Charles C. Turner, *Introduction to American Government* (Redding, CA: North West Publishing, LLC, 2003), 91.

27. Ibid., 91.

28. Judy Jones and William Wilson, *An Incomplete Education* (New York: Ballantine Books, 1987), 57.

29. Stevens, *Merriam-Webster's Collegiate Encyclopedia,* 1021. It should be pointed out that President Lyndon B. Johnson appointed Marshall to both the U.S. Courts of Appeals in 1961 and U.S. Solicitor General in 1965, before he appointed him to sit on the Supreme Court.

30. Ibid., 1021.

31. "Education standards: Best and brightest," *The Economist,* August 17, 2013, 70.

32. Meyerson, *Political Numeracy,* 98.

33. Orfield, "Dismantling Desegregation," 252.

34. Hughes, Meltzer, Lincoln, and Spencer, *A Pictorial History,* 304.

35. Bell, *Silent Covenants,* 4.

36. Meyerson, *Political Numeracy,* 98.

37. Adam Liktak, "Justice Ginsburg calls court one of the most activist in American history," *Las Vegas Sun,* September 1, 2013), 3.

Reading 1.4

What I Have Learned from Conservative Students Teaching American Politics at a Predominantly White Institution (PWIs)

Reflections of a Minority College Professor

Earnest N. Bracey, Ph.D.

Reflections

I am an African American professor at a Predominantly White College in Las Vegas; and I have been teaching political science and Black American History for almost twenty-five years. During this entire time, I have personally enjoyed teaching all these many years—that is, until recently, because of the (abrasive) caliber of some college students that are signing up for my American politics classes. Unfortunately, some conservative students are taking my political science classes for *ulterior* motives or nefarious reasons, which makes my job even harder. In fact, some of my conservative students are disruptive and disrespectful, because of who I am and what I represent. In essence, I believe that these particular students would like to quash *any* liberal voice that sees the world differently than they do, which is beyond ridiculous. They even questioned whether I should be in the classroom *at all*, because of my race. Where did these conservative students get their dyspeptic beliefs? Why can't they be reasoned with? And where do they come from? Paradoxically, many disagree with the known facts and *objective* truth if it doesn't conform to their mistaken and narrow-minded attitudes, and far-right views. It is hard enough teaching American politics without their ludicrous interferences, and sometimes reckless assumptions and disruptions. In other words, these conservative students energetically and *unapologetically* state their right-wing ideologies and positions, with the *insouciance* that is the hallmark of white nationalism and racial tribalism. Speaking the truth is *verboten* to many of them, as I always based my lectures on telling the truth. Unfortunately, some of my previous conservative students had closed their minds about the truth in politics; or they were not open-minded, because many collectively wanted *everyone* to think about the social and political issues (of the day) in the same way that they did. But clearly, we are divided by ideology in the United States.

Earnest N. Bracey, "What I Have Learned from Conservative Students Teaching American Politics at a Predominantly White Institution: Reflections of a Minority College Professor," *Communication, Society and Media*, vol. 2, no. 1, pp. 16–27. Copyright © Scholink, Inc. (CC BY 4.0).

Shockingly, some of my former conservative students were inclined to dislike progressive, liberal professors, like myself, as they saw me and others as true villains, for whatever reasons, and even un-American. Never mind that I served honorably in the U.S. Army for over twenty years. Of course, my military service didn't matter to some of these students, nor did they care about me standing up for my liberal and progressive beliefs, as if I was *unpatriotic* in some way. To be sure, I recall that some of these conservative students tried to stoke fear and loathing against liberal professors who didn't share their conservative values, or pretentious and negative ideas. Many were offended even when I told them to step back and think critically about the political issues, or their interpretation of the facts. Inevitably, these conservative students made their odd and preposterous positions known in a *scripted* and *orchestrated* way. They also believed in speaking their mind, and "out-of-turn", even when they were totally incorrect about politics and history, and not called on, which stirred their annoyance with me. I often cringed from their misperceptions and misinformation, as they trafficked in *right-wing* conspiracy theories. Nevertheless, these students thought that their "voice" should be given a platform in every classroom, in every situation, no matter what. For example, one conservative student, only nineteen years old, didn't want to believe in our common humanity. To say the least, we became completely at odds with each other, because of his perceptions about race. But every educated person knows that we (all human beings) have a common ancestor (Crystal, 1994a; Glaude, 2016; King, 1981; Fairbanks, 2015). The particular point this student made was that what I was trying to impart was "made-up", as he didn't want to plumb the depths of the truth and the evidence, as it contradicted with his misperceptions about racial or ethnic groups.

As if on cue, this same conservative student, with his political biases, would sit every day on the front row in my classroom and loudly fumble with his papers, as I tried to lecture, which was rude and unpleasantly distracting. On the surface, these conservative students seemed curious and eager to learn; but I quickly realized that nothing could have been further from the truth, as their *Modus Operandi* (MO) was to distract. Also, this particular conservative student only wanted to talk about the *Benghazi* investigation in Congress, which had nothing to do with the reading assignment and lessons of the day. This was not totally unexpected, because we are living in an academic world where some professors are afraid to speak their minds or the truth. As it turned out, many of my conservative students, as mentioned, didn't want to think critically about the political issues, because their minds were already made up, especially in our ideologically conflicted and polarized nation today. Therefore, our capacity to teach and agree on historical facts is being threatened by sometimes angry, misguided students in a coordinated way. All in all, this situation in the college classroom today is problematic, and something professors, like myself, haven't had to deal with in the past—that is, being hassled by lazy thinking students, which is certainly damning in regards to higher education and the breakdown of *civility* in our country and politics. Many also use the techniques of *whatifisms* or *whataboutisms*, because some don't put a lot of stock into what liberal professors say about mostly *anything*, especially the political issues. These conservative students also *obsequiously* asked inconspicuous questions, at awkward times—which almost never related to the various assignments—as a pretext to starting a serious classroom dispute and disruption. So they asked about *irrelevant* things, just for the sake of argument. Moreover, many didn't want to know the incontrovertible facts about American politics, especially if it was negative toward conservatives. What these conservative students also failed to recognize was that we are not a *monolithic* society. That is, conservatives and liberals don't think alike, particularly about certain public policy issues. Yet many believed that conservatives should be totally in charge (or control) of our governments, without knowing *exactly* why they felt this way, which was illogical and embarrassingly uninformed, considering that we have a two-party, democratic system.

Furthermore, many of my conservative students believed that facts were *subjective*, which was absolutely nonsense. In this regard, I told this student that made this equivocal comment that *facts* are *facts*, and can be checked for accuracy; but this abrasive student didn't want to believe it. So I asked him to give me the exact date of his birth; and he did so. I next told him that his birthday was not really a fact, and that he was born on another date, to prove to him that his birth was not *subjective*. Nonetheless, he still didn't understand the nuance of what I was explaining or imparting to him—or the truth of my argument. In general, *politics* can be a dirty business, and it is hard to point out or disseminate the truth and facts when teaching political science (in the college classroom) today, particularly for some conservative students, because some facts don't fit their ideological frame of reference (Robinson, 2018) (Note 1). Let me explain: In one of my classroom lectures about the American Revolution, I informed my students that the first person to die for the American Revolution was a black man, a patriot named Crispus Attucks, during the Boston Massacre (Stevens, 2000a). Another conservative student expressed his misgivings and opined that this fact really didn't matter. After all, he went on to *grandstand* and *argue* that no one cared about the first person to die in the Vietnam War, either. I told this conservative student that he was mixing apples and oranges, to use the metaphor, and that he was making a very *specious* argument. I went on to let him know that the Vietnam War had nothing to do with our fight for independence from Great Britain. But this same conservative student, with his confusing beliefs, would brook no criticism, mainly because of the "Mutability of the Past" theory, where he thought that a black man, sacrificing his life for the founding of our nation didn't matter; or that this truth should be ignored. It became immediately apparent to me, then, why this conservative student was registered for my American politics class in the first place. He was there to monitor what I was saying about current social issues, not to listen or to *think* and learn about the *truth* of our nation—in terms of politics. I also believed that his mission (this conservative student) was to verbally attack me personally, which he did, as he aligned himself with the far-right. And he told me so.

Some of my colleagues also knew before hand when there was a problem with a conservative student, because we discussed these matters in faculty, discipline/department meetings; but many failed to call these students out, which I thought was an appropriate thing to do. Also, at the start of each semester, I made it a point to tell my students that there was a proper and respectful *etiquette* in my classroom—or any college classroom, for that matter; but they were "put-off" by this comment from me. In addition, many of my former conservative students were offended by me addressing other controversial, social and political topics, as if I didn't have the right or authority to talk about such matters. Some students even refused to accept *uncomfortable* facts, even if the information was retrieved from a reliable news sources. They called it "fake news" (Albom, 2018; Stibel, 2018) (Note 2). Many of these same students also claimed that there was no real evidence to support the political facts that I presented to them, on a "silver platter", so to speak, and even if *everything* I imparted to them made absolute sense. Perhaps it wasn't easy for them to think critically for themselves. Or it might have been easier for them to be "spoon-fed" information from agents of their *political socialization*, like with family members, where they learned their political values. This is to say that many of my conservative students came to my classroom with preconceived, sometimes dubious notions about government and politics. And their faulty logic and warped attitudes about politics, generally, could be breathtakingly wrong. So is this a sad commentary on the state of secondary education in the United States today? (Gambescia, 2018) (Note 3) Perhaps. Moreover, I was once personally threatened by a female, conservative student in an *anonymous* phone call, as she didn't believe that I should bring up controversial topics of our political past, or inconvenient, ugly truths about our government leaders, like with the knowledge of President Andrew Jackson, a slave owner, who was responsible for the "Trail of Tears", where Native Americans were forced marched from their native lands in the 1800s (east of the Mississippi), leading to the death of over 4,000 Cherokee Indians (Stevens, 2000b; Wilkins & Stark, 2018).

Equally important, many of my older conservative students didn't believe in the Orthodox, Socratic Method of teaching, either, as they never wanted to be asked probing questions about the specific, political lessons, as they were mostly unprepared, which was totally unacceptable. Some disrespectful students also believed that they were entitled to good grades, without earning them, and even if they didn't attend *any* classes. Additionally, some took the truth for granted, or out of context, as one conservative student told me, "the truth doesn't matter". I know that I couldn't control these students and what they chose to believe, but I was actually flabbergasted when this conservative student told me this. But contrary to the opinion voiced by this student, I tried to let him know that the truth always corresponds to the facts and *reality*. In other words, *facts* are *facts*, as mentioned, and not in "the eyes-of-the-beholder". This argument had no effect on this student's thinking, however. When I began a lecture about Watergate, this same conservative student opined that we should forget that the Watergate scandal even happened in the 1970s, where the illegal activities of a conservative administration broke into the Democratic Party's National Headquarters (Crystal, 1994b; Edwards & Lippucci, 1998), to steal operational/party secrets. Eventually, President Richard M. Nixon, a conservative, had to resign, because he tried to cover up this crime, but was later pardoned by Gerald Ford, who was never elected President of the United States by the American people, as he succeeded to the office of the presidency (Crystal, 1994b), having previously been given the Vice Presidency by Nixon and the Congress. This same conservative student was outraged by this knowledge, and angry that I even brought up Watergate, as he only wanted to discuss the second amendment. Indeed, he firmly believed that *only* liberals wanted to take away the rights of the American people to keep and bear arms. However, I informed this particular student that nothing could be further from the truth, as he was a member of the National Rifle Association (NRA). I added that this was a misperception. Unfortunately, the NRA continues to push or espouse this nonsense—that is, when liberals only want our government to address sensible gun control laws. Further, the American people should know that many liberals are also members of the NRA, in good standing. I also explained to my class, and this conservative student, much to his chagrin, that the second amendment says nothing about the rights of individual citizens to have arms (Stevens, 2000c; Volkomer, 2007). College students should always know the truth about this contentious and controversial policy issue.

And more important, I have been tirelessly committed to the truth in politics, like discussing the Iran-Contra Scandal of the mid-1980s, involving illegal weapons transactions, by the Reagan administration to Iran to secure the release of U.S. hostages held in Lebanon (Stevens, 2000d). Also, at that time our government was supposed to ban *any* aid to the Contras (an enemy), and "a rebel force" that wanted to overthrow Nicaragua's legitimate government (Stevens, 2000d). These complex facts have been largely forgotten by college students, or never really talked about anymore by American citizens today. Or the American people have forgotten this politically damaging scandal. Therefore, it is hard to see "eye-to-eye" with someone who refuses to accept the facts, or those who pass off their lies as the truth, and verbally attack *anyone* that disagree with them. But as their political science professor, I always tried to understand where my conservative students were coming from, respecting their right to express their views, as they are cut from a different *political cloth*. I tried to let them know that it is okay to disagree, without being disagreeable. But their romantic views about (the goodness of all) conservative ideas, without empathy or compassion, was enough to frustrate anyone. Additionally, when it came to addressing the *abortion* issue, for example, these unnamed conservative students, who infiltrated my classes, argued that women should *never* have the right to an abortion, no matter the circumstances. However, all Americans should know that the right of a woman to have an abortion is "settled law", decided by the U.S. Supreme Court in the 1973 *Roe vs. Wade* ruling (Weaver & Mascaro, 2018; Volkomer, 2007; Edwards & Lipppucci, 1998) (Note 4). Many times, these conservative students also brought up *Planned Parenthood* and how horrible they thought that this organization was supposed to be, but without knowing the complete facts, the history, or much about this important women's group. Indeed, their weak arguments and distorted opinions could be irritating, to say the least. Yet, I felt these students should be allowed to speak out about the *abortion* issue for the sake of discussion and fairness in the classroom. But many were sometimes stressed out by their disagreements, and lack of political knowledge, which was often on shaky grounds. Or they looked for unattractive, alternative explanations (Krugman, 2018; Kazin, 2018) (Note 5).

Moreover, many of my conservative students had foul dispositions, as they seemed angry with me personally, because I didn't keep my (so-called) tongue, or sugarcoat *anything* in my political science classes, even when I was threatened by some of them, and especially when I was critical of conservative government, which was always based on the objective facts and the truth. Some saw my fearlessness in telling the truth about current politics and our political history as a threat, or an affront to their agenda, whatever that might have been. The bottom line: Many of my conservative students were being exploited and manipulated (perhaps without knowing it), and swayed by *Herd Poison*, where they conformed—to conservative notions—without thinking critically, which can be extremely dangerous and disconcerting. Indeed, some of these conservative students seemed to care only about protecting their *hate speech*, or alternative views of the world, which is slowly tearing our country apart from within, especially with the resurgence of white supremacist groups, and the climate of racial hatred in American politics today. Perhaps most tellingly, these students wanted to dissuade and marginalize professors like me, or keep me from criticizing our ugly past. They told me (in no uncertain terms) that I should focus on our *exceptionalism*, and nothing else. Furthermore, many of my conservative students didn't want to be reminded of how conservative administrations brought us the Great Depression, which "was unprecedented in its length and in the wholesale poverty and tragedy it inflicted on (American) society" (Harris & Levey, 1975, p. 1132) between 1929 to 1934. Of course, Republican Herbert Hoover, a conservative, was the President of the United States during most of this time. Conservatives were also responsible for the Wall Street disaster during the Bush administration, where the American people had to bail out the big banks—because they were (so-called) too big to fail—with taxpayers' dollars. To say the least, many of the Wall Street bankers were never held accountable. Even more important, we have a tendency to gloss over the unending wars in Iraq and Afghanistan, started by a conservative administration. Conservatives also don't like to address the 2000 Presidential election fiasco, where unfortunately, the conservatives on "the Supreme Court played a decisive role in determining who won the presidency when in a 5-to-4 ruling it halted the manual recounting of ballots in Florida", and gave conservative George W. Bush the U.S. presidency (Burns et al., 2004, p. 392). Because of an inattentive public, American citizens have quickly forgotten these important political events.

Many conservatives only want to hold liberals responsible, in some way, as if they had something to do with the second major recession in recent American history, starting in the late 2000s, during another conservative administration. In this regard, my conservative students distracted from this discussion in my American politics classes by bringing up the spectacular moral failure of President Bill Clinton, who was impeached by Conservative Republicans in the House of Representatives in Congress, because he had a consensual affair with Monica Lewinsky, a young intern, and committed perjury by initially denying the relationship (Burns et al., 2004; Tomasky, 2017) (Note 6). I let my conservative students know that their interruptions had nothing to do with the 2000 Presidential Election, or the recession brought on by a conservative government. But they didn't want to endure *any* kind of intellectual disagreement, like their denial of *Climate Change*, which is negatively affecting our environment almost on a daily basis (Albeck-Ripka & Pierre-Louis, 2018; King, 2018; Friedman, 2018; Masto, 2018), because of the rolling back of environmental regulations. Nor do conservative students want to discuss the dismissal of civil rights cases under the current conservative administration (Green, 2018), or a stolen Supreme Court seat. In fact, Senate Majority Leader Mitch McConnell, a conservative Republican, has indicated that his greatest political achievement was "to stop former President Barack Obama from filling the Supreme Court vacancy created by Antonin Scalia's death in 2016" (McConnell, 2018, p. 10A) Question: Why did senate conservatives think that it was fair to deny federal appeals court Judge Merrick Garland even a hearing? Was this uncouth action even constitutional?

I personally believe that some conservative students, as mentioned, didn't care about these finer points, or which political arguments even made the most sense, even if it was based on the *real* facts. Or they disliked the concept of "constructive engagement", which some thought was nonsense. Surprisingly, many of my colleagues have also been verbally attacked by some of these conservative students, who have accused them of *harassment* or *discrimination*, especially those professors who are originally from other countries, or who are naturalized U.S. citizens. I also firmly believed that some of these conservative students would like to disparage and silence these professors—who often pose provocative questions, and tell the earnest truth—at all cost. What is going on at our respective college is "shameful", and jaw-droppingly wrong. It has certainly been a wake-up call for some of us. Unfortunately, some colleagues at my college are not even able to teach what they know to be truth, without fear or repercussions, which is a famous *adage* expressed by Albert Einstein. In the final analysis, these conservative students know almost nothing about academic freedom. Why?

Conclusions

Unfortunately, many historians, philosophers, and political scientists today, on college campuses, are taking a *neutral* stance when it comes to teaching history or American politics, because they are unwilling to take a (righteous) stand against these disruptive and seemingly disgruntled, conservative students. But to my mind, this *capitulation* is a very cowardly thing to do. More surprisingly, many of these liberal professors are now teaching *on-line*, because many don't want to resist the lies, or be targets or bothered by these conservative students in a "brick and mortar" classroom setting *anymore*. So are their actions just a cop-out, because of differences of opinions and viewpoints? Clearly, some of these students appear to deliberately provoke certain professors with the lie that their first amendment rights are being violated in some way. To be sure, liberal professors are even afraid to confront these disruptive, conservative students—to tell them what is acceptable, *credible* and what is not. But professors today must be undeterred and not afraid to teach what is right; nor should they be intimidated or bullied by these ill-informed students, just because they don't agree with their particular points of view. This is to say that some students see things only from a conservative perspective and nothing else, like their dismissal of Affirmative Action (Stevens, 2000e), as some kind of *inappropriate* hand-out for minorities. What they should know is that Affirmative Action has tried to balance the *inequality* that continues in this country for racial minorities. Moreover, many of these conservative students dislike being censored, even if their *partisan* or ideological information is highly suspect. There is also no doubt that these students want to avoid engaging in productive, tolerant, meaningful and intellectual discussions. Therefore, I think that what these conservatives say in my classroom is deliberate and coordinated, particularly when they make baseless assumptions about American politics. And they present the same unfortunate and tired ideas, almost every semester. But more than that, many use "identity politics", to flame racial discord, to justify what they say in an effort to make other young, brilliant students in my classroom see things their way. Equally significant, their ideological "orthodoxy" is like a *train wreck* waiting to happen. Some conservative students are also dismayed and offended by me personally when I ask them to consider important parallels in political time, like the eventual failure of conservative or *autocratic* governments throughout (organized) human history.

To further complicate matters, and in an effort to affect what we teach at the higher edu-cation levels, wealthy Republicans and conservative "big shots", like the *Koch Brothers* are spending millions to influence professors and students at colleges and universities—that is, what is taught, and what these billionaires want people to believe, which is a strict conser-vative view point (Greenwald, 2012). It certainly doesn't have to be this way. But the United States is in an unhealthy situation (and environment) when it comes to higher education, and the negative implications are enormous. In light of this, it is all the more important that political science students consider all the facts and the absolute truth, like the real reasons for the American Civil War, which was essentially to maintain the cursed institution of black slavery, in perpetuity, not some state rights' issue (Crystal, 1994c; Jillson, 2005); and despite words to the contrary. To be blunt, some conservative students, in my American politics classes tried to find excuses for some of their slave-owning ancestors, while trying to justify their inhumane actions. Historically, we have had to deal with an American, slave-dominated world, but my conservative students didn't want to hear it, as they told me that it was *old news*. Essentially, I informed my students that it is hard to defend the indefensible. But this advice usually went on deaf ears. It also remained unclear if my conservative students would even learn from history, or the truth about our political system, and fragile democracy. Or perhaps many see the issues presented in this reflection as irrelevant. But contrary to what some students might think, such issues, as presented in this work, are more important than ever. To say the least, many of my conservative students wanted *everyone* to respect their values, but felt no need to respect the values of others, with different viewpoints, especially liberal students and college professors. This, of course is a serious mistake, as our nation is a diverse, multi-racial democracy, and all our opinions should be respected.

Finally, it is difficult to teach students *anything* if their minds are already made up about what they think is right, like the issue of *creationism* over *evolution* (Crystal, 1994d; Fairbanks, 2015; Toler, 2012) (Note 7). *Doubters* about evolution should know that one theory is based on faith, and the latter is based on scientific facts that can be supported by solid evidence. Many of my conservative students could have cared less about the truths of *evolution*. Toward this end, political science professors must continue to repudiate unsophisticated, *myopic* ways of thinking, because something has to give. Even more important, professors must indeed understand the malicious intentions of some of their students, while remaining vigilant, and fighting back against racial *tribalism* and the conservative politics of division and *polariza-tion* at the highest education levels, as it shows no signs of abating. Professors must also be aware of the partisan divide, and MO of intimidation by some conservative students, and reject their *divisiveness*, as it is a dangerous recipe for undermining the "teacher-student" relationship at the university level. This doesn't mean that conservative students should be shunned or banned automatically from the college classroom, because of their immaturity, but their disrespect and disruption shouldn't be tolerated. More broadly, conservative students should *never* be underestimated, either. In my role as a teacher, I often tried to tell students that they should strive to do better when it comes to understanding American politics and our political spectrum, without shooting from the hip, and without knowledge, or making things up. But I was often ignored on this front. *Racism*, for example, continues to raise its ugly head (in many ways), in our nation today; however, my conservative students didn't want to believe it. Obviously, they were not always challenged or intrigued by the topics at hand, particularly with their right-leaning political views. Keep in mind, as mentioned, that nothing has prepared some professors for such *existential* threats to their livelihood and teaching profession.

In the end, professors who are disrespected by these conservative students must *never* take what is happening to them personally in the classroom, or lying down. Further, they must not turn a blind-eye, or accept their disgraceful behavior, either, especially if they are from a minority group, like me. Conventional wisdom holds that professors should always listen to their students with respect and empathy, but their *uncouth* behavior must *never* be normalized. Furthermore, a sense of humor and understanding, with patience, is also important too; however, it is also important to remember that nothing should be taken for granted at our college and universities, when professors are being personally threatened by students. Finally, unflappable professors today must have the *stones* to push back (delicately) in higher education against the unruly, disruptive college student, no matter what, because ignoring this issue will have serious, negative implications for our long-term education future. Unfortunately, many American citizens are stubbornly ignorant about this higher education issue.

Notes

1. College students must know that you cannot make up your own facts. Perhaps this conservative student had an unconscious bias, and my factual viewpoints were unwelcomed. Of course, many conservative students want to shut down liberals with whom they disagree.

2. It should be pointed out that the truth is not whatever you want or think it should be, especially given the egregious way politicians are misinforming and lying to the American people.

3. It is a "shameful thing" that some college students today don't know a lot about "some founding principles of American government". Professor Stephen Gambescia goes on to write that such "discussions with students are important before we dig deeply into how policymaking occurs in the United States".

4. Unfortunately, some conservatives try to offer a picturesque view of Republican policies, which have been disastrous for American citizens over the years, as explained in this article/reflection.

5. Conservative students are disrupting college and university classes throughout the United States.

6. It should be noted that Clinton was never removed from office, because you need two-thirds vote in both the House of Representatives and the Senate of Congress.

7. It should be noted that creationists oppose "the theory of evolution, and some evangelical conservative Christians claim there is scientific evidence to support creationism, though this has not been supported by other scientists".

References

Burns, J. M. et al. (2004). *Government by the People* (basic version, 20th ed., p. 392). New Jersey: Pearson Prentice Hall.

Crystal, D. (Ed.). (1994a). Race. *The Cambridge Encyclopedia* (2nd ed., p. 915). New York: Cambridge University Press.

Crystal, D. (Ed.). (1994b). Watergate. *The Cambridge Encyclopedia* (2nd ed., p. 1177). New York: Cambridge University Press.

Crystal, D. (Ed.). (1994c). American Civil War. *The Cambridge Encyclopedia* (2nd ed., p. 57). New York: Cambridge University Press.

Crystal, D. (Ed.). (1994d). Evolution. *The Cambridge Encyclopedia* (2nd ed., p. 401). New York: Cambridge University Press.

Edwards, D. V., & Lippucci, A. (1998). *Practicing American Politics: An Introduction to Government* (p. 243, p. 600). New York: Worth Publishers, Inc.

Fairbanks, D. J. (2015). *Everyone is African: How Science Explodes the Myth of Race*. New York: Prometheus Books.

Glaude, E. S. Jr. (2016). *Democracy in Black: How Race Still Enslaves the American Soul*. New York: Crown Publishers.

Greenwald, R. (2012). *Koch Brothers Exposed* (DVD Documentary). Brace New Foundation.

Harris, W. H., & Levey, J. S. (Eds.). (1975). Great Depression. In *The New Columbia Encyclopedia* (p. 1132). New York: Columbia University Press.

Jillson, C. (2005). *American Government: Political Change and Institutional Development* (3rd ed., p. 362). Belmont, CA: Thomson Higher Education.

King, J. C. (1981). *The Biology of Race* (revised edition). Los Angeles, CA: University of California Press.

Stevens, M. A. (Ed.). (2000a). Attucks, Crispus. In *Merriam-Webster's Collegiate Encyclopedia* (p. 110). Massachusetts: Merriam Webster, Inc.

Stevens, M. A. (2000b). Jackson, Andrew. In *Merriam-Webster's Collegiate Encyclopedia* (p. 831). Massachusetts: Merriam Webster, Inc.

Stevens, M. A. (2000c). National Rifle Association. In *Merriam-Webster's Collegiate Encyclopedia* (p. 1132). Massachusetts: Merriam Webster, Inc.

Stevens, M. A. (2000d). Iran-Contra Affair. In *Merriam-Webster's Collegiate Encyclopedia* (p. 818). Massachusetts: Merriam Webster, Inc.

Stevens, M. A. (2000e). Affirmative Action. In *Merriam-Webster's Collegiate Encyclopedia* (p. 18). Massachusetts: Merriam Webster, Inc.

Tomasky, M. (2017). *Bill Clinton*. New York: Times Books.

Volkomer, W. E. (2007). Abortion Rights. *American Government* (11th ed., pp. 317–318). New Jersey: Pearson Prentice Hall.

Wilkins, D. E., & Stark, H. K. (2018). Indian Removals, Relocations, and Reservations (1830s–1880s). *American Indian Politics and the American Political System* (4th ed., p. 124, pp. 152–154). New York: Rowman & Littlefield.

Albeck-Ripka, L., & Pierre-Louis, K. (2018, April 22). Environmental Laws under Siege. Here's Why We Have Them. *The New York Times*, 4.

Green, E. L. (2018, April 23). Civil rights cases being dismissed as burdensome. *Las Vegas Sun*, 1–5.

Stibel, J. (2018, May 16). Fake news: It's all in your brain. *USA Today*, 2B.

McConnell says stopping Garland biggest decision. (2018, June 10). *The Las Vegas Review-Journal*, 10A.

Gambescia, S. (2018, August 3). Nation needs a reset for Civics 101. *Las Vegas Sun*, 3.

Albom, M. (2018, August 8). The press is not the enemy of the people. *USA Today*, 5A.

Friedman, T. (2018, August 18). Will Mother Nature vote in 2020? *Las Vegas Sun*, 3.

King, L. (2018, August 22). EPA plan would prolong life of coal plants. *USA Today*, 3A.

Robinson, E. (2018, August 22). Truth can't be spun from lies. *Las Vegas Sun*, 4.

Weaver, D., & Mascaro, L. (2018, August 22). Kavanaugh: Roe v. Wade settled. *Las Vegas Review-Journal*, 4A.

Krugman, P. (2018, August 24). GOP gripped by a climate of paranoia. *Las Vegas Sun*, 3.

Kazin, M. (2018, August 26). America's Never-Ending Culture War. *The New York Times*, 4.

Masto, C. C. (2018, September 1). We cannot afford to ignore climate science. *Las Vegas Sun*, 1, 5.

Toler, P. D. (2012). *The Story of All of Us: Mankind* (pp. 3–17). Philadelphia, PA: Running Press.

Part II

Civil Rights and Black Politics

Reading 2.1

Speaking Truth to the Masses
The Nonviolent Politics of Mahatma Gandhi and
Dr. Martin Luther King, Jr.

Earnest N. Bracey, Ph.D.

Introduction

When we talk about the legacies of Mahatma Gandhi and Dr. Martin Luther King, Jr., it is useful to praise and distinguish between both of these great men, especially in terms of their specific beliefs and social philosophies. Moreover, it is important to recognize Gandhi and Dr. King's "way of truth" in order to understand their militant nonviolence. Indeed, both Gandhi and Dr. King were dedicated political and social activists. Furthermore, these two luminaries, and men of color, had the same persistence, courage, and perseverance, as well as the same prophetic vision or way of hammering away at the forces of evil, racial dominance, and blatant racism, particularly against those who were unsympathetic to the plight of their respective people. This is to say that their struggle for peace, civil rights, and nonviolence played a significant and vital role in both of their similar fights for freedom against racial oppression, inflicted (in large measure) by various dominant groups. The odds against both men seemed insurmountable. However, as professor Ronald J. Terchek has stated, "Gandhi and King each [carried] a comprehensive view of autonomy" and justice, making "it the standard to judge practices, laws, and [racist] institutions"[1].

If there was one continuous thread in both men's life, it was that they took uncompromising stances against discrimination and cruel suppression, while combating *any* infringement of human rights and the interest of indigenous, dark-skinned people, while seeking liberation. And through all of their trials and tribulations, both Gandhi and Dr. King unflinchingly presented their own ideas about life and how things should be for all humans; as they both rejected bigotry and harassment toward all people. Moreover, their proactive strategies of direct action, nonviolent activism, noncooperation/noncompliance, *or civil disobedience* (against unjust laws and policies) were indeed rewarding, as their tactics became more and more evident during their activism days; but as everyone should probably know, things were also extremely difficult and dangerous for Gandhi and Dr. King during their adult lives, as those in complete authority initially refused to share power and control over racist governments or vast, imperialistic empires and important resources to help the *indigent* or needy. Impoverished people certainly identified with the struggles of both men, as there was no ambiguity in Gandhi's and Dr. King's thinking about poverty. In fact, both men were seen as bulwarks against repressive forces, as well as advocates for economic justice. Nevertheless, as professor of political science Michael J. Nojeim has written:

> As leaders and moral spokes persons, both [Gandhi and King] felt strongly about people taking the initiative for their own self-improvement. Both were extremely self-critical and tried to meet a very high standard of self improvement they set for themselves and then for others. Both used their leadership roles to reform their own people from within as much as they sought to confront oppression from without[2].

Equally important, the "powers that be" went to extreme measures, such as with intimidating tactics and unmitigated violence toward the two men, to protect their dominance and privileged lives. Perhaps Gandhi and Dr. King ignored the extent of their vulnerability to these real dangers, with their nonconformist ideas. Historically speaking, what both men were able to accomplish was unprecedented during their amazing times, with large, human outpourings against dominant and variously oppressive regimes of evil. Accordingly, one must understand the racist institutions (or the context) in which both men lived. The illustrious reputations of Gandhi and Dr. King, of course, are well-known and documented, as their brave and nonviolent actions, and devotion to social duty propelled them to international prominence and worldwide attention, as benevolent revolutionaries. Therefore, their political judgments and legacies should *never* be questioned, especially given their contributions to indigenous Asian Indians and African American people, and their rightful introduction of the techniques of nonviolence for unprecedented social change. To say the least, history will always view both men in a wholly positive and favorable light. For example, a 2011 USA Gallup Poll found that 69% of Americans have "a highly favorable view" of Dr. King, and 91% approve of his memorial on the National Mall in Washington, D.C[3]. And there are numerous statues of Gandhi throughout the world, from Bangalore Karnataka, India, to Union Square Park, New York, to Tavistock Square, London, England.

Their good works proved to be a formidable challenge, but both Gandhi and Dr. King were able to embolden a timid, hesitant and fearful people, who would believe and eventually follow the two men. Furthermore, there was no question that they almost reluctantly placed themselves in the category of self-proclaimed leaders, or spokespersons, for their particular race or ethnic groups, while giving their respective political movements the rhetorical boost and moral support needed to continue their nonviolent activities and strategic marching campaigns. Gandhi and Dr. King were also hounded, persecuted, and *scrutinized* like no other political leaders during their time. For example, both men were subject to intense criticism by different power elites or respective dominant groups, as if they had some devious or ulterior motive for doing the worthwhile things that they did. Still, Gandhi and Dr. King galvanized supporters for their cause, while explaining the efficacy of nonviolent protest. Ultimately, both men did not necessarily live their lives completely unscattered or protected; nor did they worry about the political consequences of their controversial actions. Indeed, they were faced with many perplexing problems during their remarkable and productive lives that went beyond their immediate control. For instance, Gandhi and Dr. King suffered pains of agony and mental anguish, as they were often beaten, arrested, and imprisoned by the hands of callous and heartless members of different dominant groups.

All in all, their lives were frequently intertwined with their own personal beliefs, unique responsibilities, and value systems; but neither man boasted about their many achievements, for they were modest and not especially vain. This is to say that these principled men did not show deliberate aggrandizement, or try to toot their own horns. In so many words, their flexibility of mind and unwavering determination actually helped them to achieve their respective endeavors. Nonetheless, after so much good work, and inexplicably, Gandhi and Dr. King's unusual paths through life, in the final analysis, led them to their untimely assassinations by evil madmen of unpleasant dispositions. But while they lived, they were, for the most part, fearless. This is to say that Gandhi and Dr. King didn't let anyone intimidate or scare them. They also never capitulated to racism and terrorism. Furthermore, Gandhi and Dr. King believe that human goodness could triumph almost *any* problem. Additionally, both men were fueled by the fact that they were on the right side of history, fighting brutal racial exploitation, as they inspired separate opposition movements, to the umpteenth degree. Finally, Gandhi and Dr. King worked for a better world and the benefit of *all* humanity.

Mahatma Gandhi as a Nonviolent Leader of Political Power

Mohandas (Mahatma) K. Gandhi, of course, came to be called by the moniker, "the father of Indian Independence"[4]. And he metamorphosed into both a political and spiritual leader, as he preached, taught, and philosophized with intelligence and insight, combining "the education of an English lawyer with the temperament of an Indian ascetic to lead a national resistance movement against the British"[5]. Additionally, Gandhi used Hindu ideas and asceticism, combined with his own personal philosophy of life to achieve his worthy and audacious goals in "the struggle of the Indian people for independence from Great Britain"[6]. Indeed, Gandhi amassed unprecedented political clout—that is, as the leader of his *Quit Indian Movement*—eventually toppling the British government in India. Moreover, Gandhi embraced *celibacy* and the technique of *fasting* or hunger strikes (sometimes almost to his detriment and health), and *poverty* (or a simple life), stripping himself of cursed Western notions, which he thought absolutely corrupted his people. In this respect, historian Kevin Reilly writes that, "Gandhi was extremely critical of Western culture as he witnessed the havoc British rule wreaked on his [beloved] country"[7]. The *whitish* loincloth and shawl would come to symbolize Gandhi's complete break with the trappings of Westernism.

Moreover, we might say that Gandhi led an extraordinary, noble, and complicated life, as he came to believe that the implicit act of *fasting* and *civil disobedience* (against British government officials) was the most rational or pragmatic course of action against such a formidable and vastly superior force. But many critics thought that Gandhi was too eccentric for his own good—a caricature of a starving, emaciated, funny little Indian man—an annoyance in many ways to the British colonialists. After returning home from studying law in England and unsuccessfully practicing as an attorney in India, Gandhi decided to try his luck in South Africa, where he became greatly successful, particularly in regards to the affairs of the Indian community that had settled there. And it was in South Africa and later India where Gandhi demonstrated "that nonviolence could be used effectively for solving [intractable] problems both nationally and international[ly]"[8].

So successful were Gandhi's efforts against the government's anti-Indian activities in 1914, that he "secured an agreement from the South African government that promised the alleviation of anti-Indian discrimination"[9]. We might be hard pressed further for an explanation, but it was an unprecedented agreement at that time, given the racism and harsh separatist philosophy of *apartheism*. Yet, it was in India where Mahatma Gandhi began, in earnest, his true activist mission. Indeed, Gandhi became a heroic man who helped transform India politically and socially through his nonviolent movement and bold actions. It should also be mentioned that: Although Gandhi initially supported the British government in his homeland, especially as a young man during World War I, that would drastically change upon his firm renouncement of Great Britain and prodigious advocacy of Indian Nationalism during the advent of World War II. Gandhi also committed himself to fighting racial intolerance and discrimination. And little did the British government know about the unexpected events that would soon unfold in India. Gandhi first started his *truth campaigns* (called *satyagraha*) in South Africa and later in India, where he legally fought unjust laws and discrimination against the Indian majorities.

We can easily discern Gandhi's love of humanity, as he genuinely liked people, or *all* human beings, who he thought were worthy of dignity and respect. He was also concerned with the *inhumanity* and *evil* nature of mankind, especially in regards to how some suffering people were being mistreated and exploited by the rich and powerful. Furthermore, Gandhi knew that if indigenous, dark-skinned people could be "defined as less than human, like bugs or roaches, *extermination* [could] all too easily be seen as the appropriate action"[10], in terms of committing genocide or eliminating an irritant, or human pests.

Gandhi, of course, believed that all humans were from the same life source, united under a supreme being or one God; and this bold philosophy made a lasting impression on people of all walks of life and throughout the world. According to Indian philosopher, N. Radhakrishnan:

> The Gandhian concept of reverence for all life has not been found to be a mere statement of what is true, but a useful guide to being truthful, for the Gandhian concept of truth is not a virtue or principle but a process. Gandhi himself acknowledged how in his early years he was influenced by the Buddhist and Jain traditions and how his understanding of the essential teachings of these religions helped him formulate his theories and shape his life[11].

The aforementioned passage by Radhakrishnan outlines the wonderful depth of concern Gandhi had for human life in that he believed that all human beings should prosper and flourish. Nevertheless, Gandhi made it *explicitly* clear that the British should leave India, his torn-apart, troubled, and divided country. And Gandhi was unrelenting, and without compunction on this score. Initially, the British colonizers balked, thinking of Gandhi as a crazy man, or a shady, self-proclaimed prophet of the Indian people. But eventually he became a real player in the politics of India, as mentioned. Indeed, the British began to slowly sense that *something* was different about this Mahatma Gandhi. He was certainly a magnificent piece of work, unstoppable. But as far as the British government was concerned, leaving India was an unthinkable prospect that they could not have imagined at that time during the 1930s and early 1940s. Perhaps the British laughed smugly or heartily at Gandhi and the very idea of abandoning part of their great empire. But inevitably, they would do just that—that is, acquiesce to Gandhi's request for them to peacefully leave India without bloodshed or violence. Of course, as the famous black writer John Oliver Killens once wrote: "There were enough Indian bodies to literally form a wall against the imperialistic British and stop them from functioning"[12].

Toward this end, Gandhi never really spoke harshly or with bitterness toward the British occupiers. Instead, Gandhi showed his considerable displeasure of British rule with profound messages of compassion and love. Historian Robert Jakoubek cogently put it this way:

> In Gandhi's teachings, love and nonviolence were wedded to the force of a mass movement dedicated to ending [Indian] oppression. He never talked of

hating or destroying the British. He asked his followers to love the enemy as they loved themselves. Through love, he [Gandhi] said, the oppressors would be redeemed, and they would see the error of their ways[13].

Therefore, through *fasting,* prayer, direct action, mass agitation, and nonviolent demonstrations, Gandhi was able to accomplish the impossible. However, he was unable to stop the movement to establish Hindu and Muslim nations, after the mighty British ultimately left the country. "And further," as Killens once pointed out, "India was not uniformly nonviolent". That is to say that, "even as Gandhi preached nonviolence, violence often times exploded in the hinterlands"[14]. Furthermore, the very thought of dividing the country of India disturbed Gandhi immensely, as he had worked extremely hard, tirelessly, on behalf of many, to see that such a division never happened. Yet, Mohandas (Mahatma) Gandhi was never at risk of beating himself up personally and psychologically over such negative things, as sectarian violence. But the thought of separating his beloved nation certainly filled Gandhi with (consuming) dread. We now know of these two separate countries as *India* and *Pakistan,* which have always been starkly polarized. To be sure, Gandhi thought that his efforts had been futile because of his inability to convince the Hindu and Muslim factions to unite or join forces, as they were mostly divided by religious beliefs. Gandhi also thought that failing to unite India totally was his most unfortunate defeat or failure.

But it should be noted that "one of Gandhi's greatest accomplishments was that he could take great ideas as *swaraj* and *satyagraha* [or holding to the truth] and translate them into mass action that helped repair Indians' self-esteem, helped restore their courage, and helped in recruiting a whole new constituency of activists"[15]. Moreover, and quite appropriately, Gandhi was able to get concessions from the British government regarding the fledgling, modern nation-state of India. Finally, Gandhi, who was dubbed Mahatma (which meant great soul) was able to gradually unify (before his death) the divergent factions of the Indian nationalists' movement, or the separate political groups within their traditional borders, particularly with the ideas and reality of India becoming a sovereign nation, or independent of British rule.

Martin Luther King and Nonviolent Social and Political Change

Before we can begin any discussion of Dr. Martin Luther King, Jr., we must never forget the simple act of courage from Rosa Parks, the "onetime seamstress" and the "Mother of the Civil Rights Movement" in the United States "who refused to give up her seat to a white passenger on a public bus in Montgomery, Alabama in 1955"[16]. This is to say that without her bravery and sacrifice, Dr. King's legacy might not have ever happened—that is, in terms of the young, black Baptist minister becoming the focal point or acknowledged leader of the once fledging civil rights movement in the United States. Professor of History David Levering Lewis tells us:

> When Mrs. Rosa Parks, a seamstress at a downtown Montgomery, Alabama, department store, a loyal member of the National Association for the Advancement of Colored People, and a model of personal industry and propriety, defied the city's segregated transportation ordinance by refusing to surrender her bus seat to a white person on the first day of December 1955, she inaugurated an era in the struggle for civil rights. Her [heroic] deed made King possible[17].

Clearly, had Rosa Parks not been roughly treated and arrested, which "triggered a boycott of the buses in Montgomery," where black Southerners "refused to ride the buses until the laws were changed," Dr. Martin Luther King, Jr. may have never emerged as "the prominent leader of the eventual boycott and the modern-day civil rights movement"[18]. Perhaps even more revealing, Dr. Martin Luther King, Jr., who would come to be called and reverently know as the *Black Prince of Peace*, "attained national prominence" in the United States by fiercely "advocating a policy of passive resistance to segregation," racial discrimination and white supremacy[19]. According to political historian Ronald J. Terchek, Dr. King effectively took a page from Gandhi's political "play-book," so to speak, by mobilizing "nonviolent civil disobedience to challenge racial segregation and advance the cause of racial equality in the United Sates"[20], especially in regards to despicable Jim Crow Laws in the South. Dr. King was also a racial reconciliator, as he tried to bring together several disparate black civil rights groups. Furthermore, Dr. King reminded white America that they could go beyond their preconceived ideas about blacks in order to move forward and beyond their terrible prejudices and petty racial differences. And despite words to the contrary, Dr. King was a serious advocate for economic and racial justice for *all* underprivileged people. Dr. King, moreover, kept white America off-balance with his experimental tactics and nonviolent strategies. Equally important, he was savvy enough to get his message out by effectively using the mainstream media. Dr. King's biographer Robert Jakoubek writes:

> King was most attracted to Gandhi's concept of *satyagraha,* or the peaceful defiance of government. In response to continued British rule, Gandhi led boycotts, strikes, and marches, each nonviolent but each protesting the evils of imperialism, and each making it more difficult for the British to govern. King recognized in *satyagraha* a way for black Americans to break the back of segregation[21].

Dr. King also used his clout and philosophy of nonviolence and passive resistance to achieve success during the height of the civil rights movement of the 1950s and 1960s, especially in establishing the Southern Christian Leadership Conference (SCLC), which opposed the evils of Jim Crow segregation in every respect. Professor Lewis has pointed out that the essential ingredients or formula for nonviolent civil rights campaigns during Dr. King's activism, were "perfected in Montgomery [Alabama]": where there were "unsuccessful presentation of elementary grievances; mounting of increasingly provocative peaceful demonstration[s]; gross acts of violence by white citizens and outrageous misconduct by local law enforcement and judicial bodies, relentlessly reported by the national media"[22]. In so many words, the media played a significant role in the success of Dr. King's political activities, mainly in the segregated and racist South.

However, the specific and effective tactics often used by Dr. King led to his arrest and incarceration on several occasions, particularly as the movement in the South grew to a heated, nation-wide endeavor. Ultimately, in 1956, Dr. King, as a leading voice for blacks "gained a major victory and prestige as a civil rights leader, when the Montgomery buses" were finally desegregated or integrated and everyone was treated on a first-come, first-served basis[23]. Moreover, "the Montgomery bus boycott launched the *direct action* phase of the civil rights movement"[24], which directly confronted and challenged members of the dominant group for their mistreatment of minorities. More importantly, Dr. King was able to effectively weigh the possible ramifications of encountering hard-nosed racists and other hateful White Southerners in regards to potentially explosive racial issues, because he deeply cared about the well-being of black people everywhere, of every sort. Evidently, Dr. King was not oblivious of the fact that many white Americans did not like him, and wanted to subvert and undermine the nascent civil rights and black power movements, respectively. But his quiet optimism about gaining equality for black Americans was absolutely infectious in the black community. And in a particularly profound way, the struggle for black freedom and liberation in the United States in the 1960s became an everyday thing (or serious process) for black Americans at that time. But Dr. King did become disillusioned (or despondent sometimes), because of the lack of immediate racial progress or slow pace of diversity reforms.

Dr. Martin Luther King, Jr., of course, was a towering figure who influenced many who sought the "truth" and social change by nonviolent means. Dr. King was also someone who ultimately thought he was capable of wielding effective power and authority in the black community, because of his voice, especially among black revolutionaries, who thought that violence was the answer to correct the social inequalities in the United States. Perhaps Dr. King didn't know any other way to be, as the civil rights movement became irresistible. However, many black militants during this time were hateful and jealous of Dr. King's phenomenal success. This is to say that Dr. King never tried to take the civil rights movement toward a more militant or violent direction, when he was directly challenged in the early 1960s by such black nationalist groups as the Nation of Islam (or Black Muslims) and the infamous Black Panther Party. Professor of Political Science Dennis Dalton tells us that, with righteous action, "Martin Luther King, Jr. actively demonstrated in America, as Gandhi had in India, that there [was] nothing "unreal" about nonviolence"[25]. Fortunately, many black Americans rejected the whole idea of trying to change things by violent means. Therefore, this vote of confidence in Dr. King's overall political strategy gave him the will and conviction, perhaps, to go on, to move forward with hope and faith. In addition, it allowed an "infusion of money and talent from national liberal organizations and increasing participation of non-resident whites (clergy, labor, students) in nonviolent demonstrations" against entrenched racism, specially in the South[26].

Dr. King was also willing to criticize destructive black culture, and selfish black habits and behavior—such as with some blacks' use, separately, of alcohol and illicit drugs. No doubt, Dr. King didn't think that some recalcitrant black people were of greater interest to him than those that agreed with him; it was just that he was more concerned about some of their malign, misguided, and violent intentions more than anything else. Of course, Dr. King always stood posed for action, as he keenly studied Gandhi and embraced his methods of militant nonviolent resistance and techniques of *civil disobedience* for the modern-day civil rights and black protest movements in the United States. In so many words, Dr. King "struggled to erase the color bar of stigmatization and exclusion that had relegated racial minorities to second-class citizenship"[27]. Furthermore, Dr. King's respect for Mohandas (Mahatma) Gandhi had always been profound, as he too rejected *nihilism* and violence. As the late psychoanalyst Erik H. Erikson has written, "Militant nonviolence [was at least descriptive of the attitude and the action of the *satyagraha*], but it failed "to suggest the spiritual origin of nonviolent courage in Gandhi's truth"[28], which so influenced Dr. King and other black activists during the civil rights era.

For his controversial work, mostly as a civil rights leader and activist, Dr. King was awarded the Nobel Peace Prize in 1964, making him the youngest-ever recipient. However, as Professor Stanley Wolpert explains, Gandhi didn't win the Nobel Peace Prize, perhaps, for racist reasons, as "the head of the Nobel Committee after World War II, Gunnar Jahn, blocked Gandhi from getting the prize when two other members of the committee proposed his name"[29]. And Jahn never gave a logical or sound reason for his disapproval of Gandhi's bid for the prestigious prize. It should be pointed out, however, that the indomitable Gandhi "was able to mobilize and galvanize more people in his life-time than any other person in the history of this world. And just with a little love and understanding goodwill and a refusal to cooperate with [evil laws], he [Gandhi] was able to break the backbone of the British Empire"[30].

Conversely, Dr. King was able to break the backbone of white supremacy and legal segregation in the United States, as he tried in many ways to emulate Gandhi, which allowed him to do great things (in terms of insuring racial equality) for blacks and other minorities in America. Dr. King was certainly energized by the righteous things Gandhi was able to accomplish in India. However, Dr. King did not have the support of the U.S. government behind him. For example, J. Edgar Hoover and the FBI created a smear campaign to discredit Dr. King, as he was considered a threat to the internal security of the United States. What rubbish. Such perceived treachery and subversion on the part of Dr. King was just plain nonsense, ridiculous. In the end, "multiple atrocities perpetrated by [racist] whites," led to "direct or indirect federal intervention and negotiation settlement with chastened or cowed white officials"[31]. So when it is all said and done, we have Dr. Martin Luther King, Jr. to thank for much of the progress and grandiose changes for blacks in America, but the struggle for equal rights still goes on today. In other words, we are still struggling with our racial identity in the United States.

Conclusions

Both Mahatma (Mohandas) Gandhi and Dr. Martin Luther King, Jr. were remarkable men, magnetic leaders, despite their human frailties, weaknesses, and failures, who led famous marches to protest the unequal treatment by white dominant groups. Gandhi, for example, led a famous protest march "to extract salt from the sea", mainly because of the British government's unfair salt tax in 1930, and entrenched monopolies. Professor Clayborne Carson explained this momentous event in this way:

> He [Gandhi] started ... walking with eight people. Gradually the number grew to millions and millions. Gandhi went on and reached down in the river and brought up a little salt in his hands to demonstrate and dramatize the fact that they were breaking this law in protesting against the injustices they had faced over all the years with these [unfair] salt laws[32].

Gandhi, apparently, marched with determined implacability, or undiminished purpose to achieve his goals, which were contrary to British wants and expectations. And Dr. King, as a result of his nonviolent campaigns, and an outpouring of support, orchestrated and fearlessly led the unforgettable and massively popular march on Washington, D.C., which protested how poorly and inhumanely blacks were being treated in the United States. It was also during this time that Dr. King gave his famous "I Have a Dream Speech," at the end of 1963. Such audacious but separate, momentous marches must have certainly taxed both men's strength and endurance—that is, beyond the obvious political risks. And in several complex ways, Gandhi and Dr. King were similar. Indeed, their capacity for expressing in action [certain] theories of nonviolence was not the only feature they shared. Some scholars claimed that both men were cut from the same activism cloth. N. Radhakrishnan writes:

> Gandhi's greatness lied in the manner in which he could successfully extend the principle of nonviolence from the individual to the social and political plane. He affirmed that nonviolence is the greatest force at the disposal of mankind and it is mightier than the mightiest weapon of destruction devised by the ingenuity of man[33].

Gandhi reminded us also about what it really means to be "caring" humans; as well as showing us the need for compassion and some common interdependence, for he firmly believed that mankind was put on this earth to do great things. Thus, Gandhi's philosophy can perhaps translate across all cultures, as he had extraordinary insights into the suffering of all kind of indigenous people, or people of color. It also bears remembering that, "as pastor of the Montgomery [Alabama] Dexter Avenue Baptist Church, Dr. King helped to liberate the United States from the poison [and evils] of racial discriminations and nonviolently transformed America's civil rights movement ...[34]" Many militant blacks, however, as already mentioned, did not believe in Dr. King's self righteous preaching about loving your enemies and nonviolent activism. Novelist and National Book Award winner, Charles Johnson put it this way in his brilliant novel *Dreamer*, about the life of Dr. Martin Luther King, Jr.:

> A decade after his Montgomery victory, and spiraling successes throughout the South ... in the mysterious way the [Civil Rights] Movement kept changing as he chased it, and changing him, pushing him higher and higher, beyond anything he'd dreamed possible ... from local bus boycotts to unqualified calls for integration, and finally to grander dreams of global peace and equality—a decade after his finest triumphs for nonviolence, the press, and even people who'd joined hands with him singing "We Shall Overcome ..." saw his methods as outmoded, his insistence on loving one's enemies as lunacy, his opposition to Black Power as outright betrayal[35].

These profound remarks by Johnson points out that Dr. King also had to carefully maneuver within the black community to deflect criticism of his tactical and strategic decisions of nonviolence, in terms of the black freedom struggle. Dr. King always tried to explain his motivations (for doing certain things), such as addressing issues of injustice, unfairness, immorality, and inequality with great detail. Hence, both Gandhi and Dr. King's organized resistance and brave actions were calculated, not impulsive, with high hopes for peaceful encounters and success. Gandhi, however, never thought he should be bound by British occupation laws. In many ways, Gandhi and Dr. King's ability to articulate their positions effectively was indeed commendable, as they were able to positively affect their political and social worlds. Otherwise, they might have been little more than footnotes in history. Both men were certainly courageous in their truth telling, as they said many things convincingly, always taking the high road, while talking about the political and social issues that mattered during their times. Gandhi, for example, once stated that "no one can ride on the back of a man unless it is bent"[36]. Similarly, Dr. King once wrote that: "He who is devoid of the power to forgive is devoid of the power to love"[37].

What both Gandhi and Dr. King accomplished in life (or during their unique lives) has been ostensibly good for the world. And learning about the noteworthy lives of Gandhi and Dr. King is crucially important for *anyone* living in our world today. This is to say, both men are revered because they felt that diplomacy and peace, not simmering conflict, should be given a chance (always) in settling disagreements or *any* disputes. Even so, there must have been times when Gandhi and Dr. King, perhaps like Jesus Christ, might have wondered if their missions in life were worth the effort. To be sure, both illumined men proved that if you put your heart and soul into something, as well as your mind into any endeavor, you could achieve it or *anything,* moving mountains, so to speak, and the world. In this respect, Gandhi and Dr. King were also able to face down their most vitriolic and hateful critics. To understand both of these great men, these "warriors of peace," is to discover the truth about the ideas and principles of Democracy, politics, justice, peace, and love—or what Gandhi and Dr. King tried to impart to the world. Essentially, both men loved humanity, in general, believing that humans were capable of decency and goodness. However, much of what both men achieved, for all intent and purposes, is being quietly ignored by some people today. Why? Moreover, many of us are unaware that we can actually change the world as a consequence of our actions, like Gandhi and Dr. King. Even more important, we must ask: Can the techniques of nonviolence be used to achieve whatever end in today's controversial political arena? That is—when it comes to radical politics or engaging in unjust activities. While great strides have been made in resolving human problems by nonviolent means, the causes of racial injustice, conflict, and human suffering, as well as poverty are still prevalently with us. Professor of psychiatry at Tufts University School of Medicine sums things up this way:

> Gandhi and King succeeded to a degree ... but they also failed. India was fatally
> divided because Hindus and Muslims could not accept each other; segregation

ended in the U.S., but it happened slowly and at the cost of social traumas whose consequences still afflict us[38].

Perhaps, both Gandhi and Dr. King felt that mankind should always try to understand the truth of our existence, even if they failed. And until the day that both men regrettably died, they determinedly approached or confronted adversities and finally their fate. Gandhi and Dr. King, during their controversial and notable lives, continued to envision a world of peace, hope, and harmony, as in the absolute brotherhood and sisterhood of all men and women. The two men also advocated for political and social justice for everyone, which is worthy of consideration. And like Dr. King, who was struck down by white racist and assassin James Earl Ray on April 4, 1968 in Memphis, Tennessee, Gandhi was also tragically shot down at "point-blank-range" by Nathuram Godse, on January 30, 1948. Specifically, Gandhi was murdered by Godse, an angry young Hindu radical and fanatic who believed that Gandhi had sold-out the Hindu people because of his solicitude, tolerance, and solidarity with the Muslim community. Of course, Gandhi saw Muslims as human beings and part of the global society too. Unfortunately, Gandhi was assassinated in New Delhi where he was attending a prayer meeting. Coincidentally, Dr. King was murdered in Memphis, "a day after delivering his mesmerizing "I've been to the Mountaintop" speech (like having a religious revival) to striking sanitation workers[39], who were demanding better pay and working conditions, as well as the right to unionize. Finally, the venerable Dr. King and Mohandas (Mahatma) Gandhi were able to change their oppressive and particular (and peculiar) worlds by nonviolent means; and we must all be inspired by that. We must also give praise to their glorious deeds, because they made a difference. Unfortunately, Gandhi and Dr. King's unexpected and untimely deaths have left a noticeable void in our lives (or existence), and perhaps all of us (humans) should wonder what they could have accomplished for the future of mankind had both men lived. Perhaps it was their fate to die. People loved both men because they told the truth about the oppression of indigenous people by rapacious dominant groups. As it is, we must all try to put into action the magnificent, nonviolent beliefs and ideas of Gandhi and Dr. King, especially in our everyday lives in order to achieve harmony, balance, love, and peace in the world which they often spoke so articulately and grandiloquently about.

Notes

1. Ronald J. Terchek. *Gandhi: Struggling for Autonomy* (New York: Rowman & Littlefield Publishers, Inc., 1998), p. 203. Incredibly, what made Mahatma Gandhi and Dr. Martin L. King so compelling was they both addressed injustice and inequality during their activism days, which seemed improbable given the racial times and circumstances.

2. Michael J. Nojeim. *Gandhi and King: The Power of Nonviolent Resistance* (Westport, Connecticut: Praeger, 2004), p. 263.

3. Larry Copeland, "Among Icons, A New King: Memorial on Mall honors an era's 'man of peace,'" *USA Today* (August 19–21, 2011), pp. 1A–2A.

4. Mohandas K. Gandhi, "Hind Swaraji," in Kevin Reily. *Worlds of History: A Comparative Reader, Volume Two: Since 1400,* second edition (New York: Bedford/St. Martin's, 2004), p. 339.

5. *Ibid.* See also Joseph Lelyveld. *Great Soul: Mahatma Gandhi and His Struggle with India* (New York: Alfred A. Knoph, 2011).

6. Robert Jakoubek. *Martin Luther King, Jr.* (New York: Chelsea House Publishers, 1989), p. 34.

7. Gandhi, "Hind Swaraji," p. 339.

8. N. Radhakrishnan. *Gandhi Human Security and the Soka Renaissance* (India: G. Ramachandran Institute of Nonviolence, 1997), p. 6.

9. William H. Harris and Judith S. Levey, editors. *The New Columbia Encyclopedia* (The New Columbia University Press, 1975), p. 1042.

10. Guy B. Adams and Danny L. Balfour. *Unmasking Administrative Evil* (Thousand Oaks, California: Sage Publications, Inc., 1998), p. 15.

11. Radhakrishnan, "Gandhi Human Security and the Soka Renaissance," p. 6.

12. John Oliver Killens. *Black Man's Burden* (New York: Pocket Books, 1969), p. 118.

13. Jakoubek, "Martin Luther King, Jr.," p. 35.

14. Killens, "Black Man's Burden," p. 118.

15. Nojeim, "Gandhi and King," p. 295.

16. Richard Willing, "Rosa Parks Center of Legal Storm," *USA Today* (December 28, 2004), p. 3A.

17. David Levering Lewis, "Martin Luther King, Jr., and the Promise of Nonviolent Populism," in *Black Leaders of the Twentieth Century,* edited by John Hope Franklin and August Meier (Urbana and Chicago: University of Illinois Press, 1982), p. 278. According to Journalist Larry Copeland, "Blacks in Montgomery, whose previous attempts to desegregate the buses had fizzled, rallied to her [Rosa Parks'] defense, organizing a massive boycott of the Montgomery Bus Line". See Larry Copeland, "Among Icons, A New King," *USA Today* (August 19–21, 2011), p. 2A.

18. A Modern Heroine: Rosa Parks," *Las Vegas Review-Journal* (February 1, 2005), p. 6E.

19. Harris and Levey, editors, "The New Columbia Encyclopedia," p. 1479.

20. Terchek, "Gandhi: Struggling for Autonomy," p. 201.

21. Jakoubek, "Martin Luther King, Jr.," p. 36.

22. Lewis, "Martin Luther King, Jr.," p. 278.

23. Harris and Levey, editors, "The New Columbia Encyclopedia," p. 1479.

24. Tomiko Brown-Nagin. *Courage to Dissent: Atlanta and the Long History of the Civil Rights Movement* (New York: Oxford University Press, 2011), p. 122.

25. Dennis Dalton. *Mahatma Gandhi: Nonviolent Power in Action* (New York: Columbia University Press. 1993), p. 177.

26. Lewis, "Martin Luther King, Jr.," p. 279. Dr. King also sincerely cared about the victims of exploitation and welfare of other common people.

27. Manning Marable. *Malcolm X: A Life of Reinvention* (New York: Viking, 2011), p. 482. It should also be noted, according to Marable that Dr. Martin Luther King "embodied the historic struggle waged by generations of African Americans for full equality," p. 480.

28. Erik H. Erikson. *Gandhi's Truth: On the Origins of Militant Nonviolence* (New York: W.W. Norton & Company, Inc., 1969), p. 198.

29. Stanley Wolpert. *Gandhi's Passion: The Life and Legacy of Mahatma Gandhi* (Oxford and New York: Oxford University Press, 2001), p. 265.

30. Clayborne Carson, editor. *The Autobiography of Martin Luther King, Jr.* (New York: Warner books, 1998), p. 129.

31. Lewis, "Martin Luther King, Jr.," p. 279.

32. Carson, "The Autobiography of Martin Luther King, Jr.," p. 128.

33. Radhakrishnan, "Gandhi Human Security and the Soka Renaissance," p. 6. It should be pointed out, however, that Gandhi and Dr. King never steered clear of controversy; and they sacrificed their lives for the good of less fortunate people, and against ruthlessly exploitation.

34. Carson, "The Autobiography of Martin Luther King, Jr.," p. 123 and 169. See also Dalton, "Mahatma Gandhi," p. 177.

35. Charles Johnson. *Dreamer: A Novel* (New York: Scribner, 1998), p. 6.

36. Wolpert, "Gandhi's Passion," p. 265.

37. Martin Luther King, Jr. *Strength to Love* (Philadelphia: Fortress Press, 1963), p. 48.

38. Nassir Ghaemi, "Depression in Command," *The Wall Street Journal* (July 30–31, 2011), p. C3. Although the powers-that-be didn't really care about the two men, both Gandhi and King were respected and esteemed by almost everyone; they were especially recognized as peacemakers.

39. Copeland, "Among Icons, A New King," p. 2A (pp. 1A–2A). It should be pointed out that many of the issues both Gandhi and Dr. King dealt with during their day still exist, unfortunately, in today's world.

Reading 2.2

Ruby Duncan, Operation Life, and Welfare Rights in Nevada

Earnest N. Bracey, Ph.D.

T HE NAME RUBY DUNCAN ONCE REVERBERATED throughout the Las Vegas community. For those who know her, she is a legend. For many living in Las Vegas today, however, Ruby Duncan is hardly known. More important, the nation has all but forgotten her in the national backlash against welfare mothers, a crusade fostered by the Reagan era's taunt: "the Cadillac welfare mothers." Nonetheless, Ruby Duncan has become an acknowledged and powerful figure in Las Vegas's black community over the years, and even in her well-earned retirement. In fact, this matriarch has blazed new trails in race relations in Nevada and mapped the way politically for many voiceless minorities.

Born on a sharecropper's farm in the backwoods of Tallulah, Louisiana, on June 1, 1932, she might have lived a hard and miserable life. Indeed, one has only to read Alice Walker's Pulitzer-prize-winning novel, *The Color Purple,*[1]—the fictionalized life of poor Celie, the book's main black female character—or view Steven Spielberg's movie of the same name, to get an idea of how Ruby Duncan's life perhaps might have been.

Working a dawn-till-dusk existence on the infamous Ivory Plantation in the rugged Louisiana cotton fields, her bittersweet life started out as a struggle to exist—and to survive. Even then, as a black child of the depression, Ruby Duncan would not give up. She was ambitious, street-smart, and proud—qualities necessary for the survival of poor blacks at that time. Those early years in Tallulah were filled with pain and hardship, and suffering. However, Duncan hoped for a better life, even as she was as a little girl being physically and sexually abused by trusted male relatives. Psychologically traumatized for years, and initially with low self-esteem, she struggled on.

Ruby Duncan knew neither her parents, who died before she was four years old, nor her siblings, a sister and three brothers. Little Ruby was unceremoniously shuttled from relative to relative to live. Nevertheless, she kept on striving, eking out a meager existence for herself, almost alone,

Photo of Ruby Duncan taken while running for the Nevada state legislature in 1977. (*Photo courtesy of Ruby Duncan*)

going to school when she could by walking eight grueling miles to a small, decrepit, grey wooden church that served also as a makeshift school for black children from October to December each year. According to historians Mary Frances Berry and John W. Blassingame

> Southern whites wanted to limit black education to elementary schools where the chief focus would be on industrial education, teaching trades and manual skills. The black schools [were] organized around the labor needs of southern planters and consequently close[d] during planting and harvesting times.[2]

After learning the rudiments of mathematics, reading and, writing, Ruby Duncan dropped out of school in the ninth grade, receiving no further formal education until she earned her general equivalency diploma—the GED—as an adult in Nevada. She regretted dropping out of school, but thought it was her only alternative under the harsh circumstances. Duncan had always dreamed of attending the predominantly black Grambling State College in Louisiana, now Grambling State University, but it was not to be. Therefore, it was not an easy decision, as it began a difficult time for her as a full-time waitress and barmaid for $9.50 per week for more than eighty hours a week. Unfortunately for Ruby Duncan, this was the only type of work she could find in segregated Louisiana. Pregnant, at sixteen, the result of a rape by a rejected suitor, she gave birth to her first child, a bright-eyed baby boy. Her motivation was always to do the right thing, to do a good job, to make a better life for herself and her small child. Young and naive, mostly a child herself, she could not properly take care of a new baby all by herself while trying to earn a living working long, hard hours. Therefore, to help out, Duncan's favorite aunt Mamie Lynn, in Las Vegas, took sole responsibility for raising the boy.

Sad, lonely, tired, and missing her beloved child, Ruby Duncan later took her Aunt Lynn's welcomed suggestion (or advice) that she move immediately to the sprawling city of lights, where the wages were considerably better than in the racist and segregated South. Indeed, in Las Vegas blacks could earn fair wages for an honest day's work. And the lure of decent work became almost irresistible. In fact, many blacks were seeking their fortunes and opportunities outside the South. The black community in Las Vegas, for example, increased from just two hundred in 1940 to more than sixteen thousand in the 1950s. Historian Nell Irvin Painter explains:

> Leaving the sexual abuse, poverty, and multifaceted disabilities that plagued them, the [black] women and men who made the break from their bad "Old Country"—the rural South—were seeking their fortune (with all the meanings of the word in folklore) in the way of other immigrants to the United States. Southern [black] migrants exercised their freedom and reached a better land.[3]

Consequently, and without more thought, Ruby Duncan set off in 1952 for the unknown desert of Las Vegas, only to be disappointed as she debarked from the broken-down Greyhound Bus. To her absolute amazement, and perhaps humiliation, Ruby Duncan found racism and discrimination against blacks just as virulent and prevalent in southern Nevada as in the Deep South, with similar segregated black and white communities, and private prejudices. Nevada was even called the Mississippi of the West, because of its unofficial and unwritten discriminatory policies toward blacks and other minorities.[4]

Moreover, Duncan discovered that her Aunt Lynn lived in a surprisingly dilapidated, ramshackle hotel building of sorts in the hot desert east of Las Vegas, where poor black people had to share communal bath facilities, sometimes with unknown neighbors. Equally important, water had to be carted to that black community in rusty steel drums from ten miles away in Henderson, a neighboring and thriving city today.

Las Vegas was not the promised land she had hoped for and expected. But even with the debilitating effects of racism and discrimination in downtown Las Vegas and elsewhere, Ruby Duncan got busy and started working right away to make a decent life for herself and, after reuniting with her son, for him.

Racial divisions and Jim Crow laws were the order and business of the day in the glittering city. Black businesses and black clientele and tourists were barred even from the infamous Strip at that time. But Ruby Duncan was resolute and never discouraged. From her point of view, anywhere was better than the back-breaking labor of picking cotton in the backward South. She wanted to build a new life in Las Vegas and quickly forget her terrible past and unremarkable existence in Louisiana.

But Ruby Duncan did not escape the heavy toil and physical labor of menial tasks. She worked as a hotel maid in many of the best of Las Vegas's posh casino-resorts. After five years of continuous back-breaking labor and an inhuman workload, as well as a disabling physical injury, Ruby Duncan had all but given up. Her harsh work experiences in casino hotels led her to say, "Slavery is not over," to anyone who would listen. Along the way, Ruby Duncan married an airman from Nellis Air Force Base, but eventually divorced him, and ended up on the Nevada welfare rolls. By this time, her family had grown to five boys and two girls.

Reluctant to become a welfare mother, Ruby Duncan believed she had no other option after a life-threatening accident: She slipped on hot cooking oil on the polished kitchen floors of the Sahara Hotel. Incapacitated for almost a year because of the accident, she still somehow had to take care of her little children. Swallowing her considerable pride, Ruby Duncan accepted welfare for the first time in her life. Meanwhile, she began to acquire a political education of sorts after her slow medical recovery. For example, she spoke up about welfare rights when no one else would in the black community; and she attended political meetings to voice her opinion about the inequality of Nevada's meager welfare offerings to the poor.

In 1974, Duncan was a candidate for the State Assembly from District 17 in Las Vegas.[5] She lost that election. But, in 1977, Ruby Duncan spoke before Nevada State Senate and Assembly committees advocating full employment, food stamps for the poor, and even welfare reform. And in 1980 she also served as a Nevada delegate to the National Democratic Convention.[6]

Although Ruby Duncan has been ridiculed for her strong southern accent and squeaky little voice as well as a lack of higher education and public speaking acumen, many listened to her solemn pleas and candid statements about the rights she and other welfare recipients thought they deserved. And never did she lose her opinionated voice, even when critics dubbed her a violent militant and false messiah.

Ruby Duncan became an important social activist and organized many of the welfare fights and demonstrations in the state of Nevada, particularly in Las Vegas, serving as the president of the Clark County Welfare Rights Organization.[7] She later became involved in the National Welfare Rights Organization, becoming a dedicated and devoted member of the executive board, which was chaired by the late George Wiley, the first black research chemist for DuPont.[8] Wiley was extremely proud of Duncan's political savvy and activism in the state and her stance on welfare and right for recipients. He often praised her stellar performance.[9] Although Duncan was on welfare for approximately six years, she was never ashamed of having received help when she needed it the most. After all, the state welfare system was designed to help needy mothers and poor Nevada families, and their battle cry for entitlements became a rallying point for many disadvantaged mothers. They became known as the welfare mamas.

During the late 1960s the state of Nevada, despite the righteous cry of Ruby Duncan and other single mothers, cut benefits for the so-called welfare mamas. This action by the state ultimately incited Duncan and other welfare mothers to action. They even marched in front of the state capital in Carson City to protest the lowering of welfare grants, as welfare benefits were called then.[10] But politicians and other Nevada leaders initially paid them no heed. And to add insult to injury, the state essentially waged a campaign against the recipients in 1970, to stop "welfare cheating." Unfortunately, during these trying and tumultuous times "many welfare recipients sought anonymity rather than notoriety, and feared (with justification) that any protests on their part would make it even more difficult for them to regain their income."[11]

In response, Ruby Duncan helped organize a protest march on the Las Vegas Strip in 1971, aided by the National Welfare Rights Organization (NWRO) and George Wiley. It became a defining moment for the issue of welfare in Nevada. According to historians Nick Kotz and Mary Lynn Kotz,

> The effort had taken two months of groundwork, with Wiley orchestrating every move. The lawyers filed suit in federal court, charging that Nevada officials had violated the rights of the state's welfare recipients, depriving them of due process. The organizers carried out the painstaking work of locating the seventy-five hundred persons whose checks had been cut off or cut down, and then, with lawyers, interviewing them to determine the details of their individual cases, and at the same time trying to convince them that they should join the demonstrations and become members of NWRO. This was the most difficult part.[12]

Nonetheless, many welfare mothers attended the demonstrations and thousands of poor people came to that first Strip march. They were joined by Jane Fonda, Sammy Davis, Jr., and the leader of the Southern Christian Leadership Conference, the Reverend Ralph Abernathy.[13] An unwieldy group of angry, but peaceful demonstrators, led by Ruby Duncan herself, slowly marched down the Las Vegas Strip, chanting songs of righteous protest—and finally stopping at Caesars Palace, shouting loudly and repeatedly in unison, "We are in Caesars Palace. ... We shall not be moved." Tourists, Strip casino workers, and the like, were flabbergasted and no doubt annoyed. Other hotels on the Strip closed their doors, outraged and disgusted.

To say the least, this disrupted the tourist trade and the gaming businesses on the Strip, and made for Duncan some dangerous enemies. In the turmoil, she received her first death threat.[14] But Ruby Duncan persisted. The fear of an all-out riot on the Strip and the loss of business effectively quashed the idea of actually doing her harm. She was only lambasted and excoriated. But Ruby Duncan hadn't finished with protesting. Another massive demonstration on the Las Vegas Strip took place in 1972, and included hungry, disadvantaged children. The enthusiastic group of black children and their parents formed a human chain of determined marchers, ending up at a four-star restaurant in the famous Stardust Hotel.

The late Rev. Ralph Abernathy with Dr. George Wiley, Director of the National Welfare Rights Organization during the march on the Las Vegas strip. (*Photo courtesy of Ruby Duncan*)

For this outlandish and defiant act, Ruby Duncan and many other black welfare mothers were ultimately detained, manhandled, and arrested.[15]

Duncan was always proud that before her actual arrest, these neediest of black kids were served some of the finest gourmet dinners at any Las Vegas casino, which she helped order for them. When it came to paying the enormous tab for the very expensive meals, Duncan fondly recalled telling the Stardust casino bosses to take the bill and shove it.[16]

The demonstrations and protest marches on the Strip eventually produced positive results, because in 1975 the Nevada state government reinstated the grant benefits denied to welfare mothers and other needy families in the state. In fact, many Nevada leaders and gaming executives "met secretly and passed their strong judgments to state officials: The demonstrations must stop. Let the poor have their dole."[17] The state finally and reluctantly agreed.

Ruby Duncan became more emboldened by the demonstrations. Her struggles for the disadvantaged poor identified her as a sincere and committed community leader, as well as an important social activist in Las Vegas. The state of Nevada and even the nation began to take notice of this personable, heavy-set, formidable, black former welfare mother. Ruby Duncan never sought notoriety. It came as a price of leadership. In 1972 her job as the founder and later president of Operation Life put her in direct competition with the bureaucrats who ran the state welfare department. Operation Life was noted for being a Westside community self-help organization that organized poverty programs. Originally, according to journalist Bob Palm, Operation Life "was a small operation dedicated to helping the poor in West Las Vegas get the bare necessities of life,"[18] and which ran a "phalanx of programs that [catered] to the most needy ... the poor, the sick, the ill-housed, those without health care, [and] those without warm clothes."[19]

Needless to say, Ruby Duncan has never had a great love for the Nevada Welfare Division. This was one of the reasons she decided to establish Operation Life, a private, nonprofit corporation. Operation Life was also designed to help the poor and underprivileged everywhere in Southern Nevada, even beyond the black community. An unpublished account of the organization points out:

> Operation Life started in 1972 with one silver dollar donation and ten volunteer workers, welfare mothers with a mind to achieve economic independence. Within the first year, the women ... negotiated with First Western Savings Association for the rent-free occupancy of a five story former hotel [the Cove] in the heart of the low income community [the Westside].[20]

Duncan started out her operation under the auspices of the Welfare Rights Organization, which she chaired in Nevada, in one of the many offices at the famous Moulin Rouge resort in Las Vegas. But her group was ordered to vacate the premises, in her words, by "the white owners at the time," and without a full explanation.[21] Later, however, Duncan set up shop for Operation Life in the abandoned and now defunct Cove Hotel. It was noted for housing black entertainers who performed on the Strip in an earlier incarnation of Las Vegas—singers such as Lena Horne, Pearl Bailey, and Sammy Davis, Jr. They could not stay at the various white casino-resorts until the first integrated hotel in Las Vegas, the Moulin Rouge, was opened in 1955.[22]

After convincing the board members of the First Western Savings and Loan to give her fledgling organization the outright lease for the boarded-up Cove, at D and Jackson streets on the Westside, Ruby Duncan became one of the first black women in the state to operate a viable self-help organization. But the dilapidated building was no gem. It was an eyesore, an empty shell of its former glory. This did not deter Ruby Duncan, however. She helped renovate the place with the strong support and help of loyal friends, volunteers, and later, paid employees. An Operation Life newsletter explained:

> In 1973, the women [volunteer workers and welfare mothers] purchased and renovated a 10,000 square foot [part of the] building for $84,000, with 100% financing provided by a team of four local lending institutions. At the same

time, a commitment was secured from the Clark County Library District to lease the renovated building for the first branch library in West Las Vegas. Monthly lease payments service[d] the debt and continue[d] to build equity for Operation Life.[23]

Duncan still had to fight the establishment to keep the place going, insuring that the building had heat in winter, and air conditioning during the stifling summer months. Duncan pressed on, ensuring also that the Westside community had a reliable day-care center for poor working mothers, recreational facilities, a much-needed swimming pool, a youth program, and a black-run, locally written, community newsletter—all operating or functioning in and around the depressed property located at the Cove Hotel.

Duncan brushed aside her detractors. With the help of hired consultants, she learned how to write proposals for federal economic development grants. She was able to provide local welfare mothers with "intellectual (educational) training" and emotional support to empower them to take care of themselves and their many children and to stand up for their guaranteed and appropriate rights.

Ruby Duncan outside the Operation Life Headquarters building in Las Vegas, Nevada. (*Photo courtesy of Ruby Duncan*)

When it came to lobbying and fund raising, Ruby Duncan became a sort of Zen master. Her gentle suasion enabled Operation Life, over the years, to receive millions of dollars in contributions, grants, and other funds. Duncan even applied directly, and successfully, to the Nevada state government for grant money. She also received money from wealthy white philanthropists who believed in her cause. "Remarking on Ruby Duncan's lobbying ability," the unofficial story of Operation Life reports that "Nevada's former United States Senator Howard Cannon once advised the late Senator Hubert Humphrey, 'Don't ever get her mad.'"[24] Clearly Ruby Duncan was a human dynamo and a force to be reckoned with. With several city, state, and federal grants, plans for a new building emerged for Operation Life on West Owens Avenue on the Westside. Thanks to the personal supervision and careful administration of Ruby Duncan, the building eventually was constructed. Later, the Cove Hotel mysteriously burned down. Fortunately, the new facility on Owens Avenue had already been occupied, but invaluable historical files were destroyed in the Cove Hotel fire.

The new facility housed the first Westside community medical center, in 1973, for low-income and welfare families, and it was also federally funded. In fact, as "The Operation Life Story" notes:

> Health and nutrition programs have consistently been the core of Operation Life's strategy'. With its clinic, WIC program, summer feeding program, day care center and library, Operation Life ... consistently served the victims of poverty and dependent children who were malnourished and anemic, and therefore undereducated, and adults who were underemployed.[25]

Operation Life lost its protracted battle to operate the medical clinic independent of city government, Carson City, and the federal government. The state of Nevada eventually took over the organization's medical efforts. Ruby Duncan's big success, however, came in 1973, when her organization brought the Early Periodic Screening program to Las Vegas. The overall goal of the program, which was federally funded, was to improve health care for the poor. Operation Life has also been credited with helping to define welfare standards for the state. Eventually, the organization leased some of its larger offices to the now embattled local Las Vegas NAACP, and to many other beneficial Westside community entities. The place has also become a focal point for the entire black community, as it continues to provide health care information, food, self-help guidance, advice, and business assistance programs for thousands of residents. It should be noted that at one point, Operation Life was Westside's largest property owner. The building it erected on Owens Avenue is still owned by the operation.

Ruby Duncan has no regrets, especially as she remembers being charged, along with Operation Life, with corruption and fraud by Nevada state prosecutors in the 1980s. She believes the campaign against her was "well planned and organized."[26] During one memorable court session, Duncan was verbally attacked, abused, ridiculed, called an "animal," mocked and pronounced guilty before the evidence was even presented.[27] But one day, in an act of sheer bravado and outright defiance, she rose before the Nevada state court and prosecutors and loudly exclaimed, "Yes, your honor, I am guilty ... guilty as charged for helping poor people."[28] Such is the heart and character of Ruby Duncan. Orleck explained it another way:

> Prosecutors were so abusive—going so far as to call Duncan "an animal"—that after one cross-examination, Duncan collapsed and had to be carried out of court. One Judge accused prosecutors of playing not to the jury but to state higher-ups, and ordered them to tone down their attacks.[29]

Duncan and her organization were exonerated every time they were taken to court, because they had apparently done no wrong, and because of the organization's accurate bookkeeping. Perhaps the powers that be were frustrated that they could not cow this poor, marginally educated—but highly motivated and intelligent—black woman, or close down her Operation Life. Perhaps state prosecutors at the time had no great love for Ruby Duncan, either.

Or maybe they were jealous of her phenomenal success in administering the multi-million-dollar, self-help programs under Operation Life?[30] Who can say? Confronting the sometimes one-sided court system helped Ruby Duncan understand that not everyone in Nevada believed in the ability of Operation Life's high ideals and solutions to motivate poor people to improve their lives. Nonetheless, as "The Operation Life Story" clearly maintains:

> One of the most acknowledged strengths of Operation Life over its lifetime has been its ability to garner support for its programs and proposals. The first believers were the Clark County Legal Services programs, and the Catholic Church. In short order, health providers, day care professionals, educators, politicians followed in lending their support to the Operation Life experiment.[31]

Thinking in terms of her own situation, Ruby Duncan is especially disturbed about the state of things regarding welfare mothers for the future, particularly what she perceives as the continuing disparities and inequities of the welfare reform measures instituted by the Republican majority in congress and signed by President William Clinton. She is extremely concerned with the long-term effect of the recently passed Welfare Reform Bill; she asks,

"How can poor people start out with nothing and be expected to obtain jobs without training and education?" And more important, "Who will take care of the children?"[32]

The fight in the Nevada state courts took its toll on Duncan's time and energy, perhaps even dampened her spirits a bit, but she still never gave up. Unfortunately, however, her recurring health problems and medical complications forced her finally to resign as the president of Operation Life, which by that time was a $3-million community-development corporation with approximately a thousand members.[33] Today Duncan fights a different battle with serious medical difficulties.

But Ruby Duncan will always be associated with welfare rights and the Operation Life organization. She persevered in her love of her enemies and the poor. Moreover, Duncan is prominent in other ways. In 1971, *McCall's Magazine* named her as "first among women making the most significant [life-changing] contributions to our nation" that year.[34] In heart, robust size, energy and demeanor, Duncan is comparable to the late and remarkable Fannie Lou Hamer of Mississippi, who also rose to national prominence as a civil rights activist and crusader to empower the poor through collective action.[35] In a personal letter to Duncan, Earl G. Graves, editor and publisher of *Black Enterprise* magazine, who featured her in a March 1981 issue, writes:

> Your tireless efforts to promote and develop new ideas and change—in the wake of decreasing government influence—have proved most significant in the fight to provide meaningful opportunities for all Americans. Hence, your inclusion as one of the 30 Future Leaders [for the 1980s] in America ...[36]

It must also be pointed out that Duncan served six years as second vice-chair of the Clark County Democratic Central Committee, and as President Jimmy Carter's appointee both to the National Advisory Council on Economic Opportunity and to the White House Conference on American Families in the late 1970s.[37] Ruby Duncan was also described in the Las Vegas press as the poor people's Black Santa Claus because of the help and benefits she provided to the poor and indigents of Las Vegas in the past."[38] Furthermore, as recently as 1996, she was presented with an honorary associate's degree from the Community College of Southern Nevada, and, in 1999, a Distinguished Nevadan Award from the Nevada State Board of Regents.[39]

Ruby Duncan is a remarkable woman, a living community and cultural icon. She has certainly stepped on some people's toes to get what she wanted, but ultimately she believed it was necessary. And Duncan is still not afraid to tell others about her hard life. Yet Duncan is not angry or bitter with the world. In the final analysis, Ruby Duncan's life is a compelling story that must be told, if for no other reason, to point out and inform the public that welfare mothers past and present, as American citizens living in the United States, have (and have had) rights under the law.

Although Duncan was extremely busy during her activist days, it did not keep her from rearing her seven children. All of them have been educated and have become productive citizens. The best known of her children is a prominent and popular criminal attorney in Las Vegas, David Phillips, who also served a term as an elected member of the Board of Regents of the University and Community College System of Nevada.

There are images of Ruby Duncan that are burned indelibly into the collective memory of some Las Vegas old-timers—and perhaps those who know her from the historical record. Many of these individuals had believed that welfare mothers were supposedly lazy and did not want to work. Nothing could have been further from the truth. Indeed, as journalist Ned Day explains,

Ruby Duncan received the Distinguished Nevadan Award from the Nevada Board of Regents in 1999. Her son David Phillips, himself a former Regent, is second from the right. (*Photo courtesy of Ruby Duncan*)

The stereotype of welfare mothers ... as shiftless, lazy and incapable of caring for themselves was a cruel hoax. She [Duncan] ... prove[d] that given adequate financial resources, welfare mothers possessed the determination, guts and industry necessary to take care of themselves and their children.[40]

Ruby Duncan was once asked what would have happened if she had sat on her hands and done nothing to turn the tide for welfare mothers and the poor in Nevada. And she replied, "It may not have made any difference, but I believe the results of my efforts and all those who helped me and Operation Life would not have been the same."[41] Though no longer actively involved in the black community or Operation Life, Duncan occasionally confronts hostility from old enemies and strangers with perhaps a score to settle. But she has never been harmed by anyone. And she has no regrets, because from her point of view, it was the right thing to do to improve the conditions and hopeless lives of the poor and destitute in Nevada, particularly in Las Vegas.

Finally, Ruby Duncan stated that if she had her life to live over again, she would do it the same way—a remarkable life, an indomitable spirit, and a remarkable woman. For Ruby Duncan the struggle and life goes on.

Notes

1. Alice Walker, *The Color Purple* (London: Women Press, 1983).

2. Mary F. Berry and John W. Blassingame, *Long Memory: The Black Experience in America* (New York: Oxford University Press, 1982), 264–65. Note that this period was usually during the months of October, November, and December.

3. Nell Irvin Painter, forward to *The Great Migration in Historical Perspective: New Dimensions of Race, Class, and Gender,* Joe William Trotter, Jr., ed. (Bloomington and Indianapolis: Indiana University Press, 1991), viii–ix.

4. Elmer R. Rusco, "The Civil Rights Movement in Nevada," *Nevada Public Affairs Review* (1987), 75.

5. "Elect Ruby Duncan - 1980 National Delegate," political flyer, undated. In author's possession.

6. *Ibid.*

7. *Ibid.*

8. Nick Kotz and Mary Lynn Kotz, *A Passion for Equality: George A. Wiley and the Movement* (New York: W.W. Norton and Company, Inc., 1977). See also Nicholas Lehman, *The Promised Land: The Great Black Migration and How It Changed America* (New York: Alfred A. Knopf, 1991), 212. Lehman writes that the National Welfare Rights Organization was considered a left-wing organization for liberal goals and, of course, racial equality.

9. Kotz and Kotz, *Passion for Equality,* 19–21.

10. Jackie Brett, "Strengthening the Community," *Las Vegas City Magazine* (January 1986), 39.

11. Kotz and Kotz, *Passion for Equality,* 20.

12. Kotz and Kotz, *Passion for Equality,* 19–20.

13. Earnest N. Bracey, "A Shock to the System: Vegas Changed for Good After Ruby Duncan Gave Silent Minorities a Voice," *Las Vegas Life Magazine* (April 1999), 55.

14. Bracey, "A Shock to the System," 55–56.

15. Ruby Duncan, author's interview, 24 February 1998.

16. *Ibid.*

17. Kotz and Kotz, *Passion for Equality,* 18.

18. Bob Palm, "Poor Mother's Struggle Leads to Success," *Las Vegas Sun* (27 January 1980).

19. Ned Day, "A Real-Life Santa Claus Brings Cheer to Vegas Poor," *Las Vegas Review-Journal* (25 December 1985), 15B.

20. "Operation Life: Community Development Corporation Newsletter," undated, p. 1. In author's possession.

21. Duncan interview.

22. See Earnest N. Bracey, "The Moulin Rouge Mystique: Blacks and Equal Rights in Las Vegas," *Nevada Historical Society Quarterly,* 39:4 (Winter 1996).

23. "Operation Life," 1.

24. "The Operation Life Story," draft, in the author's possession (19 March 1979), 3.

25. *Ibid.*

26. Duncan interview.

27. Orleck, *Politics of Motherhood,* 114.

28. Duncan interview.

29. Orleck, *Politics of Motherhood,* 114.

30. "Thirty New Leaders for the Eighties," *Black Enterprise* (March 1981), 35.

31. "The Operation Life Story," 3.

32. Duncan interview.

33. "Thirty New Leaders," 35.

34. Brett, *Strengthening the Community,* 39.

35. See Chana Kai Lee, *For Freedom's Sake: The Life of Fannie Lou Hamer* (Urbana and Chicago: University of Illinois Press, 1999).

36. Earl G. Graves, letter, dated 6 February 1981. In author's possession.

37. "Elect Ruby Duncan."

38. Day, "Real-Life Santa Claus," 15B.

39. Bracey, "A Shock to the System," 56.

40. Day, "Real-Life Santa Claus," 15B.

41. Duncan interview.

Reading 2.3

A Political and Credibility Crisis for the Future

Black Democrats and Black Republicans in Conservative America

Earnest N. Bracey, Ph.D.

Introduction

We must remember that African Americans (or black Americans) voted primarily as Republicans after the Civil War and during Reconstruction, but have "turned away from the party of Abe Lincoln since Franklin D. Roosevelt's New Deal." (Page, 2005) Political scientist James MacGregor Burns explains it this way:

> African Americans had little political power until after World War II. Owing their freedom from slavery to the "party of Lincoln," most African Americans initially identified with the Republicans, but this loyalty started to change with Franklin Roosevelt, who insisted on equal treatment for African Americans in his New Deal programs. [Consequently], after World War II, African Americans came to see the Democrats as the party of civil rights. (Burns et al., 2004)

Given these facts, will there ever be another "critical election," where a complete reversal of how black people vote in elections will take place—that is, in terms of African Americans switching their political parties from Democrat to Republican? Probably not. Former Secretary of Education, Rod Paige, a black man, and Republican, under George H. W. administration, said that he became an enthusiastic Republican, at an early age, because mostly white Southern Democratic-segregationists were responsible for many of the "lynchings" his fellow black brethren endured—that is, black people were murdered, not at the hands of Republicans. Another former Black Democrat, the late Pollster Patrick Caddell, in explaining why he became a Republican stated that the Democratic Party was no longer "a party of the people but had been *hijacked* by elites, the well-educated, Wall Street and interest groups." (Lester, 2019) What nonsense. Indeed, how exactly can poor people, the middle-class, the less fortunate and disadvantage be considered *elitist*? Or how can this so-called leftist alliance that caucus with the Democratic Party be a part of Wall Street? Of course, black Democrats fundamentally disagree with *any* assertion that the Republican Party is now "the party of the people," when this major political party identifies "with big business rather [than with] unions, and with white Anglo-Saxons rather than [with] ethnic minorities." (Crystal, 1994) And what is so powerful about the Democratic Party coalition today? What Caddell should have known is: The *paradox* of being a black Republican is that they are in *cahoots* with a political party that is *elitist* in its purist form. Or they are *elitist* in the purest sense of the word.

Nevertheless, the Republican Party "has been especially aggressive in urging African Americans to consider a return to the "party of Lincoln." (King, 2005) Yet, the U.S. Republican Party today, unfortunately, is more aligned or akin to the *Dixiecrats*, or States' Rights Democrats, which was "a right-wing" Democratic splinter group" of white supremacists that broke away from the main Democratic Party, "in the 1948 election." (Stevens, 2000a) In essence, White Southerners "objected to the democrats' civil-rights program," (Stevens, 2000a) and their progressive agenda moving forward. Still, big government-Republican conservatives, perhaps, believe that even a disingenuous effort to recruit more black people and other minorities would only broaden the Republican Party and its desire for a bigger tent. (Stewart, 2005) But how can *any* black voter even entertain the idea of becoming a Republican today? This question essentially says that the Republican Party does not give black people *any* power, or a real sense of belonging. So there is no need to support this political party. And this is, unfortunately, the current dilemma of the Republican Party; and the blacks who have joined are, for the most part, in lock-step with the "right-wing" extremists in the party; as well as with Tea Party Republicans in Congress and state governments. And it seems like only a small number of black Republicans, unlike Democrats, are elected to higher office, even if they have *marquee* (political) billing, like Lynn Swann, a black man, who ran for governor of Pennsylvania in 2006, and lost to incumbent Ed Rendell, a white Democrat. (Will, 2006) As a black Republican, Swann had only to look in the mirror to know that the Republican Party is more *elitist* of the two major political parties; and that he wouldn't win the Pennsylvania governorship as a Republican. In this regard, the Republican Party has credibility issues *galore*, especially when it comes to inequality and not embracing *all* American citizens/voters.

Hence, being a black Republican today is out of the ordinary, and evocative, eliciting Democratic dread. Which is to say that the current Republican Party employs harsh election campaign tactics, such as Voting Suppression and *surgically* staged gerrymandering strategies—to win elections. Is this because such political measures are the *only* way the GOP can win campaign elections, at all levels? We must also be reminded of former President Nixon's "southern strategy," where he was able to pilfer or rip off the votes of white southern Democrats, and realigned conservatives in both political parties, as well as blacks, and independents. President Ronald Reagan, who was a former Democrat, masterfully employed this "southern strategy" to make hard-core conservative Democrats change their party affiliation to Republican. (Stevens, 2000b)

However, the late Senator Jesse Helms, a Republican and former Democrat (from South Carolina), "spurned black voters and their causes in order to curry favor with working-class white." (Judis, 2002) Moreover, "by identifying Republicans as the "white party," men like Jesse Helms helped the party revive Republican fortunes in the Deep South and in border states." (Judis, 2002) The radical Republicans at that time also "increased racial polarization and even ethnic hatred," (Judis, 2002) especially among white southerners who resented the callousness, and supposed heavy-handedness of the Democratic Party. Journalist James P. Gannon, a Republican Conservative, also made the point that, "The Democrats have bent over backwards to please minority groups—blacks, gays, angry feminists and atheists—at the expense of ... old white guys." (Gannon, 2005) But what Gannon fails to mention is: African Americans have experienced *cursed* racism and discrimination from both the Democratic Party and the Republican Party. It wasn't always the Republicans fighting against the *progressive* Democrats. For example, the Democratic Party turned its back on African Americans in the South, allowing racial abuses against them, and the bloody reign of terror by white hate groups, domestic terrorists, and white supremacists in the 1800s through the 1960s. So why did African Americans join or associate with a political party that was in many ways against their own best interests? What are we to make of this?

One-time presidential candidate and former Democratic National Committee Chairman, Dr. Howard Dean, predicted that there wouldn't be a big erosion of the "black vote" *anytime* soon, but he is concerned about Blacks "staying at home on Election Day[s]." (Lester, 2005) Finally, it should be noted that, "Republicans [sometimes] out hustle Democrats in getting their [base and] supporters to the polls" (Drinkard, 2001)—to vote in many critical elections, unlike Democrats who sometimes fail to do the same in many campaign elections. But in the end, if African American voters feel under-appreciated or *slighted* in some profound way, they will absolutely stay away from the polls and voting booths during *any* election, even for Democratic candidates. See Table 2.3.1 for partial list of black Congressional Democrats over the years.

Blacks and the Democratic Party versus the Republicans

Several years ago, while teaching public administration as a visiting professor at the University of Nevada, Las Vegas, one of my former graduate students, a smart, very ambitious black woman and former life-long Democrat, unceremoniously changed her political party affiliation and became a hard-charging Republican in the late 1990s, in order to run for local, state and national political offices in Nevada. Did she believe that the *only* way to win an election was to run as a black Republican? Probably so, given the circumstances of why she switched political parties. No doubt, today there is a *vacuum* of constructive black leadership in the Republican Party, as they try to appeal to black voters. So what are the alternatives?

Indeed, my former graduate student changed her political party, when she was *outright* rejected by the Democratic Party of Nevada (that didn't take her seriously). Therefore, she decided to get actively involved in conservative-Republican politics, causing her to regrettably make the unfortunate comment: "From my perspective, there is one last plantation in America, and it's called the Democratic Party." (Rake, 2004a) So do black Democrats have a *slave-master* mind-set after all? My former graduate student's disparaging comment and poor choice of words were surprising and perplexing to me, given that the modern-day Democratic Party and previous Democratic presidential administrations have been responsible for passing much of the major legislation that has helped not only women, but other minorities, in general, and all American citizens as well (e.g., Social Security, Medicare, the Voting Rights Act of 1965 and the Civil Rights Act of 1964, etc.). On the other hand, under Republican leadership, "unemployment reached its highest point in 1994, and black unemployment was up 26 percent when [George W.] Bush took [the presidential] office in January 2001." (Rake, 2004b) Unfortunately, the Republican Party, in recent history, hasn't passed *any* major national legislation that has really helped the average American worker, or black people, in particular. So can black Republicans even offer an accurate assessment of the black community, without some kind of political bias?

And what does it matter to African Americans who consider themselves Democratic? To be sure, many Republicans think that they have a better understanding of our nation's racial politics—that is, in terms of the two political parties. But some Democrats today try hard to tackle contentious political issues like racism, inequality, injustice, homophobia, toxic ideology, and racial discrimination of all kind. These are the inherent struggles. The Democratic Party today has also tried *unyieldingly* to give voice to the voiceless people in our society, whereas the Republican Party essentially wants to shut down voices that don't agree with them. Or so it seems. Also, many white southerners (today) are Republicans, mainly because they became disaffected "with the national Democratic policies on civil rights, segregation, and economic issues." (Harris, 1975)

Furthermore, the Democratic Party is more progressive than ever, because of a change in ideology, where they address issues of concern that might negatively affect people of color. And although the conservative Democratic Party of the past (in the 1850s), "called for protection of [black] slavery in the [US] territories," (Stevens, 2000c) it is now "the party of black voters [and] the party that promotes black presidential candidates and black candidates for Congress and governor, even in fairly conservative parts of the country." (Bacon, 2018) Therefore, black voters (today) caucus more with politicians that have ideas of social liberalism, while supporting the middle-class and the rights of poor people, and the less fortunate.

Of course, "the modern Democratic Party represents an uneasy alliance among labor, urban, and ethnic minority groups, intellectuals and middle-class reformers, and the traditional Southern Democrats;" (Harris, 1975) and this association is critically important in a *multi-racial* Democracy such as ours. The reality is that the Democratic Party today is not that concerned about political warfare or raw political power. Not surprisingly then, Democrats connect with more black people and other minorities than the Republicans. And although they might take the "black vote" for granted, we can understand the multiple dimensions of black Democrats. According to Democratic strategist and former *interim* Democratic National Committee chairman, Donna Brazile, "The Democratic Party isn't perfect and has not served us [blacks] perfectly, but since the Civil Rights Movement, it remains the best vehicle for Black political participation, representation and empowerment." (Brazile, 2006) Rightly, my former Republican graduate student later apologized to the black community in Las Vegas (which was reluctantly accepted), after initially stating incredulously that she stood by "her [previously mentioned] comment and [saw] no need to apologize for her characterization of a rival political party," (Neff, 2004) or the Democratic Party. However, she finally explained to the local public (in Las Vegas) that her harsh comments were made "within the context of explaining her conversion from Democrat to Republican in the late 1990s." (Rake, 2004a) This might have been true; but perhaps she wasn't aware that:

> The Republican Party's capacity for effective self-governance [has] degraded slowly, over the course of a long chain of rhetorical excesses ... corruptions and philosophical betrayals. Basically, the [Republican] party abandoned traditional conservatism for right-wing radicalism. Republicans [have come] to see themselves as insurgents and revolutionaries, and every revolution tends toward anarchy and end up devouring its own. (Brooks, 2015)

New York Times columnist David Brook is absolutely right in his assessment. Unfortunately, some black voters, for whatever reasons, believe that they are benefiting in some way by being Republican today. Black Republicans have also made a calculated risk, asserting that they are on the right side or political team—and that there is more money in being a Republican. Some even believe that the Democratic Party "exploit the problems of the less fortunate, promoting a sense of entitlement rather than self-sufficiency and hope," (Setmayer, 2006) without providing any evidence. So does the Republican Party actually acknowledge the Haves and Have nots? Or are Republicans concerned about what is in the best interest of all its citizens? Perhaps not. This is to say that the needs of black people and other minorities are not an overriding priority for the Republican Party. In other words, over the years, the *inequities* between blacks and whites and other social matters concerning people of color are ignored. Moreover, "a few ambitious black politicians," like Republican Allen West, "have figured out that one of the best ways to get ahead is to separate themselves from the black mainstream and present themselves as right-wing extremists." To be sure, "they don't waste time trying to convince other blacks to go along with their [kooky] ideas because they know that most of us are not crazy enough to support them." (White, 2014) Black Republicans are also "out-of-touch" with most issues and concerns of the black community. Furthermore, black Republicans, unfortunately, look past the despicable actions of black Republicans, like with Allen West; and they don't have a lot of political power within the Republican Party either. Or why can't the most ardent black supporters of the Republican Party walk away from liars, cheats, or deceitful individuals; or believe in the truth or the *experts*? We may never know.

Nevertheless, some African Americans have changed their political party identification, because of some elusive or unfathomable ideas about religion and family values (or loyalty to "the party of Lincoln"). Conservative commenter Tara Setmayer, a black woman, writes that, "the strong influence of the church and the importance of family structure are just a few reasons why" black people should become Republican. (Setmayer, 2006) But this is not the case today, because the Republican Party (today) remains in the dark when it comes to the terrible plight of the black community; and their actions in normalizing unconstitutional things, like limiting the voting rights of blacks and other minorities—through Voter ID laws—suppress "the black vote" in most elections throughout the United States.

Indeed, some black Republicans just don't want to hear it, nor are many receptive to something different when it comes to public policies that are enacted by the Democratic Party. Equally important, the false narrative by some black Republicans that "conservative policies are beginning to resonate with both the Black middle class, as well as with the disadvantaged," (Setmayer, 2006) must be rejected, because it perpetuates a *lie*. Perhaps some believe that joining the Republican Party is the right thing to do, all things considering. Is this because the Republican Party has a better plan or *moral compass*? Absolutely not. Or is it just fashionable to join them because they are in power throughout the country? Some black Republicans contend that they are able to keep things into perspective; and see the Republican Party as the "wave of the future" for blacks and other minorities, instead of working with the Democratic Party to make the Republicans more appealing, sustainable and stronger for all ethnic groups. Is this just wishful thinking?

Black Republicans also express their strong belief in our Democracy and the American Dream; but so does the Democratic Party. In fact, "even historically, Democrats have elected more than three times as many African-Americans to Congress than Republicans, and three-quarters of the Republican African Americans were elected before 1900." (Brazile, 2006) In truth, the best understanding of black Republicans is: the national Republican Party maintains a tight leash on them, demanding fealty, and respect, which they crave, but don't necessarily deserve. According to Brooks, American "citizens may fall into different political factions," but Republicans "still are joined by chains of affection that command ultimate loyalty and love." (Brooks, 2015) So are Republicans intellectually smarter? Probably not. Or is it because they are *exclusive* of the so-called "others?" Perhaps. According to Dr. Howard Dean, who was (as mentioned) a one-time presidential candidate and former Democratic National Committee chairman, the Republicans are a pretty *monolithic* party. (Wickham, 2005) However, Professor Lucius J. Barker, and *et.al.* tell us:

> The views of the new black [Republican] conservatives, like those of other groups, *are not* monolithic. Nevertheless, we can identify certain positions that constitute the core of their creed. What distinguishes them from the more traditional black leaders and thinkers is their belief that rather than being a positive force, government and government sponsored social welfare programs are primarily impediments to black progress. Like their white counterparts, black [Republican] conservatives are generally opposed to the interventionist state. They deride social welfare programs and claim that government and government-created dependence are among the major problems confronting African Americans. (Barker, 1999)

So does Barker's accurate and extensive quote explains why some black voters join the Republican Party, which has been historically hostile to African-Americans in the recent past? And how exactly do their repressive actions humanize all ethnic groups, let along steer them in a certain direction that might *benefit* the Republican Party? It must be difficult for some black Republicans to organize their political thoughts, as they accept a doctrine or philosophy that is foreign to many African Americans. For example, black Republicans have a tendency to pretend that we don't live in a racist society, which is based on "white privilege." More importantly, some black Republicans believe that there is nothing more important than their short-sighted ideology, which reaches the level of almost religious conviction. But how can black Republican *commensurate* and *enable* an unprincipled, conservative administration?

TABLE 2.3.1   Partial List of Prominent, Congressioal Black Democrats from the early 1900s to Today

1. Carol M. Braun
U.S. Senator from Illinois
(1993–1999)
(1st Black woman to serve as a
U.S. Senator in Congress.)

2. Barack H. Obama
U.S. Senator from Illinois
(2005–2008)
(Elected as the 1st Black President
of the United States, 2008–2016.)

3. Roland Burris
U.S. Senator from Illinois
(2009–2010)

4. Cory Booker
U.S. Senator from New Jersey
(2013–present)

5. Mo Cowan
U.S. Senator from Massachusetts
(Feb 2013–Jul 2013)

6. Kamala Harris
U.S. Senator from California
(2017–present)

12. Augustus F. Hawkins
House - California 21st (1963–1975)
House - California 29th (1975–1991)

13. John Conyers
House - Michigan's 1st (1965–1993)
House - Michigan's 14th (1993–2013)
House - Michigan's 13th (2013–2017)

14. Shirley Chisholm
House - New York's 12th
(1969–1983)

15. Louis Stokes
House - Ohio's 21st (1969–1993)
House - Ohio's 11th (1993–1999)

16. Ron Dellums
House - California's 7th (1971–1975)
House - California's 8th (1975–1993)
House - California's 9th (1993–1998)

17. Parren Mitchell
House - Maryland's 7th (1971–1987)

22. Andrew Young
House - Georgia's 5th (1973–1977)

23. Harold Ford Sr.
House - Tennessee's 8th
(1975–1983)
House - Tennessee's 9th
(1983–1997)

24. William H. Gray III
House - Pennsylvania's 2nd
(1979–1991)

25. Harold Washington
House - Illinois's 1st (1981–1983)
(Elected as the 1st Black Mayor of
Chicago.)

26. Mike Espy
House - Mississippi's 2nd
(1987–1993)
(Ran for MS Governor in the 2018
election.)

27. John Lewis
House - Georgia's 5th
(1987–present) (Civil Rights Icon.)

32. Bennie Thompson
House - Mississippi's 2nd
(1993–present)
(Serves on the Committee of
Homeland Security in Congress.)

33. Maxine Waters
House - California's 35th
(1993–2013)
House - California's 43rd
(2013–present)

34. Sheila Jackson
House - Texas's 18th (1995–present)

35. Jesse Jackson Jr.
House - Illinois's 2nd (1995–2012)

36. Elijah Cummings
House - Maryland's 7th
(1996–2019)
(Chairman of Investigative
Committee in Congress.)

37. Harold Ford Jr.
House - Tennessee's 9th
(1997–2007)

7. Arthur W. Mitchell
House - Illinois's 1st (1935–1943)

8. William L. Dawson
House - Illinois's 1st (1943–1970)

9. Adam C. Powell Jr.
House - New York's 22nd
(1945–1953)
House - New York's 16th
(1953–1963)
House - New York's 18th
(1963–1971)

10. Charles Diggs
House - Michigan's 13th
(1955–1980)

11. Robert N. C. Nix Sr.
House - Pennsylvania's 4th
(1958–1963)
House - Pennsylvania's 2nd
(1963–1979)

18. Charles Rangel
House - New York's 18th (1971–1973)
House - New York's 19th (1973–1983)
House - New York's 16th (1983–1993)
House - New York's 15th (1993–2013)
House - New York's 13th (2013–2017)

19. Yvonne B. Burke
House - California's 37th (1973–1975)
House - California's 28th (1975–1979)

20. Cardiss Collins
House - Illinois's 7th (1973–1997)

21. Barbara Jordan
House - Texas's 18th (1973–1979)

28. Kweisi Mfume
House - Maryland's 7th (1987–1996)
(Served as leader of the NAACP in
the 1990s.)

29. Jim Clyburn
House - South Carolina's 6th
(1993–present)
(Currently serving in the House of
Representative leadership.)

30. Cynthia McKinney
House - Georgia's 11th (1993–1997)
House - Georgia's 4th (1997–2003)
House - Georgia's 4th (2005–2007)

31. Bobby Rush
House - Illinois's 1st (1993–present)
(Served as a member of former
Black Panther Party.)

38. Gregory Meeks
House - New York 6th (1998–2013)
House - New York 5th
(2013–present)

39. Al Green
House - Texas's 9th (2005–present)

40. Yvette Clarke
House - New York's 11th
(2007–2013)
House - New York's 9th
(2013–present)

NOTE: In modern American (political) history, more Black Democrats, including Black women have been elected and served, or are currently serving in the U.S. Congress today.

For some, it is almost comical and tragic at the same time to watch black Republicans give in to a philosophy that they don't really share, either; and despite all of their hard-scrabble hopefulness. More than anything else, they have a morally bankrupt view of the world. It is as if black Republicans have very low expectations. Also, to say the least, the United States today is a more demographically diverse nation, so it is a surprise that black Republicans can put aside their *misgivings*, where the truth lies, particularly about their political party. Or they seem to have thick-skin about so-called *hackneyed*, political matters. Moreover, the Republican Party, in general, is notorious when it comes to playing the "race card" in campaign elections. For example, when Democratic candidate Harold Ford, Jr., a black man, sought the vacant, Tennessee Senate seat in the 2006 election against Bob Corker, a white man, Republicans launched and broadcasted an *ad* that sent a blatant, racist message. Essentially, the *ad* showed "a white woman with blond hair and bare shoulder who says she met Ford at a playboy party and whispers, "Harold, call me." ("RNC pulls," 2006) This highly charged, defamatory *ad* made "an implicit appeal to racial fears about black men and white women." ("RNC pulls," 2006) This negative campaign *ad* was later pulled from TV stations in Tennessee, but the damage had been done, which was *manifestly* wrong.

But Republican campaign officials, at that time, indicated that Harold Ford Jr. couldn't win such a conservative state as Tennessee, so he would likely lose anyway, despite the racist, senatorial campaign advertisement. Or it might have been "a tall order" if Ford had *any* chance of winning. (York, 2006) Harold Ford, Jr. lost that particular election to Bob Corker, and he later left the State of Tennessee (entirely) for New York. We should also mention President George H. W. Bush's uncharacteristically racist and infamous, but "successful campaign for the presidency in 1988," which was tainted and "marked in part by racially charged politics of crime that continues to reverberate [in our society] to this day." (P. Baker, 2018) Indeed, it was this racist stench of the Willie Horton episode that was shamefully introduced in U.S. presidential politics. According to journalist Peter Baker: "Mr. Horton was an African American prisoner in Massachusetts who, while released on a furlough program, raped a white Maryland woman and bound and stabled her boyfriend. Mr. Bush's campaign and supporters cited the case as evidence that his democratic opponent, Gov. Michael S. Dukakis of Massachusetts, was insufficiently tough on crime." (P. Baker, 2018) So will the Republican Party do almost *anything* to win elections, short of assassination? How can such unforgivable, uncouth actions be acceptable or good for our Democracy?

Blacks and the Republican Party versus the Democrats

Apparently, black Republicans sometimes believe in whatever sweeping, racist and dishonest schemes that the Republican Party might present? What they should know is that some hard-right extremists and white supremacists in the Republican Party have a disdain for black people and other minorities, as well as a disregard for the notion of fair play, in terms of sustaining Democratic institutions. Furthermore, Republican conservatives tend to favor *order* and *control*, "and consequently are inclined to be somewhat *sanguine* about inequalities of outcomes." On the other hand, Democratic "liberals tend, however, to infer unequal opportunities from the fact of unequal outcomes." (Will, 2007) Bluntly speaking, and as mentioned, the Republican Party is not really concerned about the welfare, or best interests of African Americans, or *all* American citizens, for that matter; and despite words to the contrary. This is to say that "the Republican Party is not serious about tackling *racism* because *racism* is an effective tool in their electoral politics." In other words, "the path to Republican victory requires exploiting stereotypes and prejudices." (Foster, 2018) So are black Republicans paying attention? It is as if they are ignoring a strong stench that permeates the entire Republican Party, while it festers into a *fetid* pool of ignorance and racial animosity.

To back up this harsh comment, we only have to look at the twisted activism of black Republican Niger Innis, the son of the late Roy Innis, who was once the celebrated director of CORE (or the Congress of Racial Equality). Niger Innis has no shame, and is now the spokesperson of the group, appearing "on Fox News and other conservative media outlets throughout the country denouncing Black Lives Mater and claiming to be a representative of the civil rights movement." (Fang, 2015) But Niger Innis *is not* really a representative of the famed and venerable civil rights movement today, but only a "mouthpiece" for the white victimhood faction of the Republican Party. And the CORE organization, according to Nekima Levy-Pounds, a professor and Black Lives Matter activist, "provides rhetoric that reinforces a "white supremacist view" of Black Lives Matter." (Fang, 2015) Perhaps it is time for the disagreeable Niger Innis to look deep into his soul and learn that law enforcement officials should be held accountable for the *plethora* of "shooting deaths of numerous unarmed black people across this country," (Fang, 2015) as the Black Lives Matter movement has tried to expose. Question: Should black Republicans totally ignore these serious matters, or pretend that they are not occurring? For some African Americans, the Republican Party has become a "right-wing" nightmare. Many black Republicans think of themselves as moderates, but this is not the direction that the Republican Party is going these days; and being a "Republican in name only," or a RINO, is not tolerated, for the most part, in the Republican Party today. Also, identifying the social and political issues (that hurt people) is very difficult for some black Republicans to acknowledge. And, "when an African American signs on with the GOP [or the Republican Party], he's often belittled as an Uncle Tom, a Stepin Fetchit, or, more malevolently, an Alan Keyes." (Labash, 2006) Keyes has been a *perennial* candidate for higher office, as a black Republican, whose extremist views brook no compromise when it comes to the abortion issue. Accordingly, Keyes is outright dismissive of political "candidates who espouse other conservative issues but support abortion rights as "unfit to lead the country." (Keen, 1995) Keyes also had the gall to say that black Republican and retired Army General Colin Powell "ended his chances of winning" the presidency when he confirmed his support for abortion rights." (Keen, 1995) Perhaps Keyes has forgotten that the right to an abortion is constitutionally mandated.

Many African Americans also see being a Republican is like a "double-edged" sword in that this political party does not represent or address the legitimate concerns of black people, as mentioned earlier. So is it a false choice to be a black Republican? Indeed, can we say that the black Republican is "the lawn jockey of American politics?" (Labash, 2006) Labash also tells us that the black Republican is "largely regarded as exploited and ornamental, a toady showpiece that enables mister [white] Charlie to say, "See, we have some, too." (Labash, 2006) Equally important, can we say that African Americans "vote Democratic based on tradition, [and] not [because of some specific] ideology?" (S. Carter, 2004) Dr. Howard Dean, a Democrat, believes, as well as many others in the Democratic Party, that "taking black voters for granted is a long-standing problem for the party that dates to the 1960s." (Lester, 2005) This is to say that the Democratic Party is good at "talking the good talk, yet failing to offer meaningful reform in [minority] communities." (S. Carter, 2004) Black Republicans, moreover, believe that the Democratic Party has black voters by the *heartstrings*, blinded, perhaps, to the obvious: That is, what the Democratic Party (really) represents and stands for in terms of power politics. And for years, "Republicans have been stressing to black voters (rightly, if not cynically), that there is no surer way to be taken for granted than to reflexively pledge allegiance to the same [political] party in perpetuity." (Labash, 2006)

To be sure, taking "the black vote" for granted must not stand if the Democratic Party is to be successful in the future—that is, in political elections; and if long-standing ethnic groups are to gain complete confidence and trust in the political party. Former Republican Governor Robert L. Ehrlich Jr. even claims "that democrats are racist for assuming that blacks should belong only to their party." (Bellantoni, 2004) But Ehrlich's statement is, of course, ludicrous. What Ehrlich should know is that, "The Black community continues to vote [Democratic], simply because of party allegiance," and because Republican officials "do not create an environment in which innovative [and progressive] policy-making can happen." (Ali, 2015) Additionally, we must ask: Are African Americans systematically marginalized and isolated from the power centers of the Democratic Party today? The answer is no. However, "the experience of blacks with the Democratic Party can be seen, at its best, as mixed." (Barker, 1999) But this does not mean that loyal black Democrats should abandon their party and run-out and join the ranks of the Republican Party. But black, hard-nose conservatives have seriously suggested that, "the Republican Party might be worth another look, especially if the GOP more directly addresses issues of concern to blacks." (Gilgoff, 2005) Nevertheless, would a change in political party affiliation even be possible? Probably not. That is, given that blacks make-up *only* a minority of the Republican Party faithful. Of course, the dominant Republican Party must sustain and maintain its power-base of white Christians and white Southerners to be successful in the future. Therefore, this coalition of white Americans will always be the Republican Party's first priority in *everything*. Moreover, John Eisenhower, the son of the late President Dwight D. Eisenhower has written that, "The current Republican Party leadership has confused confident leadership with hubris and arrogance." (Eisenhower, 2004) He goes on to scathingly point out that the Republican Party no longer emphasizes *fiscal responsibility*, which has been a part of their platform for years, nor have they balanced "the budget whenever the state of the economy [allows] it to do so." (Eisenhower, 2004) Keep also in mind that "after years of *hysteria* about the evils of debt, establishment Republican economists endorsed a [recent] budget-busting tax cut." (Krugman, 2019) In this sense, the Republican Party has sadly failed its constituents; and African Americans, in particular—that is, with the possible exception of the wealthy, or *plutocrats*, just as much as the Democratic Party has failed its "power base" in recent history. In this regard, according to black American economist and arch-Black Republican, Thomas Sowell:

> The black vote today goes automatically and overwhelmingly for the Democrats, just as the old "solid South" voted Democratic for more than a century. But nothing political is eternal and Democrats today have to scramble to try to win victories in the south, which they could once take for granted. (Sowell, 2004)

What Sowell suggests is that the Democratic Party's grip on African American voters can be eventually broken with time and patience. But can critically thinking, black voters *really* feel differently or favorably about the current Republican Party? Indeed, can black people join the Republican Party if they don't generally share the same beliefs, opinions, xenophobic goals and racist philosophies? Perhaps not. For some people of color today, the Republican Party is a constant reminder of elitism, "white privilege" and support for big businesses, and the wealthy. Although this embrace of such plutocratic entities has kept conservative voters intrigued and supportive, it has been a nightmare, as mentioned, for the poor and downtrodden. And to make things even harder, black Republicans, for whatever reasons, put up with the racist and fundamentally discriminatory treatment of black people and other minorities that occurs all around them (in the Republican Party). Or needless to say, black Republicans grudgingly accept whatever the main Republican Party does—that is, for the sake of *unity*. Therefore, it is reasonable to conclude that very few African Americans will join the ranks of the Republican Party, even if they see opportunity as being the most paramount thing in their lives. See Table 2.3.2 for a short, but complete list of black Republican members of Congress over the years.

TABLE 2.3.2 Complete List of Prominent, Congressioal Black Republicans from the 1800s to Today

1. P.B.S. Pinchback
U.S. Senator-Elect from Lousiana
(Denied seat because of his race; served briefly as the 1st Black Governor in the United States from Louisiana.)

2. Hiram R. Revels
U.S. Senator from Mississippi
(1870–1871)

3. Blanche Bruce
U.S. Senator from Mississippi
(1875–1881)

4. Edward Brooke
U.S. Senator from Massachusetts
(1967–1979)
(1st U.S. Senator elected after Reconstruction.)

9. Jefferson F. Long
House - Georgia's 4th
(Jan 1871–Mar 1871)

10. Benjamin S. Turner
House - Alabama's 1st
(1871–1873)

11. Josiah T. Walls
House - Florida's at-large
(1871–1875)
House - Florida's 2nd
(1875–1876)

12. Richard H. Cain
House - South Carolina's at-large (1873–1875)
House - South Carolina's 2nd (1877–1879)

17. John A. Hyman
House - North Carolina's 2nd
(1875–1877)

18. Charles E. Nash
House - Louisiana's 6th
(1875–1877)

19. Robert Smalls
House - South Carolina's 5th
(1875–1879)
House - South Carolina's 5th
(1882–1883)
House - South Carolina's 7th
(1884–1887)
(Smalls was a River Boat Captain and Naval hero during the Civil War.)

20. James E. O'Hara
House - North Carolina's 2nd
(1883–1887)

25. George H. White
House - North Carolina's 2nd (1897–1901)

26. Oscar S. De Priest
House - Illinois's 1st
(1929–1935)

27. Melvin H. Evans
House - Virgin Islands' at-large (1979–1981)

28. Gary Franks
House - Connecticut's 5th
(1991–1997)

5. Tim Scott
U.S. Senator from South Carolina (2013-present)
(1st Black Republican to be elected after Reconstruction and modern Congressional history from South Carolina. Also served in the House of Representatives - South Carolina's 1st District, 2011-2013.)

6. Joseph Rainey
House - South Carolina's 1st (1870-1879)

7. Robert C. De Large
House - South Carolina's 2nd (1871-1873)

8. Robert B. Elliott
House - South Carolina's 3rd (1871-1874)

13. John R. Lynch
House - Mississippi's 6th (1873-1877)
House - Mississippi's 6th (1882-1883)

14. Alonzo J. Ransier
House - South Carolina's 2nd (1873-1875)

15. James T. Rapier
House - Alabama's 2nd (1873-1875)

16. Jeremiah Haralson
House - Alabama's 1st (1875-1877)

21. Henry P. Cheatham
House - North Carolina's 2nd (1889-1893)

22. John M. Langston
House - Virginia's 4th (1890-1891)

23. Thomas E. Miller
House - South Carolina's 7th (1890-1891)

24. George W. Murray
House - South Carolina's 7th (1893-1895)
House - South Carolina's 1st (1896-1897)

29. J. C. Watts
House - Oklahoma's 4th (1995-2003)

30. Allen West
House - Florida's 22nd (2011-2013)

31. Will Hurd
House - Texas's 23rd (2015-present)

32. Mia Love
House - Utah's 4th (2015-2019)
(Although Love was the 1st Black woman to be elected from Utah as a Republican, she was defeated in her re-election bid.)

NOTE: After the Civil War and Reconstruction, Black males were predominantly Republicans, and were elected to the U.S. Congress. However, Black Democrats are overwhelmingly elected to the U.S. Congress today. Additionally, Black women were not given the franchise until 1920, with the passing of the 19th Amendment to the U.S. Constitution.

Conclusions

Unfortunately, the Democratic Party and the Republican Party will probably always be apart on the many racial/social, economic and political issues today, especially as the nature and ideologies of the two major political parties have (drastically) changed. Black conservatives have indeed changed their party affiliation, too, as they try to come to grips with joining a political party of racists, and embracing white supremacist fantasies. The Republican Party today, however, would like to distant itself from their "sordid legacy," (Judis, 2002) and dubious past. And one thing is certain: The (new) Republican Party has become "a haven for southern Segregationists and Northern "white flight" conservatives." (Page, 2005) So is the Republican Party fascist, *elitist*, or even racist? And why do white supremacists join this intrepid political party? Perhaps even some American citizens believe that the so-called Grand-Old Republican Party is "begotten by and raised on racism." (Lambus, 2005) And still others believe that newly-minted, black Republicans, especially in the South "are just disgruntled ... former Democrats." (Lambus, 2005) Obviously, though, something has to change if the Republican Party is intent on courting blacks and other minorities. Conversely, according to political commentator, Steve Rozman:

> The Democratic Party has already been criticized by some party loyalists for previously abandoning some party principles. If it were to throw in the towel on key social issues for short-term gain, such opportunism would probably provoke the flight of many of the party's core supporters and financial contributors—with no guarantee that large numbers of former Democrats would return to the party fold. (Rozman, 2005)

Even more important, according to political science professor Ross K. Baker: "Democrats, as a [political] party, have always been better at soul searching ... than winning elections," (R. Baker, 2005) especially in state elections in recent years. Therefore, the Democrats have "ample cause ... to lament its fate and search for miraculous cures" (R. Baker, 2005) after losing streaks in significant state and local elections throughout the United States. Hence, with such doubts, and losses, the Democratic Party must *never* forget its political base, or turn its back on African Americans, particularly when it comes to inclusion and basic, political rewards. Additionally, the Democratic Party must not let Republicans define the political issues, by relentlessly pressing home their progressive agenda, without retrenchment, embarrassment or feeling guilty about where they stand. Finally, Democrats must remain on the offensive, while taking a page from Newt Gingrich's Republican playbook, where the *real* truth is told about corrupt Republican politicians of all stripes. Newt Gingrich, of course, was the former Speaker of the House of Representatives, and "conservative firebrand who won control of

Congress [over two] decade[s] ago by campaigning against an entrenched, arrogant and all powerful Democratic majority." (Toner & Hulse, 2005) But political things haven't really changed for the better under the current Republican leadership. We must also ask: Does the Republican Party want to always control *every* aspect of our government? Unfortunately, the now, all powerful and dominant Republican Party is following in the same dangerous path as the Democratic Party (once did) by being also *overbearing*, exclusive and *rapacious*. Can Republicans ever understand this point? The contradictions are almost endless. Indeed, "the fragile credibility of the [Republicans in] Congress is [still] facing a severe test." (Broder, 2005) As Journalists Robin Toner and Carl Hulse have written: "Republicans are keenly aware of the dangers, having ridden to power themselves on the promise of reform, and they say they will not stumble into a landslide defeat the way the Democrats did in 1994." (Toner & Hulse, 2005) The promises made by the Republican Party do not always come to fruition, as these commitments take center stage in our society. As economist Paul Krugman writes: "Unable to make good on its promises, the GOP, like other failed revolutionary movements, [try] to maintain its grip by exploiting its position of power." (Krugman, 2006) The racial element of it all has not been lost on black voters, either. Black Republicans are also ideologically "in-sync" with the Republican Party, promising the world (so to speak) to small businesses, but not really following through (on some successful future). More specifically, black Republicans cozy up to *any* of the disastrous policy ideas of the Republican Party, like privatizing Social Security or Medicare, or tax cuts for the wealthy and denying minority citizens their Constitutional rights to vote.

Presumably, we have a fragmented political system that rewards party loyalty above almost anything else. And many are keenly aware that, "Democrats, [and] Republicans just can't get along [especially] these day," (Mean, 2005) as suspicions mount between the two major political parties. The intent, of course, is to ensure that the Democratic Party or the Republican Party maintain their political power in government at all levels. In this respect, there is still a serious disconnect between the two major political parties.

Also in this context, should "we-the-people" be satisfied that the Democratic Party and Republican Party can't work together to get things done for all the American people, no matter their background? Or will this always be the case, because "neither has *anything* to say that the other side is interested in hearing?" (Mean, 2005) Perhaps these differences are why a lot of substantial legislation is not being passed in Congress—to solve the many social and economic problems of the United States today. Nevertheless, there are black Republicans that believe, "Republican policies can lead to a better life for blacks, if given a chance." (Setmayer, 2006) Although the Republican Party is adamant about having the right (financial) policy ideas to help all Americans, there is insufficient evidence that their policies are any better than Democratic fiscal policies. We only have to look at the abject failure of former Republican Governor of Kansas, Sam Brownback, and his "trickle-down ideology," which tested a bankrupt government policy at the state level. Columnist Eugene Robinson said it best when he wrote:

> All Brownback did was apply what passes for mainstream Republican ortho-doxy these days: cut taxes, eliminate regulation, shrink government, then stand back and watch as economic growth soars. It just didn't work. It never works. Republicans cannot point to an instance in which this prescription has led to the promised *Valhalla* of skyrocketing [financial] growth. (Robinson, 2017)

So how exactly can "supply-side tax" policies help the black community, and other people, in general, if it doesn't work? Journalist Michael Mazerov concluded that "Kansas revenues plunged, leading to cuts to education and other vital services and downgrades in the state's bond rating." (Mazerov, 2018) And this misguided policy measure wasn't good for *anyone* living in Kansas, as it was pure folly. For these aforementioned reasons and many other prob-lems as well, the Republican Party should aggressively court and include African Americans and other minority voters in their election strategies—that is, if they want to remain in polit-ical power, or control of government at all levels. But does the Republican Party have the capacity to handle challenges in every ethnic community today? Probably not. At least the Democratic Party is trying to be more inclusive of blacks and other minorities. However, black Republican and economist Thomas Sowell once boldly predicted:

> If the share of the black vote that goes to the Democrats ever falls to 70 per-cent, it may be virtually impossible for the Democrats to win the White House or Congress, because they have [already] lost the white male vote and their [fervent] support among other groups is eroding. (Sowell, 2005)

Sowell's dire warning, as a staunch Republican, should give black, liberal Democratic Americans cause for alarm and serious concern. But Sowell's predictions on the result and direction of national elections have been stunningly wrong. Furthermore, black elected officials and lawmakers also see a racial shift in black, democratic voting districts between African Americans and the larger, growing Hispanic populations. This is to say that black Democrats will—in the near future—face Hispanic challengers, who may be running under the Republican Party banner—that is, in several Congressional Districts, (J. Carter, 2001) after they have been possibly converted to the Republican Party. Nonetheless, with all the major and intractable political problems presented in this paper, is it *any* wonder that some black Americans might make the hard decision in joining a major political party that operates in their own *worse* interests. Moreover, does the so-called "infighting" between the Democratic Party and Republican Party leave an opening for an independent party to take hold in the black community? In other words, will *alienation* motivate or make black Americans abandon their major political parties, and become registered independents? This remains to be seen. However, we must bear in mind, as political scientist Robert A. Dahl has written: "Political parties and party competition are essential to representative democracy; we can be pretty sure that a country wholly without competitive parties is a country without democracy." (Dahl, 2002) Unfortunately, the Democrats and Republicans will continue to play "identity politics," or political warfare in its purist or rawest form. When it is all said and done, however, one political party must *never* control all branches of our national and state governments in perpetuity. And what about the related racial matters? Although this might seem improbable, we should know that multiple parties are necessary, because such political systems give us choices, unlike with *totalitarian* or autocratic government systems. In the final analysis, we must seriously note that "if inclusiveness is the true goal" of the Democrats and Republicans, "then both [political] parties must work harder to rid themselves of political paternalism that makes black voters feel slighted." (King, 2005) Otherwise, they (black Democrats and black Republicans) will be left in the cold, and pushed away from the proverbial economic and political table.

References

Ali, O. (2015, June). Independents' Day (as told to Matt E. Stevens). *Ebony.com*, 31.

Bacon, P. Jr. (2018, December 11). Have Republicans Given Up On Winning Black Voters? *Five thirty Eight* (https://five-thirtyeight.com/features/have), 5. According to journalists Martin, J. (2019, March 1), *Las Vegas Sun*, 5, "there is a growing school of thought that democrats should not spend so much time, money and psychic energy tailoring their message to a heavily white, rural and blue-collar part of the country, when their coalition is increasingly made up of racial minorities and suburbanites." See also: Martin, J. & Burns, A. (2019, March 1). Rust Belt, Sun Belt, both? Route to White House flows many directions. *Las Vegas Sun*, 4.

Baker, P. (2018, December 3). Bush Made Willie Horton an Issue in 1988, and the Racial Scars Are Still Fresh. *The New York Times*, 10. See also: Harris-Perry, M. (2011, December 5). Note to Hermain Cain: What Lynch Mob? *The Nation*, 10.

Baker, R. K. (2005, April 20). Soul-searching within the Democratic Party. *USA Today*, 21A. For years, juxtaposing the truth, we have been hearing about how blacks will join the Republican Party in droves. But this hasn't happened, nor is it our reality.

Barker, L. J., Jones, M. H., & Tate, K. (1999). *African Americans and the American Political System* (4th ed.). New Jersey: Prentice Hall. It should be pointed out that more white Americans benefit from social welfare programs, like "food stamps," not black Americans. Also, many black Republicans believe that it is their God-given right to be Republican if they want.

Bellantoni, C. (2004, September 6–12). Democrats' claim on blacks is 'Racist,' Ehrlich says. *The Washington times*, National Weekly Edition, 23. Ehrlich also stated that "the Democratic attitude toward race opens a window for Republicans to show the diversity of the party." But clearly this remains to be seen.

Brazile, D. (2006, November). What is the Real Political Party for Black America: Democrats Offer Blacks Hope and Opportunity? *Ebony Magazine*, 182.

Broder, D. S. (2005, April 11–17). The Heat is on the GOP. *The Washington Post*, National Weekly Edition, 4.

Brooks, D. (2015, October 16). GOP has created caucus that breeds incompetence, hates compromise. *Las Vegas Sun*, 2.

Burns, J. M., et al. (2004). *Government by the People* (basic version, 12th ed., p. 118). New Jersey: Pearson Prentice Hall. See also: Wexler, S. (1993). *The Civil Rights Movement: An Eyewitness History*. New York: Facts On File, Inc.

Carter, J. (2001, May 20). Latinos after dynamics of 'black' house district. *USA Today*, 6A.

Carter, S. D. (2004, November 5). Blacks should reflect on conservatism. *USA Today*, 15A.

Crystal, D. (ed.). (1994). Republican Party. *The Cambridge Encyclopedia* (2nd ed., p. 933). New York: Cambridge University Press.

Dahl, R. A. (2002). *How Democratic Is the American Constitution?* New Haven & London: Yale University Press.

Drinkard, J. (2001, August 31). The two major parties may be losing grip on voters. *USA Today*, 4A. Once upon a time, Republicans were more liberal than they are today. But the Republican Party has now taken on the philosophy and reign of the former conservative Democratic Party of our past. Additionally, nothing crystallize the racial policies of the Republican Party today than denying that racism even exists. Furthermore, there is nothing black Republicans fear more than black Democrats voting in droves during election days.

Eisenhower, J. (2004, October 3). This is not your father's Republican Party. *Las Vegas Sun*, 3D. It should also be noted that the Republican Party "was founded in 1854 to establish the principle of liberty and justice for all Americans, regardless of race." However, "in recent years, Republicans have lost their connection to that tradition." See also: Roy, A & Yoo, J. (2019, March 25). Eastern Americans. *National Review*, 33.

Fang, L. (2015, August 17). The Long Sad Slide from Leading Civil Rights Organization to Anti-Black Lives Matter Group. *The Intercept*, 2. See also: How Roy Innis Turned CORE into a Critic of Black Lives Matter. (2015, August 17). https://the intercept.com/.../core-went ... Being a Republican today is not traditionally how the black community participates politically. And black Republicans know this. So will black Republicans even understand the true horrors of colluding with a political party that really (and generally) don't respect them? Or could we be wrong on this point? Unfortunately, black Republicans ultimately embrace the radical, new, right-wing direction of the Republican Party. In this regard, it is hard to gauge what black Republicans really believe; and how they might vote.

Foster, K. (2018, December 28). 2018 Was the Year (Some) Black Republicans Finally Came to Their Senses. *Opinion*, 2. https:/www.hufingtonpost.com/.../opinion. ... Republicans attempt to make it more difficult for black people to vote and other people of color; therefore, extreme voter suppression measures, and other discriminatory practices, as well as racial harassment continue *unabated* in the United States.

Gannon, J. P. (2005, June 16). Confessions of a white Christian Republican. *USA Today*, 19A. It should be noted here that, "Right-wing politicians and their media allies pretend to the point of farce, that the primary racial injustice in America involves white people unfairly accused of racism." What nonsense. See also: Goldberg, M. (2019, March 5). Racing to the bottom in the Republican Party. *Las Vegas Sun*, 3.

Gilgoff, D. (2005, March 21). A Courtship worth watching: Conservatives come calling, and blacks may be listening this time. *U.S. News & World Report*, 29. It should be pointed out that both, "mainstream [political] parties turned a blind eye to Jim Crow," particularly in the South. See also: Goldberg, J. (2019, February 24). Democrats shift on race. *Las Vegas Review Journal*, 1.

Harris, W. H., & Levey, J. S. (eds.). (1975). Democratic Party. *The New Columbia Encyclopedia* (p. 744). New York: Columbia University Press. The completely dogmatic—"my way or the highway"—take no prisoners, scorched earth, political philosophy of the conservative Democratic Party, in the past, against the Republican Party is something that cannot be easily glossed-over, or forgotten.

Judis, J. B. (2002, November 11). Can the GOP convince blacks not to vote soft sell? *The New Republic*, 12. "Mimicking the segregationist Democrats of the past," according to columnist E. J. Dionne, "Republicans have of late used the unfounded specter of voter fraud to justify voter ID laws and other measures squarely aimed at impeding access to the ballot box by blacks and the young." See also: Dionne, E. J. (2019, February 27). Republican Party has come to a crossroads. *Las Vegas Sun*, 3.

Keen, J. (1995, September 15). The heart of Keyes' message: Responsibility. *USA Today*, 7A. Black Republicans, like economist Thomas Sowell, make the unsupportive claim that "congressional democrats really do practice the same *kind* of ethnic politics that resulted in the *Rwandan* genocide and the Sri Lankan civil war, even if they do not practice them to the same extent." *What Rubbish*. Democrats in congress (today) haven't advocated killing anyone. See also: Williamson, K. D. (2011, December). Thomas Sowell: Peerless Nerd. *Commentary*, 45.

King, J. (2005, May 13). 'Party of Lincoln' wants blacks back. *USA Today*, 11A & 19A. Unfortunately, black Republicans seem to ignore the extreme factions of the Republican Party in our political culture, as if it doesn't matter, or fit with their mistaken beliefs. So what are their political influences in trying circumstances?

Krugman, P. (2006, December 31). Republicans won't let voters, facts get in the way of their revolution. *Las Vegas Sun*, 5.

Krugman, P. (2019, January 1). Bad faith, pathos and GOP economics. *Las Vegas Sun*, 3. According to economist Paul Krugman, "Republicans never actually cared about debt; they just pretended to be deficit hawks as a way to hamstring [Democratic] President Barack Obama's agenda." See also: Krugman, P. (2019, February 14). Debt double standard hamstrings Democrats. *Las Vegas Sun*, 3.

Labash, M. (2006, October). The Black Republicans. *Esquire Magazine*, 208. We must keep in mind that there is no empirical evidence that the "hard-right" philosophy of the Republican Party today has benefited *any* poor person of color. This knowledge should be cringe-worthy for *any* young, black person contemplating joining the Republican Party. Black Republicans don't like the name-calling, even if there is a semblance of truth in what critics say about them. Moreover, they don't like any criticism of a Republican, in whatever field of endeavor. Unfortunately, some black conservative Republicans are also seen, or "regarded as inauthentic, self-loathing, [and] soulless race traitors." See also: Williamson, K. D. (2011, December). Thomas Sowell: Peerless Nerd. *Commentary*, 46. But we must also note that it is a myth that there is real political power in being a Republican for African Americans.

Lambus, G. O. (2005, July 18). Retzer wrong for Tanzania service. *The Clarion-Ledger*, 6A. We should keep in mind that, "Some white [Republican] conservatives ... seem convinced that you can't be racist if you have an affectionate relationship with a person of color." See also: Goldberg, M. (2019, March 5). Racing to the bottom in the Republican Party. *Las Vegas Sun*, 3. No doubt, "there's been a *schism* on the left between those who argue that class and economic equality should be the dominant *prism* for social and political reformers and those who say that race and identity should be the primary consideration." *Las Vegas Review Journal* (2019, February 24), 1E.

Lester, W. (2005, May 25). Party taking blacks lightly, Dean says. *Las Vegas Review-Journal*, 19A. It is inconceivable now that blacks will become Republicans any time soon. And this reality, or subject matter is really the news.

Lester, W. (2019, February 17). Carter campaign strategist Caddell dies at age 68. *Las Vegas Review-Journal*, 5B.

Mazerov, M. (2018, January 22). Kansas Provides Compelling Evidence of Failure of "Supply-Side" Tax Cuts. *Center on Budget and Policy Priorities*, 1. https://www.cbpp.org/.../ kansas.../2/16/19. It should be understood that although Republicans consider themselves as economically conservative and fiscally responsible, they are really not. In other words, there is no real evidence to prove their claims today.

Mean, M. (2005, March 10). Democrats, Republicans just can't get along these days. *Las Vegas Sun*, 25A. According to journalist Margaret Talev, "Republicans say the Democrats have kept them out of the loop ..., making them skeptical of Democrats' promise of a new era of bipartisanship." See also: Talev, M. (2006, December 31). Democrats have ambitious agenda. *Las Vegas Review*

Journal, 12A. This is a preposterous argument for our future, because our two main political parties are still competing against one another for black voters. And it is overwhelmingly unlikely that the Democratic Party or Republican Party will suspend their rivalry.

Neff, E. (2004, September 25). Boggs McDonald play race card, draws democrats' fire. *Las Vegas Review Journal*, 1A. Despite what's been said about the Democratic Party, it "is perceived by blacks and others as being more welcoming to and supportive of blacks, although it has been criticized for taking black voters for granted in past elections." Moreover, "the nomination and election of Barack Obama have reinforced the view of the Democrats as being more amenable and open to blacks." See also: McClaim, D. & Tauber, S. C. (2020). *American Government in Black and Whites: Diversity and Democracy*. New York: Oxford University Press.

Page, C. (2005, March 9). Blacks seeing GOP differently. *Las Vegas Sun*, 14A. According to political scientists McClain and Tauber, "On issues of race, the current Republican Party is viewed by blacks and other individuals as hostile to blacks and other non-white groups, and the party has had a tortured history with race throughout most of the twentieth century." See also: McClain, P. D. & Tauber, S. C. (2020). *American Government in Black and White: Diversity and Democracy*. New York: Oxford University Press. Bear in mind that "since the 1980s," the Republican Party has become "more conservative in outlook," with an "Interventionist foreign policy stance," while "advocating for limited central government," and the so-called "protection of states' rights." See also: Crystal, D. (ed.). (1994). Republican Party. *The Cambridge Encyclopedia* (2nd ed., p. 933). New York: Cambridge University Press.

Rake, L. (2004a, October 1). Commissioner apologizes to black group for comments. *Las Vegas Sun*, 1B & 2B.

Rake, L. (2004b, September 24). Boggs McDonald's remark angers blacks. *Las Vegas Sun*, 1B.

RNC pulls *ad* in Tenn. amid racism charges. (2006, October 27). *USA Today*, 8A. Because of such despicable election antics and racist tactics, columnist Clarence Page tells us that it "remains to be seen" if "Republicans can change black or Hispanic minds" about the Republican Party. See also: Page, C. (2014, August 1). Can GOP 'ideas' lure minorities back in '14? *Las Vegas Sun*, 3.

Robinson, E. (2017, June 14). As experience in Kansas has shown, Trump/GOP plan will cause pain. *Las Vegas Sun*, 3.

Rozman, S. (2005, July 21). Dems must not give up on issues. *The Clarion-Ledger*, 8A. Democrats are progressive today, whereas Republicans are all about maintaining the status quo, while mostly rejecting the idea of political compromise. So is this why black Democrats are not switching to the Republican Party—to so-called get ahead?

Setmayer, T. (2006, November). Liberals' relationship with blacks is like a bad marriage. *Ebony Magazine*, 183. However, it should be noted here that "Democratic lawmakers say their "big tent" party must embrace varying degrees of liberal ideology to match the House [of Representative] districts they hope to represent." See aslo: Cochrane, E. (2019, February 24). Liberal Group Is

Seeking Its Next Ocasio-Cortes (Or Two, Or Five, Or Ten). *The New York Time,* 15. We must keep in mind that black Republicans aren't pulling any financial strings in the Republican Party, all things considering. Some might also argue that black Republicans are essentially *powerless,* because of a lack of inclusion in the power circles of the Republican Party.

Sowell, T. (2004, August 30–September 5). Relieving the democrat stranglehold on the black vote. *The Washington Times,* National Weekly Edition, 33.

Sowell, T. (2005, May 26). Black voters must be kept frightened. *Las Vegas Review Journal,* 9B. Some black Republicans are even calling "on black people to escape from the country's [so-called] liberal ideology." However, "according to some polls, 92 percent of black voters ... are overwhelmingly democrats," and disapprove of the current Republican administration in the White House. See also: Shear, M. D. (2019, March 9). Trump's black supporters: Inside a small, divided world. *Las Vegas Sun,* 1.

Stevens, M. A. (ed.). (2000a). Dixie Crat. *Merriam-Webster's Collegiate Encyclopedia* (p. 475). Massachusetts: Merriam Webster, Inc. The Republican Party "as a whole has abandoned the embrace of civil rights and voting rights that had been, from the Lincoln era to Rockefeller's time, the GOP's calling card." See also: Dionne, E. J. (2019, February 27). Republican Party has come to a crossroads. *Las Vegas Sun,* 3.

Stevens, M. A. (ed.). (2000b). Reagan, Ronald W. *Merriam-Webster's Collegiate Encyclopedia* (p. 1352). Massachusetts: Merriam Webster, Inc.

Stevens, M. A. (ed.). (2000c). Republican Party or GOP (Grand Old Party). *Merriam-Webster's Collegiate Encyclopedia* (p. 453). Massachusetts: Merriam Webster, Inc.

Stewart, J. (2005, April 28). Rasta Republican. *Wall Street Journal,* A19.

Toner, R. & Hulse, C. (2005, April 11). Democrats are turning to Gingrich's playbook. *Las Vegas Sun,* 9A. It should be noted here that the Republican Party was soundly defeated in the 2018 midterm Congressional elections by the Democratic Party.

White, J. (2014, July 12). Allen West: Not Lazy, Just Crazy-Like a Fox. *The Root,* 6. http://www.theroot.com/article/culture/2012/04. ...

Wickham, D. (2005, June 14). Democrats, don't put muzzle on Dean. *USA Today,* 11A.

Will, G. (2006, July 24). Swann swims upstream in governor's race. *Las Vegas Sun,* 5. See also: Kinnon, J. B. (2006, November). The New Black Power (Election 2006). *Ebony Magazine,* 165.

Will, G. (2007, May 31). Conservatism is a much better route for Americans to take. *Las Vegas Sun,* 5. Black Republicans favor policies that identify with the dignity of work. This is a good thing. But black Democrats also believe in the same thing (about hard work). So is this one of the major things the two political parties want to think about? Probably not.

York, B. (2006, November 9). Ford, Driven: Harold Ford, Jr. goes against a Corker of a candidate in Tennessee. *National Review,* 30 & 60. Also see: Lawrence, J. (2005, December 23). Family legacy cuts both ways for candidate. *USA Today,* 8A.

Reading 2.4

The Continuing Significance and Relevance of the Congressional Black Caucus (CBC)

A Political Group in Transition

Earnest N. Bracey, Ph.D.

Introduction: The Beginning of the Congressional Black Caucus (CBC)

In 2005, the Congressional Black Caucus (or the CBC) met in Mississippi, one of the "hot-bed" States of the Confederacy and white supremacy,[1] as well as a state of the modern-day (black), civil rights movement. The meeting was held in Jackson, the capitol, where the CBC members reconfirmed their commitment, as an "all-black" group in the U.S. Congress, "to eliminate unequal treatment minorities [still] receive in many parts of [American] life."[2] This is important to understand, because if the U.S. Congress, as a whole, fails "to deal responsibly with national [racial] problems," particularly in regards to African Americans, "the explanation [is] in part with the design of the [supreme legislative] institution."[3] Therefore, the Congressional Black Caucus (CBC) was created "in 1969 when the 13 black [members of the] House of Representatives joined together to strengthen their efforts to address the concerns of blacks and other minority citizens."[4] For a long while, black members of Congress were just beating their heads against the wall, so to speak, and not getting much done, by way of legislation, because of their small numbers (see Table 2.4.1).

However, it should be pointed out that, "following the Civil Rights Act of 1964 and the Voting Rights Act of 1965, black membership in Congress [has risen] steadily."[5] Though it might be said that the Congressional Black Caucus (CBC) is relegated to only a small part of the American political system, the group's profile is now extremely high, because they can now address almost *any* kind of crisis that might involve their growing minority constituents. Of course, establishing the Congressional Black Caucus (CBC) was not seen as a very radical idea in the beginning; but presently, some members have introduced controversial bills and legislation that seeks to *right* some of the *wrongs* perpetrated against minority people over the years, or in our *ugly* past.

We must also keep in mind that the original members of the Congressional Black Caucus (CBC) wanted to act and speak with one voice, as well as provide the necessary leadership, direction and "political visibility far beyond their numbers."[6] Indeed, members of this black group continue to bring a much needed perspective (in the U.S. Congress) to the urgent concerns of black people and other people of color; like: gun violence, health-care, education, income inequality, employment, affordable housing, and prison reform and *unjust* incarcerations. Hence, "one of the major objectives of the Congressional Black Caucus (CBC) is to push Congress to deal with these [aforementioned and] persistent problems,"[7] in our society. In this regard, the Congressional Black Caucus (CBC) has been debatably successful in American political life; but members have had to be prudent in considering their specific Congressional goals, given the criticism levied at them by the white members of Congress. This is to say that many white members believed that the U.S. Congress (itself) was already complicated enough without having such a distinctive (black) group from within its ranks. But, "the move of the CBC to concentrate (and restrict) its attention [only] to legislative matters [appeared] to [have been] a good strategy."[8] Moreover, some white members of Congress from the very beginning saw the Congressional Black Caucus (CBC) as a sort of perverse (political) idea. This is to say that some believed that the CBC was just an advocacy group for *only* the black community. So what? Lucius J. Barker and others write that the CBC operates, and "resembles the expressive interest groups that people join to symbolize and express more effectively their values and opinions with respect to certain [political] causes."[9] Question: What is so wrong about CBC members wanting to advance the unique problems and causes of their constituents, especially when it came to bipartisan agreements to fund programs (for the poor and less fortunate) by the federal government? Nothing. In a nutshell, the Congressional Black Caucus (CBC) was established by black members, "to positively influence the course of events pertinent to African Americans," and to "achieve greater equity for persons of African descent in the design and content of domestic and international programs and services."[10] More crucially, the Congressional Black Caucus (CBC) shares a common set of political beliefs with the National Democratic Party, and is organized, generally, into a powerful "voting block" that can sway other members to their point of view (or a minority point of view), when it comes to voting on legislation, like passing education and *anti-poverty* bills, or providing federal aid for those needing healthcare.

According to political scientists David V. Edwards and Alessandra Lippucci, the Congressional Black Caucus (CBC), as with other informal Congressional groups, initially got support from the Congressional body itself. And, before Republican conservatives in Congress—

> stopped the practice in 1995, some [CBC members] managed to get their own paid staff and office space by collecting dues from [other] members or by inviting interest groups and other outsiders to fundraisers. Some [even had] coordinated activities with outside [lobbying] groups funded by [big] businesses, labor groups, or other special interests.[11]

Consequently, many CBC members, today, are completely justified in what they have been doing over the years, while *never* putting politics above or ahead of principles, or what they deem is necessary for their constituents. For example, black journalist and political commentator, Alex Poinsett explained it this way:

> Bursting on the national scene in January 1969, the [Black] Caucus sought to respond collectively to distress calls from [needy] citizens who, though living hundreds of miles from their congressional districts, saw them [the CBC] as congressmen-at-large, [and] as national caseworkers for the nation's black, poor and disadvantaged.[12]

Although the Congressional Black Caucus (CBC) is governed by the respective rules in the House of Representatives and Senate, its members have always wanted the flexibility to get tangible, legislative things done in the U.S. Congress. However, they can't just do *anything*, or do things in their own imaginative way if it goes against these Congressional rules—in both houses. In either case, the Congressional Black Caucus (CBC) has moved deliberately forward to change congressional laws and policies for the betterment of all American citizens.

CBC members also focus on the criminal justice system, as well as the Civil Rights Act of 1964, which essentially prohibits discrimination based on race, color, or national origin. Even more important, the Congressional Black Caucus (CBC) continues to meet around the country to show *avid* support for the "Have-Nots" in our society, and to establish the appropriate means and, "an agenda that [will hopefully] close the gap of disparities they see between blacks and other Americans."[13] Such notable and commendable efforts are especially significant today since "civil rights legislation has not fared well" under Republican control and leadership.[14] And without spouting wild propaganda, the Congressional Black Caucus (CBC), therefore, provides a crucial role or *cog* in the political wheel in American politics that represents the interests of African Americans, and "the African American members of

Congress."[15] Also, it is important to note that the Congressional Black Caucus (CBC) makes a convincing case for passing social legislation that is most important to the entire nation, like trying to prevent the lead (poisoning) that's in some of our (contaminated) drinking water throughout the United States (e.g., Flint, Michigan). In this respect, the Congressional Black Caucus (CBC) tries to put these issues into context, no matter the cost or circumstances.

Some past and current CBC members are immensely popular, like the legendary John Lewis, a Civil Rights Icon from Georgia, who is widely regarded as one of the great leaders of the black freedom and civil rights movements in this country. Or we might consider the formidable Shirley Chisholm from New York, who in 1968, "became the first black woman to be elected to the U.S. Congress, where she served until 1983." Additionally, the late Shirley Chisholm "cofounded the National Women's Political Caucus," and ran "for the 1972 Democratic Presidential nomination."[16] In hindsight, establishment of the Congressional Black Caucus (CBC) was the right thing to do, as it has "become an institutionalized part of the Washington and national scene."[17] But there are those who may strongly object or argue that the Congressional Black Caucus (CBC) is irrelevant and no longer necessary in today's high-pace and sophisticated political culture. Furthermore, some conservative black lawmakers have even contended that, "caucuses based on race have largely outlived their usefulness,"[18] especially given that "the diversification of the constituencies CBC members represent—a development largely brought on by [congressional] redistricting in the early 1990s."[19]

To be sure, the revived, congressional redistricting process throughout the United States has also contributed to diluting some black representation in Congress. This means that the number of majority–black districts have decreased significantly, because they have been ruled *unconstitutional* by the U.S. Supreme Court. Currently, however, political party *gerrymandering* has not be totally eliminated. Nevertheless, *majority-minority* districts were significant; and as journalist Jeremy Derfner writes:

> The 1992 majority-minority districts were some of the most integrated districts in the country. And after most of them were scaled back in response to the Supreme Court's *Shaw v. Reno* decision outlawing racial redistricting, they became even more integrated than before.[20]

But proportionately, this famous decision by the Supreme Court has not fixed the problem of racial or ethnic representation in the U.S. Congress.

1.	Shirley A. Chisholm	House of Representative	New York	Democrat
2.	William L. Clay, Sr.	House of Representative	Missouri	Democrat
3.	George W. Collins	House of Representative	Illinois	Democrat
4.	John Conyers, Jr.	House of Representative	Michigan	Democrat
5.	Ronald V. Dellums	House of Representative	California	Democrat
6.	Charles C. Diggs, Jr.	House of Representative	Michigan	Democrat
7.	Augustus F. Hawkins	House of Representative	California	Democrat
8.	Ralph H. Metcalfe	House of Representative	Illinois	Democrat
9.	Parren J. Mitchell	House of Representative	Maryland	Democrat
10.	Robert N. C. Nix, Sr.	House of Representative	Pennsylvania	Democrat
11.	Charles B. Rangel	House of Representative	New York	Democrat
12.	Louis Stokes	House of Representative	Ohio	Democrat
13.	Walter E. Fauntroy	Congressional Delegate	Washington, D.C.	Democrat

Majority-Minority Congressional Districts and The CBC

Put another way, redistricting based on political party or ideology has not been banned by the Courts. Why? Unsurprisingly, *shrewd* and self-serving white Congressmen, like former Republican Majority Leader, Tom DeLay (from Texas) took maximum advantage of this failure to decide or act decisively on the part of the U.S. Supreme Court, to ban political *gerrymandering*, which further undermined or eroded African American representation in the U.S. Congress. Indeed, DeLay's "long [nefarious] journey reached the political "promised land" in 2003—a redistricting delegation [in Texas] from a 17–15 Democratic majority, to a 21–11 Republican majority."[21] DeLay's "direct actions" were also extremely damaging to the "black vote" in Texas elections, particularly in areas where there is a high concentration of African Americans, in their respective districts. Constitutionally, such a redrawing of Congressional district lines should have been accomplished after the "census [or after every 10 years] to ensure that each district has an equal number of residents."[22] However, this knowledge (or policy) did not deter DeLay's outright, political biased *plot*, as he successfully orchestrated the redistricting plan in Texas before the census, which was later implemented by the state legislature. So was this plan an illegal act on the part of DeLay and the predominantly Republican state legislature in Texas? Perhaps. Politically speaking, we must understand that, "majority-minority districts [allowed] black candidates to gain the toehold of incumbency," and has had "a small but discernible transformative effect on white voting patterns."[23] Even so, the question is whether white Americans are willing to vote for black Congressional candidates with a different ideological bent. Or can African Americans really be elected in predominantly white districts?

Unfortunately, our nation is still not *color-blind*. Therefore, can we say that white voters in *majority-white* districts are more likely to elect *only* white, Congressional candidates, rather than African Americans, because of some loyalty to a *color line*? Who knows exactly? According to journalist Jeffrey McMurray, however, it has been "largely due to redistricting, [that] some blacks are [now] elected from majority white suburbs, Southern farmlands or thriving business hubs, forcing the [Black] Caucus to refocus its mission."[24] But what does this all mean? Keep in mind that such *majority-white* districts are not necessarily equal to majority-black districts/populations; and white voters *may* or *may not* elect an African American person to Congress. So can black Congressional candidates possibly win in *majority-white* districts? Perhaps. Or does it depend on the party affiliation of the black candidate? Eventually, voting for black members of Congress—disregarding a person's race, or political affiliation—might tell us that racial prejudices and "election polarization" is not always the rule, but it is the *exception*. In other words, white constituents might possibly vote for liberal, black candidates when it might suit their ends or needs, or further their power base (somehow) in Congress. Therefore, as Lucius J. Barker and *et.al.* write:

> Black influence in Congress ... depends upon more than how many blacks happen to be members at any given time. As the dynamics of power in Congress now operate, it is not enough to gain membership in that body; members must be able to remain there for a long time. They need to gain seniority. By doing so, a [black] member can normally become a committee chairman, and such positions provide crucial influence in the congressional power system. Obviously, members wish to gain seniority on the right committee, that is, a committee that is important to the interest of the [black] member's constituents.[25]

We must also bear in mind that, "While many blacks also stereotype white candidates [for Congress] negatively, they are far less likely to do so in terms of a white candidate's ability to achieve important societal goals and far more likely to report that blacks vote more on the basis of qualifications rather than race."[26] Incredibly, however, some white members of Congress are "tone-deaf" about tackling social and political problems facing minority communities. More importantly, American citizens must ask: Will Congressional districts throughout the United States, with black liberal majorities, *always* elect black representatives to the U.S. Congress, no matter what? Perhaps. However, it must also be understood that not all *majority-black* districts will automatically elect an African American to Congress—that is, because of his or her skin color. Moreover, "black representatives [in Congress today] are being pulled" in different directions, and by "different interests."[27] This means that African Americans or black members of Congress must be vigilant and absolutely sensitive to the variations of minorities that are in their new political districts (or in their own backyards), and realize how exactly they are being elected to the U.S. Congress. In particular, this recognition might indicate that members of the Congressional Black Caucus (CBC) must represent not only blacks in their (expanding) districts, but others as well. Further, many CBC members must understand that, they "represent the vast majority of Americans."[28] Former black Congressman Ronald V. Dellums has poignantly written that the Congressional Black Caucus (CBC), in its infancy, was "bound together by race—and the experience of race in American," believing that they needed "to work with each other to more forcefully advance [their] common agenda."[29] However, we should be cognizant that, "a central element in the [Congressional Black Caucus today] is the increasing importance of *biracial politics* and political coalitions."[30] Dellums goes on to write that the original Congressional Black Caucus (CBC) was:

> Largely made up of urban-based members ... [and the CBC] was fairly uniform in its focus on securing funding for housing, transportation, healthcare, education, and economic development—on solving the problems of the cities and addressing the crisis of urban decay. But [they] were aware of other issues, and did [their] best to be advocates for rural blacks and those in the South. [Furthermore], civil rights and social justice goals constituted [the CBC] "non-budgetary" portion of [their] domestic priorities focus. And [the CBC was] determined to raise the profile of Africa and the Caribbean in the debate on United States foreign policy.[31]

Political Alliances and Evolution of the CBC

Perhaps most importantly, as discussed by Dellums, it might be wrong to argue that a new racial alliance and constituency between the Congressional Black Caucus (CBC), and almost everyone else actually exist, because it can be politically *misleading*. Still, members of the Congressional Black Caucus (CBC) are being elected today (in Congressional elections) because of their strong *biracial* appeal.[32]

As mentioned, white voters will help elect black representatives (in white districts) if they believe they have *something* to gain economically or politically. Unfortunately, the Republican Party frowns upon black Republicans in Congress joining the Congressional Black Caucus (CBC), primarily because of ideological differences and political reasons (see

Table 2.4.2). Specifically, black Senator Tim Scott (from South Carolina) *is not* a member of the Congressional Black Caucus (CBC), nor is House of Representative Will Hurd of Texas; nor was former Congresswoman Mia Love from Utah.[33] We must ask why? Of course, members become a part of the Congressional Black Caucus (CBC) because they want to be a part of something larger than themselves; but this is not the case with the current crop of black Republicans in Congress today. Moreover, depending on your point of view, the constituencies of several Congressional Black Caucus (CBC) members have "put them on different sides of legislation from to time,"[34] disrupting the unity they (the CBC) supposedly have. This means that some CBC members now vote on national and international bills or legislation that is contradictory to the core mission and/or goals of the whole group. Therefore, several Congressional Black Caucus (CBC) members focus more on issues that are not necessarily "race specific," because their constituencies are not entirely of one racial or ethnic group, nor do they represent "majority-minority" districts, or fall in line with the National Democratic Party. It is predicted that the make-up of CBC constituencies will definitely move along *biracial* or *multiracial* lines in the future—and as black Democrats change toward the ideological center. Is this because African Americans are not voting in the necessary numbers to get black candidates elected or reelected to the U.S. Congress? Probably. Indeed, American citizens today must not ignore the demographic shifts that are even now playing a role, (or serious factor) in state or general elections; and especially in terms of electing Black Congressional representatives. But the CBC *cannot* do *everything* for everyone, or "be all things to all people."[35] Some scholars and political scientists have even suggested that the Congressional Black Caucus (CBC) *cannot* be both "a legislative organization and a civil rights organization,[36] because of the obvious conflicts of interest. But many black members of Congress are inclined to disagree, as it is not so simple a dichotomy to decipher.

Furthermore, Congressional critics and other *political pundits* might incorrectly argue that, "an ideological muted biracial politics will keep the CBC from leading on issues that affect African Americans," as well as other minorities.[37] But this might not be exactly true, either, given the Congressional Black Caucus' traditional or historical role in Congress. Additionally, *all* Americans should consider the CBC of today, compared to when it was first started. It is fair to say that the Congressional Black Caucus (CBC) was also established to actually frame many of the controversial discussions about racism, discrimination and Civil Rights, as our nation was in a different place in the past—that is, in the sense that African Americans didn't have many social or political rights. That said, it should be pointed out that our nation was "less racially diverse [politically] and [blacks were] truly marginalized,"[38] and mistreated. The Congressional Black Caucus (CBC), therefore, tried to "give groups [and organizations] outside the [U.S.] Congress a clearer and more realistic view of what [the CBC] could and could not do and what their responsibilities" should be.[39] In this way, the Congressional Black Caucus (CBC) will continue to address our present race-relation problems. On the other hand, however, journalist Poinsett believes that the Congressional Black Caucus (CBC) should be grounded politically, and only "focus on the legislative process, [which is] the one specific area where it [possesses] the greatest expertise."[40] This simply means that the Congressional Black Caucus (CBC) should "provide a black perspective for any legislation that [comes] through the [House of Representatives], especially through its [Congressional] committees,[41] and subcommittees. And this might be the CBC's greatest strength. Indeed, it is one of the things that the Congressional Black Caucus (CBC) prides itself on. Furthermore, many political scholars fundamentally believe that, "a very black and urban-centric political agenda"[42] is counter-productive, and could be the "Kiss-of-Death," so to speak, for some CBC members, particularly running for the U.S. Congress today, because of the increase in diversity in their changing districts or communities.

Federal Elections and the CBC

Increasingly, black voter participation, because of "voting behavior" can also make a significant difference in federal elections when minority candidates are involved, and the "black vote" is *unjustly* diluted, or if elections are outright stolen, as was alleged in the 2000 Presidential Election. According to journalist Greg Palast, "the U.S. Civil Rights Commission looked into the smelly pile of spoiled ballots [from the 2000 Presidential election] and concluded that, of the 179,855 ballots invalidated by [Republican] Florida officials, 53 percent were cast by black voters."[43] And therein lies the problem with African Americans having the right to (participate and) vote in the United States. Or whether their votes are even counted in their continuing *disenfranchisement* by racist, partisan forces in this country.

Palast goes on to write:

> An apartheid vote-counting system [present in the 2000 Presidential Election was] far from [being] politically neutral. Given that more than 90 percent of the black electorate votes Democratic, had all the "spoiled" votes been tallied, Gore would have taken Florida in a walk, not to mention fattening his popular vote total nationwide. It's not surprising that the First [Bush] brother's team, informed of impending rejection of black ballots, looked away and whistled.[44]

As for changes in the size of the Congressional Black Caucus (CBC), or in order for the intrepid group to grow in membership, black voter participation is, essentially, the key. So how can we make our national election systems better for African Americans running for the U.S. Congress? Unfortunately, like our divided nation, the black and white members of

Congress live separate lives, without a lot of behind-the-scenes or personal interaction, or intimate, political contact. Furthermore, "blacks have yet to achieve political power commensurate with their numbers." Clearly, "for blacks to reach proportionality in elected office and, more specifically, for blacks to increase their membership in Congress, it seems clear that more whites will have to start voting for black candidates."[45]

Furthermore, the Congressional Black Caucus (CBC) must create sound legislation to prevent (white) "voter fraud" and the rejection of black votes in *any* State or federal election; otherwise our Democracy should be considered a *sham*. Moreover, a return to *majority-minority* districts, and a "just ruling" by the Supreme Court in regards to *gerrymandering*, should render Congressional districts—drawn along political lines—*unconstitutional*, which is another way to grow minority voting—that is, if we are to be serious about this political matter. Meaning, we should draw Congressional district lines in a non-partisan manner. It is also important to note again that African Americans *must not* "remain under-represented in [the U.S. Congress] compared with their share of the total population."[46] Yet, also keep in mind that the CBC's clout is considerable, given its small size. Indeed, Congressional Black Caucus (CBC) votes can actually save a president's agenda. For example,

> in 1993 [former] CBC chairman, Representative Kweisi Mfume of Maryland, and the highest-ranking black congressman [at that time], Representative John Lewis [of Georgia], delivered the [crucial Black] Caucus vote that saved [President] Clinton's $500 billion economic budget in both the House and Senate.[47]

This specific congressional vote (at that time) is important to understand, because the Clinton administration, in return, provided support "for inner cities, poor families, children, and the elderly."[48] In this respect, the Congressional Black Caucus (CBC) *did not* present a *discordant* message, and got more than they even bargained for. In other words, this particular negotiation on the part of the CBC with the Clinton administration was a winning formula, or brilliant strategy. It is also quite evident that the Congressional Black Caucus (CBC) has a legislative agenda, but its "long tradition of focusing on the politics of moral resistance"[49] cannot be summarily dismissed either. Therefore, "since 1971, the Congressional Black Caucus (CBC) has promoted African American members for leadership positions and has pushed for legislation beneficial to African Americans,"[50] as mentioned. It is also important to understand that black voters are not necessarily given *any* guarantees, but they firmly believe in the promises made or offered by CBC incumbents and *newly-minted* black candidates that represent their respective districts—that is, with a majority population of African American voters.

TABLE 2.4.2 Current Members of the Congressional Black Caucus April 2019

#	Name	Title	State	Party
1.	Cory Booker	Senator	New Jersey	Democrat
2.	Kamala Harris	Senator	California	Democrat
3.	Alma Adams	House of Representative	North Carolina	Democrat
4.	Colin Allred	House of Representative	Texas	Democrat
5.	Karen Bass	House of Representative	California	Democrat
6.	Joyce Beatty	House of Representative	Ohio	Democrat
7.	Sanford Bishop	House of Representative	Georgia	Democrat
8.	Lisa B. Rochester	House of Representative	Delaware	Democrat
9.	Anthony Brown	House of Representative	Maryland	Democrat
10.	G. K. Butterfied	House of Representative	North Carolina	Democrat
11.	Andre Carson	House of Representative	Indiana	Democrat
12.	Yvette Clarke	House of Representative	New York	Democrat
13.	William L. Clay Jr.	House of Representative	Missouri	Democrat
14.	Emanuel Cleaver	House of Representative	Missouri	Democrat
15.	Jim Clyburn	House of Representative	South Carolina	Democrat
16.	Elijah Cummings*	House of Representative	Maryland	Democrat
17.	Danny Davis	House of Representative	Illinois	Democrat
18.	Antonio Delgado	House of Representative	New York	Democrat
19.	Val Demings	House of Representative	Florida	Democrat
20.	Dwight Evans	House of Representative	Pennsylvania	Democrat
21.	Marcia Fudge	House of Representative	Ohio	Democrat
22.	Al Green	House of Representative	Texas	Democrat
23.	Alcee Hastings	House of Representative	Florida	Democrat
24.	Jahana Hayes	House of Representative	Connecticut	Democrat
25.	Steven Horsford	House of Representative	Nevada	Democrat
26.	Hakeem Jeffries	House of Representative	New York	Democrat
27.	Eddie B. Johnson	House of Representative	Texas	Democrat
28.	Hank Johnson	House of Representative	Georgia	Democrat
29.	Robin Kelly	House of Representative	Illinois	Democrat
30.	Brenda Lawrence	House of Representative	Michigan	Democrat
31.	Al Lawson	House of Representative	Florida	Democrat
32.	Barbara Lee	House of Representative	California	Democrat
33.	Sheila J. Lee	House of Representative	Texas	Democrat
34.	John Lewis	House of Representative	Georgia	Democrat
35.	Lucy McBath	House of Representative	Georgia	Democrat
36.	Donald McEachin	House of Representative	Virginia	Democrat
37.	Gregory Meeks	House of Representative	New York	Democrat
38.	Gwen Moore	House of Representative	Wisconsin	Democrat
39.	Joe Neguse	House of Representative	Colorado	Democrat
40.	Eleanor H. Norton	Congressional Delegate	District of Columbia	Democrat
41.	Ilhan Omar	House of Representative	Minnesota	Democrat
42.	Donald Payne	House of Representative	New Jersey	Democrat
43.	Stacy Plaskett	Congressional Delegate	U.S. Virgin Islands	Democrat
44.	Ayanna Pressley	House of Representative	Massachusetts	Democrat
45.	Cedric Richmond	House of Representative	Louisiana	Democrat
46.	Bobby Rush	House of Representative	Illinois	Democrat
47.	Bobby Scott	House of Representative	Virginia	Democrat
48.	David Scott	House of Representative	Georgia	Democrat
49.	Terri Sewell	House of Representative	Alabama	Democrat
50.	Bennie Thompson	House of Representative	Mississippi	Democrat
51.	Lauren Underwood	House of Representative	Illinois	Democrat
52.	Marc Veasey	House of Representative	Texas	Democrat
53.	Maxine Waters	House of Representative	California	Democrat
54.	Bonnie W. Coleman	House of Representative	New Jersey	Democrat
55.	Frederica Wilson	House of Representative	Florida	Democrat

*Elijah Cummings died in 2019.

Conclusions

The results of the Congressional Black Caucus (CBC) has been undeniably productive, as the group has made invaluable contributions to our U.S. Congress and our nation, particularly with underrepresented black and minority communities. Indeed, the Congressional Black Caucus (CBC) could have been a *disruptive* force, but it has made a positive difference in the lives of many, providing greater opportunities with the mantle of the nation's supreme legislative body. And that is nothing to sniff at. So should we respect the mission of the black members of Congress? The CBC has changed a lot in the U.S. Congress today—that is, in terms of its *make-up*. The challenges are many, however, given that the group has grown, mainly because more African Americans are being elected from their home state and mixed districts (see Table 2.4.2). It is unlikely, however, that some white American voters will ever let go of their political biases, race-based predispositions, or racial prejudices anytime soon. To be sure, some Congressional districts that are predominantly white will continue to divide themselves along racial and ideological lines. So the questions that remain are: Can African Americans from *majority-white* districts be elected across the nation? Probably. Or can black, political candidates, from mixed neighborhoods/ communities, continue to be elected to the U.S. Congress? Perhaps. Still, what are we to make of these election contradictions? These political questions must be seriously addressed, given the (proportionately) low percentage of African Americans still serving in Congress today? It is also necessary that members of the Congressional Black Caucus (CBC) should change with the times, and "broaden their [horizon or] vision beyond race,"[51] in order to be more politically competitive and helpful to all their constituencies and supporters; but the traditional agenda of the CBC is still "shaped by the liberal causes of urban black Americans."[52] Also, the current argument that is popular with some African Americans is that, the Congressional Black Caucus (CBC) "will continue to drive the agenda from the left or integrate themselves more fully into the [Democratic, political] party apparatus."[53] Recent critics of the Congressional Black Caucus (CBC) tell us that this black group cannot be viable in today's political (polarizing) climate, or even survive as a separate, parochial group. If this is true, will the Congressional Black Caucus (CBC) be able to accomplish its many, varied political goals? And although there are *only* Democratic CBC members in Congress today, many have conservative morals and conservative, political leanings, like their Congressional (Republican) counterparts. And one more thing: Congressional Black Caucus (CBC) members are not just limited to only a liberal agenda today, as in the past.

Equally importantly, the Congressional Black Caucus (CBC) is not only needed, but this independent group is vital to our modern-day politics, in terms of race-relations, because it is the driving force behind protecting the Constitutional rights of *all* poor Americans, as well as serving as the political voice for those without a *forum* for elucidating their displeasure with our federal government, particularly when it (government) is repressive toward minorities, and others that need moral support and financial help. In this respect, the Congressional Black Caucus (CBC) "has [also] cast itself as the [moral] conscience of [the U.S.] Congress, making up for a lack of votes with claims to legislative purity."[54] Furthermore, the Congressional Black Caucus (CBC) must continue to stand firm against the tide of some state legislative plans (by predominantly conservative Republicans) to redraw district lines, to favor their political party's standing, making for a permanent majority in Congress. No doubt, if such unconstitutional measures are not challenged, the representation of African Americans in the U.S. Congress will be limited, or flounder. Moreover, the Congressional Black Caucus (CBC) plays, as Poinsett astutely explained in 1973, and is relevant today, "a prophetic role in congress, functioning as the spiritual, political and moral leader of America's niggers. [And] under [Black] Caucus leadership, perhaps all niggers—the black ones, the brown ones, the yellow ones, the red ones, the white ones—may yet force this nation to fulfill its promise,"[55] to do the right thing for *all* Americans.

Finally, the Congressional Black Caucus (CBC) bodes well for the diversity in our U.S. Congress and our future. To say the least, there is absolutely a need for the Congressional Black Caucus (CBC). Consider: The CBC is not only focusing on *civic* responsibility, but also proposing legislation to reduce the wealth gap, and providing help for low-income families throughout the United States. Also, the Congressional Black Caucus (CBC) has held up surprisingly well as an independent, Congressional group over the years; and it has gained a lot of traction. As to its longevity, the Congressional Black Caucus (CBC) is at a crossroads; but it will be around as long as there are African American members in the U.S. Congress. Many CBC members are excited for the next chapter of this serious black group. Unfortunately, most Americans don't know very much the Congressional Black Caucus (CBC); and why it is necessary, or exist at all.

Notes

1. Mississippi is the only state in the nation or the Deep South that has incorporated the Confederate battle flag in its state flag. Fortunately, the Congressional Black Caucus (CBC) tries hard to understand all sides to a racial problem, regardless of where they might hold their meetings.

2. Emily Wagster Pettus, "Members of black caucus visit Mississippi," *The Clarion Ledger*, August 9, 2005, 2B.

3. Thomas R. Dye, *Politics in America*, brief edition, 2nd edition (New Jersey: Pearson Prentice Hall, 2007), 67.

4. Congressional Research Service, "Report on Black Members of Congress," http:// www.house.gov/cummings/cbc/cbchistory.htm (9/12/05), 1.

5. Dye, *Politics in America*, 267.

6. Dye, *Politics in America*, 267. The very fact that the Congressional Black Caucus (CBC) exists at all is a small miracle, because (at one time) there wasn't always enough black members—to even make a *forum*.

7. Lucius J. Barker, Mack H. Jones, and Katherine Tate, *African Americans and the American Political System*, 4th edition (New Jersey: Prentice Hall, 1999), 278. Recently, African American Senator and presidential candidate, Cory Booker has suggested "a commission to explore reparation proposals for African American descendants of slavery." See: Rodrigo Torrejon, "Sen. Booker to introduce slavery reparations bill," *USA Today*, April 10, 2019, 3A.

8. Barker, Jones, and Tate, *African Americans*, 288. African Americans in Congress today are in a stronger position than ever before. This is why the Congressional Black Caucus (CBC) has staying power. However, the founding members were thought of as delusional for wanting to find a way to overcome the adversity of blacks in the U.S. Congress.

9. Barker, Jones, and Tate, *African Americans*, 287. The Congressional Black Caucus (CBC) members make other members in Congress better, because of their righteous beliefs. CBC members also provide moral support to other members.

10. John J. Coleman, Kenneth M. Goldstein, and William G. Howell, *Understanding American Politics and Government*, 2nd edition (New York: Longman, 2011), 312. Members of the CBC also spend a lot of energy talking or dialoguing with other political party members, even with the opposition party, where they can influence votes on legislative matters in the U.S. Congress.

11. David V. Edwards and Allessandra Lippucci, *Practicing American Politics: An Introduction to Government* (New York: Worth Publishers, 1998), 44. Bear in mind that, "Despite being stripped of its staff and funding by the new republican majority in late 1994," its role and purpose remained consistent and well recognized, which is to serve as "a more effective catalyst for the economical, educational, and social concerns of Blacks and other underrepresented Americans." See: Barker, Jones, and Tate, *African Americans*, 287.

12. Alex Poinsett, "The Black Caucus: Five Year Later," *Ebony Magazine*, June 8, 1973, 69.

13. Emery Carrington, "Healthcare focus of [CBC] meeting," *The Clarion Ledger*, August 10, 2005, 1B.

14. Victoria Valentine, "Civil Rights Report Card," *Emerge*, volume 8, October 1996, 53.

15. Carrington, "Healthcare focus," 1B.

16. "Chisholm, Shirley," in *Merriam-Webster's Collegiate Encyclopedia*, ed. Mark A. Stevens (Massachusetts: Encyclopedia Britannica, Inc., 2000), 337.

17. Barker, Jones, and Tate, *African Americans*, 187. To be sure, the Congressional Black Caucus (CBC) *never* tries to ignore divisive, cultural issues, as this goes against the entire CBC mission. And within the vast halls of the U.S. Congress, controversial, racial issues, throughout our nation, still matter to CBC members.

18. Jeffrey McMurray, "Black Caucus looks beyond racial issues," *Las Vegas Review-Journal*, November 30, 2003, 11A.

19. Jeremy Derfner, "The New Black Caucus," *The American Prospect*, March 27–April 10, 2000, 16.

20. Derfner, "The New Black Caucus," 16.

21. Jonathan Gurwitz, "Have Things Gone Sour in Sugar Land?" *The Wall Street Journal*, March 24, 2005, A15. The Congressional Black Caucus (CBC) must not give up or relent, when it comes to its important role to

challenge such unorthodox, voting methods (by Tom DeLay) of Texas—that is, manipulating or wrongly changing districts, to win Congressional seats.

22. Jon Sarche, "Colorado redistricting case gains nationwide audience," *Las Vegas Review-Journal*, September 8, 2003, 7A. Unfortunately, such successful redrawn, districting plans have denied African Americans and other minorities their right to select and elect their own candidates to the U.S. Congress.

23. Derfner, "The New Black Caucus," 17.

24. McMurray, "Black Caucus," 11A.

25. Barker, Jones, and Tate, *African Americans*, 289.

26. Linda F. Williams, "White/Black Perceptions of the Electability of Black Political Candidates," *National Political Science Review*, vol. 2, 1990, 62.

27. Derfner, "The New Black Caucus," 17.

28. McMurray, "Black Caucus," 11A.

29. Ronald V. Dellums and H. Lee Halterman, *Lying Down with the Lions* (Boston, Massachusetts: Beacon Press, 2000), 94. The CBC also expressed a need to unify members to a common, political purpose. CBC members also provide a sort of social outlet for each other.

30. Derfner, "The New Black Caucus," 17.

31. Dellums and Halterman, *Lying Down*, 94. The Congressional Black Caucus (CBC) has also advocated for creating congressional legislation, to help states that assist low-income neighborhoods, while redirecting attention to eradicating white supremacy and racial hatred.

32. Derfner, "The New Black Caucus," 17. With a renewed drive, the CBC is positively addressing the myriad of issues facing our nation during many legislative sessions in Congress. All that being said, the CBC does not want to be on the sidelines, doing nothing, particularly with the prodigious energy of its members today.

33. Paula D. McClain and Steven C. Tauber, *American Government in Black and White: Diversity and Democracy*, 4th edition (New York: Oxford University Press, 2020), 184. The CBC would like all African Americans in Congress to join the caucus, but over the years, black Republicans find it hard to let go of their political party affiliation, and join the political group.

34. McMurray, "Black Caucus," 11A.

35. Poinsett, "The Black Caucus," 72. Now, more than ever, the CBC is necessary because of the diversity and changing demographics of their constituents, which might increase the number of African Americans in Congress.

36. Derfner, "The New Black Caucus," 16. All the while, this *conundrum* about the CBC is sparking further debate. Furthermore, the collective goals of the CBC, as expressed, have changed considerably in today's politics, because of changing racial constituencies, and the redrawing of district lines to benefit one political party over the other.

37. Derfner, "The New Black Caucus," 19. One could also argue that such *biracial* districts in the political landscape are, perhaps, inevitable in the near future due to the unconstitutionality of redrawing district lines to favor just Republican conservatives.

38. McMurray, "Black Caucus," 11A. We should also consider the shift occurring toward a more conservative agenda in this country, and a continuance of white nationalism.

39. Dellums and Halterman, *Lying Down*, 104. The CBC believes that it is proper and important that American citizens see the group as more than just some black organization. Nevertheless, the issues that the CBC is confronted with today are from our recent and distant past.

40. Derfner, "The New Black Caucus," 16. It is clear that the CBC wants to address such racial matters in a timely and an effective manner, to achieve maximum impact for political socialization.

41. Poinsett, "The Black Caucus," 72.

42. Derfner, "The New Black Caucus," 16.

43. Greg Palast, "One Million Black Votes Didn't Count in the 2000 Presidential Election," *Common Dreams News Center*, June 22, 2004, 1. http://www.commondreams.org/views. ...

44. Palast, "One Million Black Votes," 1.

45. Barker, Jones, and Tate, *African Americans*, 291.

46. Julie Rovner, "Record Number of Women, Blacks in Congress," *Congressional Quarterly Weekly Report*, vol. 46, November 12, 1988, 3293.

47. Darlene C. Line, William C. Hine, and Stanley Harrold, *African Americans: A Concise History* (New Jersey: Pearson Prentice Hall, 2009), 595.

48. Line, Hine, and Harold, *African Americans*, 595.

49. Derfner, "The New Black Caucus," 16.

50. McClain and Tauber, *American Government in Black and White*, 185. Keep in mind that the CBC retains "its unwritten rule to limit membership to [only] African-American legislators; but it briefly allowed [in 1988, 41] white members to join as nonvoting associates." This policy was later abandoned, as there are currently no white members in the CBC. See: "Creating and Evolution of the Congressional Black Caucus," 3. https://history.house.gove. exhibitions-and. ...

51. McMurray, "Black Caucus," 11A.

52. McMurray, "Black Caucus," 11A.

53. Derfner, "The New Black Caucus," 19.

54. Derfner, "The New Black Caucus," 16. It should be understood that, "the moral role of government is to ensure that no one set of sectarian or narrow definition of morality is imposed by the [federal] government on unwilling citizens." See: James P. Pfiffner, "The Paradox of Governmental Power," *Society*, September/October 2000, 23.

55. Poinsett, "The Black Caucus," 72. Fortunately, the CBC will remain engaged with their (diverse) constituents, as well as with other members of the U.S. Congress and the nation as a whole.

Bibliography

Baker, Lucius J., Mack H. Jones, and Katherine Tate. *African Americans and the American Political System.* New Jersey: Prentice Hall, 1999.

Carrington, Emery. "Healthcare focus of [CBC] meeting." *The Clarion Ledger*, August 10, 2005.

Coleman, John J., Kenneth M. Goldstein, and William G. Howell. *Understanding American Politics and Government*. New York: Longman, 2011.

Congressional Research Service. "Report on Black Members of Congress." http:// www.house.gov/ cummings/cbc/cbchistory.htm (9/12/05).

Dellums, Ronald V., and H. Lee Halterman. *Lying Down with the Lions*. Boston, Massachusetts: Beacon Press, 2000.

Derfner, Jeremy. "The New Black Caucus." *The American Prospect*, March 27–April 10, 2000.

Dye, Thomas R. *Politics in America*. New Jersey: Pearson Prentice Hall, 2007.

Edwards, David V., and Allessandra Lippucci. *Practicing American Politics: An Introduction to Government*. New York: Worth Publishers, 1998.

Gurwitz, Jonathan. "Have Things Gone Sour in Sugar Land?" *The Wall Street Journal*, March 24, 2005.

Line, Darlene C., William C. Hine, and Stanley Harrold. *African Americans: A Concise History*. New Jersey: Pearson Prentice Hall, 2009.

McClain, Paula D., and Steven C. Tauber. *American Government in Black and White: Diversity and Democracy*. New York: Oxford University Press, 2020.

McMurray, Jeffrey. "Black Caucus looks beyond racial issues." *Las Vegas Review-Journal*, November 30, 2003.

Palast, Greg. "One Million Black Votes Didn't Count in the 2000 Presidential Election." *Common Dreams News Center*, June 22, 2004. http://www.commondreams.org/views. ...

Pettus, Emily Wagster. "Members of black caucus visit Mississippi." *The Clarion Ledger*, August 9, 2005.

Poinsett, Alex. "The Black Caucus: Five Year Later." *Ebony Magazine*, June 8, 1973.

Rovner, Julie. "Record Number of Women, Blacks in Congress." *Congressional Quarterly Weekly Report*, vol. 46, November 12, 1988.

Sarche, Jon. "Colorado redistricting case gains nationwide audience." *Las Vegas Review-Journal*, September 8, 2003.

Stevens, Mark A., ed. "Chisholm, Shirley." *Merriam-Webster's Collegiate Encyclopedia*. Massachusetts: Encyclopedia Britannica, Inc., 2000.

Valentine, Victoria. "Civil Rights Report Card." *Emerge*, volume 8, October 1996.

Williams, Linda F. "White/Black Perceptions of the Electability of Black Political Candidates." *National Political Science Review*, vol. 2, 1990.

Part III

Blacks and Social Justice in the United States

The Racist American Eugenics Program

A Crime Against Humanity

Earnest N. Bracey, Ph.D.

Introduction

The story of the American eugenics program (or "good breeding" movement) has been a history of lies, deception, evasion, and *racism*. But the eugenics movement did happen. It was not some abstract idea, or theoretical measure. Quite obviously this sad story, riddled with complexities, is a burden for the descendents of eugenic stalwarts. I suspect that the descendents of eugenic activists do not like being reminded of their ancestors' terrible eugenic deeds, moral degradation and depredations, and the horrible things they inflicted upon the *weak* and *powerless*—like involuntary sterilization. Although the eugenicists "advocated compulsory sterilization for criminals, sex deviants, and the feebleminded,"[1] many poor women were sterilized for the simple or flimsy reason as "being considered [too] lazy or [too] promiscuous."[2]

Take for example North Carolina's sterilization/eugenics program, which singled-out women—who never had it easy—on welfare. According to Journalist Rebecca Sinderbrand, "Over the last 15 years of its operation, 99 percent of the victims were women; [and] more than 60 percent were black" women.[3] It is crucial to remember that many of the black women, who were unknowingly sterilized, did not volunteer for these horrendous medical procedures. Indeed, these women were treated with utter disregard. More importantly, black women (or women of color) in America were unduly affected by the various eugenics programs.

In truth, racists and eugenic activists, and even governmental policymakers all wanted to jump on the sterilization band-wagon, and the eugenics floodgates opened. Many state officials and governments even adopted the curious habit of literally performing *invasive* operations on black women, Native American women, and poor white women for no good reason, and against their will, and without their knowledge, arguing that such people or *ingrates* deserved what

Earnest N. Bracey, "The Racist American Eugenics Program: A Crime Against Humanity," *Forum on Public Policy,* vol. 2007, no. 2, pp. 1–15. Copyright © 2007 by Forum on Public Policy.

they got, as it kept them from reproducing, or procreating; and bringing into the world defective children.

In certain respects, these awful eugenicists were *totally* engaged, relentless, and supported the racist and discriminatory idea of doing harm to less fortunate human beings, or those they called—and considered—mentally retarded, morons, relative idiots, the unfit, or deplorable persons. But what happened to the idea of caring for our most unfortunate citizens? There was certainly nothing *humane* about forced sterilization. Unfortunately, many of these American eugenicists found their way into positions of power that gave them access to public policy-making, and the wheels of government, which enabled them to influence and affect the establishment of eugenical programs in almost every state in the nation.

It is no exaggeration to say that even while these heartless eugenicists thought that what they were doing was righteous and noble—and would do the human race some good—it was actually an evil *manifestation*, a cursed plot, or conspiracy, and deliberate act to manipulate human evolution. But what gave them the absolute gumption to lead such a dehumanizing movement? Their obsequious orchestrations and emphasis on the importance of creating a better race of humans was, of course, nonsense, eugenical *hucksterism*. However, eugenical programs were created, nonetheless, and even "ruled constitutional in *Buck v. Bell*, a 1924 Supreme Court decision that is still the law of the land" in the United States.[4]

It is striking and supremely wrong that such an *immoral* piece of legislation still exists in American society today, even as some states like Georgia have introduced "a resolution apologizing for forced sterilization ... between 1937 and 1970,"[5] where eugenicists denied some people their rights to life and liberty. So it seems almost unbelievable that our national eugenics program has not really disappeared.

Furthermore, over the years, the American eugenics program has been fraught with controversy, but extremely popular with members of the elite or dominant group (past and present); even the wealthiest, philanthropic American families, such as the financial support given by John D. Rockefeller; Mrs. E. H. Harriman (who gave much of her time and finances, with unprecedented zeal to the Eugenics Record Office), supported the eugenics movement. Additionally, John Harvey Kellogg (brother to the famous cereal magnate), as well as Philadelphia soap manufacturer Samuel Fels—and even Theodore Roosevelt, considered one of our greatest Presidents—were known as ardent eugenicists.[6] The eugenics movement, therefore, was helped perversely by such important men and women, without *any* ramifications.

The New Eugenics Movement

With wealth and power and almost unlimited resources available to these eugenicist monsters, such men and women were able to carry out their web of intrigue, incomprehensible actions, and master plan of racial purity and genocidal destruction—which negatively and adversely affected the livelihood and well-being of countless Americans—with mental disabilities and physical deformities—or our most vulnerable citizens. It was as if these eugenicists had a disdain for life and basic human rights.

Indeed, these groups of evil, misguided men and women were given more legitimacy than they actually deserved, if you ask me; but many racist thinkers today are carrying on the eugenics legacy or new eugenics movement by joining and becoming active members, and financial contributors to several racist foundations (that span the political and social spectrum), like the Pioneer Fund, established in 1937 by Nazi sympathizers, Frederick Osborn and Harry Laughlin, which blatantly "promotes theories of black inferiority."[7]

The secretive Pioneer Fund, however, is blinded by their own self-interest, and importance in that this parochial group only uses *selective perception* and *selective exposure* when it comes to understanding human genetics and advancing their twisted and reprehensible, racist agenda. The Pioneer Fund has also given enormous sums of money to high-level academic professionals to propagate racial misconceptions, or to put forth the myth that "whites are inherently smarter than blacks,"[8] or dark-skinned people. Perhaps the Pioneer Fund would serve our world best if it would use its tremendous wealth to eliminate human suffering, rather than singling out an ethnic group for some kind of genocidal punishment or extermination. Indeed, why does the powerful Pioneer Fund advocate such racist-hereditary foolishness? What exactly does this group hope to accomplish? Or what do they think can be achieved by their racial/ethnic divisiveness—some exquisite torture-sterilization program for our future?

Academic or scientific racists, moreover, like Professor Richard Lynn at the University of Ulster in Northern Ireland tries to suppress our knowledge and essentially the genetic truths about humans, by justifying the modern-day eugenics movement, which represents deeply-rooted prejudices, and "the intellectual backbone of modern fascism,"[9] by shooting from his ignorant, racist-intellectual hip, so to speak, especially when it comes to the actual racial facts.

Lynn, for example, incorrectly writes in the 2002 edition of the white separatist newsletter, the *American Renaissance*, that black Americans have a proclivity for criminal behavior, or commit more crimes because they are "more psychopathic than whites."[10] What rubbish.

Lynn makes this outrageous claim or accusation without providing a shred of evidence, however. To be more accurate, or the truth is that more white Americans commit certain types of crimes, especially white-collar crimes and corporate crimes. White Americans are simply not arrested and prosecuted with the same zeal, frequency, and sheer doggedness as with black criminals. And often white Americans are given probation and lesser prison sentences. Lynn could have simply checked the Sentencing Project Website, or reviewed the FBI crime statistics for the last decade to verify the validity of these facts.

Furthermore, the conviction rate is greater for black Americans, than with white Americans, especially when it comes to *all* crimes in the United States, including penalties for illegal drug use, where black Americans are not given the benefit-of-doubt or shorter prison sentences by the criminal justice system. And Lynn's statements (or language of ignorance) about blacks' propensity or penchant to commit crimes, and whites' intellectual superiority are racist, pseudo-scientific nonsense. Must we exclude or ignore *any* environmental factors that might have caused such aberrant or criminal behavior on the part of poor black Americans?

As already noted, the powerful and vile eugenicists aggressively (and faithfully) pursued a most dangerous and most inhumane endeavor, a path of almost no return until the late 20th century. But before this time, almost 70,000 American citizens were involuntarily and sometimes summarily sterilized until the damaging and damning practice fell out of vogue, because it was linked "in the public's mind to Hitler's Germany after World War II,"[11] and beyond. However, American eugenicists sadly laid the groundwork for Hitler, [his mostly Jewish] death camps and his [Aryan] breeding farms."[12]

Indeed, these diabolical eugenicists—voracious mad-men and women—*never* really strayed far from what they were trying to accomplish—that is, the eugenical sterilization and (possible) elimination of a subordinate group of people—or fellow human beings—the eugenicists considered undesirables. It is a fact that these eugenicists were fiercely enthusiastic, exuberant even, for such a racist and discriminatory program, as they imagined the "perfect race" possibilities, insisting on the sterilization of people-of-color with mental illnesses, or mostly uneducated poor women, starting between the 1900s, and continuing into the late 1970s.

But what gave these eugenicists the moral right to create and implement such devious genocidal programs? Can their deceitful and hideous behavior be justified? To my mind, there can be no legitimacy to their *immoral* acts. Such were the consequences of abandoning the principles of humanity, and what was/is fair and decent.

The Consequence of The Racist Eugenics Movement

It has also been argued that the eugenics program in America is still alive in some form, and continues to this day with the involuntary sterilization of some hereditary flawed and mentally disabled people, including mental patients; but clearly this matter is being avoided, or simply ignored by some state governments. Recently, for example, an unnamed hospital in

Seattle, Washington, acknowledged breaking state law by performing "a hysterectomy on a severely developmentally disabled girl whose growth was medically stunted," to appease her care-taking parents.[13]

Let me give you another example. Journalist Janet Elliot, writing recently in the *Houston Chronicle*, revealed that "186 mentally retarded and disabled residents died at state facilities [in Texas] over an 18-month period,"[14] in 2007, which demonstrates more than just a *systematic* problem. This is to say that eugenical deaths happen with astonishing regularity at state run facilities in Texas and in many other states in our nation.

Professor of political science and history, Edwin Black calls the involuntary sterilization of unsuspecting women and men—*eugenicide*, or the systematic annihilation of a group of hapless people through eugenical-sterilization. Black goes on to write that "American eugenicists saw mankind as a biological cesspool,"[15] which had to be completely purged, or cleansed from so-called *imbecilic*, nitwit persons. It must also be remembered that in a contrived and indirect way, "the old eugenics movement, [which] actually began in England [but] was led [almost assuredly and solely] by Americans,"[16] was nothing really to be proud of, because it was vulgar in its respective renditions, and deadly in its execution and consequences.

American eugenicists also felt that it was their fundamental duty to march boldly forward and supposedly purify the entire human race. But what gave eugenicists the sanctimonious audacity to establish such depraved pogroms? The American eugenics program, of dubious purpose, was a constructed system of human irresponsibility in that such men and women, who physically administered such ideological plans, refused to treat everyone involved *humanly*.

Whatever else that may be said about the American eugenics program, it is not quite clear whether the eugenicists even lived up to their own deceptive ideals and principles. For instance, did they put their own crippled children and disabled off-spring to death (as did Hitler with some disabled Germans and countless gypsies and Jews); or did they have their own autistic or imperfect sons and daughters sterilized and obliterated? Absolutely not. After all, such mentally disabled people "are individuals with their [own hearts] and minds."[17] In the final analysis, developmentally disabled people "are locked up in themselves, like in a prison, just because of their own biology."[18] But keeping such individuals from being born, through eugenics-sterilization, was/is not the answer either.

It is important to reiterate that the history of eugenics in America was a time period that was something more than a little crazy. It is not difficult to understand what happened. Maybe we expect more of an explanation? We should at least demand elucidation on the part of surviving eugenicists. Or *any* answers must begin by first acknowledging that the American eugenics program happened, because it can never be erased from our inglorious history.

Moreover, and as the story of the American eugenics movement begins to unravel, we are left to wonder how our national government was complicit in its development. But the real question we need to ask is how did we allow such a *fiendish* thing to occur? Or why did we allow this kind of thing to happen in the first place? Unfortunately, most Americans today are oblivious or blithely ignorant about the eugenics issue, as it is not even taught or mentioned in many of our history text books.

Perhaps some do not think that this controversial issue has any significance or relevancy right now in our history, where we live in a dangerous world that is dominated by war, terrorism and violence. Or many Americans (politicians especially) simply don't like to be bothered by such a harsh episode in our political and historical life. But to ignore the sins of our nation's past is a recipe or invitation for another similar disaster in the near future to happen, especially when it comes to violating human rights.

Conclusions

Maybe it is fair to say that the American eugenics program is imperfectly understood. It has been only recently that the eugenics program in America has truly revealed itself in all its horror and ugliness. Clearly, the United States has had its share of human wrongs, but the outrageous eugenics program was probably one of the worst things (in human events) that could have happened to our country, besides black American slavery—or comparatively, the American eugenics program can only be surpassed by the genocidal past events of Cambodia, Rwanda, the Jewish Holocausts—or the millions of deaths meted out to the Russian people during Stalin's Soviet Gulag. Indeed, the American eugenics program should be considered the number one horrific and deplorable act, inflicted on some of its black citizens, by our government.

Perhaps the tragic Tuskegee experiment runs a close second when it comes to our collective nation's crimes—where unsuspecting black men in Alabama, infected with syphilis, were sterilized and eventually died, by not getting proper treatment for a curable disease, and with the full knowledge of our government. No one can doubt, then, or deny that the eugenics program in the United States happened.

In fact, we must be fully aware that the fundamental rights of people were seriously violated. Indeed, the more we study and read about the American eugenics movement, the more we begin to understand and learn about the unmitigating, dehumanizing impact and disaster that it truly was—and represented. Therefore, we must take the old American eugenics movement more seriously, in part because it unnecessarily hurt people; and also because of the monstrosity and complexity of the respective eugenics programs themselves (from state-to-state) in America.

There may have been a time when American eugenicists thought that it was necessary to destroy the lives of some poor women-of-color and their unborn offspring, but we must reject such dangerous notions today. After all, the eugenicists' grotesque actions to create a perfect race through eugenics-sterilization and death are unforgivable, abhorrent and shameful. The American eugenicists were definitely irrational, chomping at the bit, so to speak, as they tried to legitimize their whole dirty business, while ruining innocent lives.

The mainstream view today is to ignore this heartbreaking issue, if possible. But we should all regard this holocaust of sorts as obscene, unspeakable, and unforgivable. And the actions of the American eugenicists were abominable, unimaginable, as well as irresponsible. Unless we fully understand this crime against humanity, it most assuredly might happen again. Today, and for the most part, our government simply tell us that it was regrettable, but the reasons used to inflict so much pain on black women and others, who the eugenicists thought were fair game, was nonsensical, as many of these women (as victims), we now know, were perfectly normal, *sentient* human beings, not retarded or emotionally damaged, or mentally unbalanced.

Fortunately, the eugenicists of the past look less and less like heroes and legitimate scientists, but more like unconscionable, blood-lusting fools. Some racist thinkers today, however, believe that those in the early American eugenics movement are really underappreciated. Unfortunately, moreover, those who try to raise the curtain, sound the alarm, or speak-out against this painful period in our history, are often marginalized and effectively muzzled by the conservative media and the unconcerned academia, as many supporters and scholars try to inform, or set the record straight about racialist eugenics in the United States. But their voices will never be silenced.

We must finally start with the belief that nothing should be taken for granted regarding the matter of eugenics. But more than anything else, we must not try to forget, minimize, or ignore that this terrible American eugenics history happened. Such a matter deserves our undivided attention. In any event, unless we understand the cultural, social, and political context of what happened during the early American eugenics movement, we cannot truly empathize with those who suffered. Nor will we be able to make sense of why *everyone* should abhor or be appalled at what happened.

For some Americans, the eugenics movement was a nightmare and perhaps a death sentence for others. Many of these emotionally scarred women, however, have been strong enough—mentally and physically—to beat the odds. Nonetheless, these survivors continue to suffer the emotional and psychological distress of whether or not they will receive some kind of monetary settlement. So how exactly can we make things right by the survivors, instead of waiting around for our government to do something? Should we wait for them to just die of old age? More importantly, we must not lay blame for such a horrendous historical event on these surviving women.

We must also make it clear, as many know, that, "no one who underwent forced sterilization in America has received assistance for it,"[19] which shows you the mercilessness and *indignity* of humankind, and our capacity for unadulterated evil. Unfortunately, our government continues to low-ball the idea of giving *any* compensation awards to *anyone* affected by the various eugenics programs in America. But the survivors must continue to endure, like the thousands of Asian women who suffered in Japan's World War II military brothels, where they were essentially forced into sexual slavery. The fight for these surviving women, affected by America's eugenics programs, goes on.

Further, the survivors of American eugenics must never give up, back-down or become discouraged when they submit claims against the government, and are turned down, or rejected. This particular issue, of course, stirs more raw emotions than almost any other current social or political problem, when it is revealed. The eugenics movement in America, therefore, will become even more of an issue when all the facts are eventually learned. So there should be a constant reminder that long-delayed compensations or restitutions are in order for these deserving and mostly surviving black women. Demanding to be heard and asking for compensations will give more eugenic survivors the chance to at least have a piece of mind before their deaths, as they have been through so much.

Failing to do *anything* by ignoring the issue of compensations for eugenics-exploitation—and hoping that this tragic history may simply go away is unconscionable, and definitely not the answer. This is to say that we must deal more resolutely with the eugenics issue. A simple, unambiguous apology by our government is also not enough. Someone must clearly acknowledge that these horrific activities occurred. Someone must also be held accountable, and give answers to these poor old women for the pain and suffering, horrible anxiety, traumatic anguish, humiliating ridicule, as well as the emotional damage rendered against and upon them by the American eugenicists.

Finally, we must guard against this kind of depraved and outlandish activity in the future, or such evil and repugnant actions on the part of humans will rear their ugly head again, and be possibly unleashed upon the world once again.

Notes

1. Barry Mehler, "The New Eugenics: Academic Racism in the U.S. Today," *Science for the People*, Vol. 15, Issue 3 (1983), p. 18 (pp. 18–23).

2. Rebecca Sinderbrand, "A Shameful Little Secret: North Carolina confronts its history of forced sterilization," *Newsweek* (March 28, 2005), p. 33.

3. *Ibid.*

4. *Ibid.*

5. "One Word Politics Try to Avoid: Sorry," *Time* (February 19, 2007), p. 20. Georgia's issuance of a resolution of apology for participation in the eugenics movement and the injustices done under the wrong-minded eugenics laws is commendable; however, to add insult to a very sad occurrence in our history, Georgia wants to pass a measure that would "designate April as Confederate history and Heritage month." To my mind, traitors to our remarkable Constitution should *never* be held up as heroes, nor praised in a misguided state Heritage month. See "Georgia may apologize for sterilization," *USA Today* (Friday 2, 2007), p. 3A, and "Georgia considers apology for slavery," *USA Today* (March 20, 2007), p. 3A.

6. Philip R. Reilly, "Involuntary Sterilization in the United States: A Surgical Solution," Volume 62, No. 2, *The Quarterly Review of Biology* (June 1987), p. 157 (pp. 153–170).

7. Mehler, "The New Eugenics," p. 19.

8. Lawrence Mower, "Researchers tied to hate groups get invitations," *Las Vegas Review-Journal* (March 11, 2007), p. 8B (pp. 1B and 8B).

9. Mehler, "The New Eugenics," p. 23.

10. Mower, "Researchers tied to hate groups get invitations," p. 85.

11. Sinderbrand, "A Shameful Little Secret," p. 33

12. Mehler, "The New Eugenics," pp. 22–23.

13. "Hospital admits breach in girl's hysterectomy," *Las Vegas Review-Journal* (May 10, 2007), p. 12A

14. Janet Elliot, "Report: 186 died at state facilities for the retarded over 18 months," *Houston Chronicle* (March 24, 2007), p. B2

15. Edwin Black. *War Against the Weak: Eugenics and America's Campaign to Create a Master Race* (Four Walls Eight Windows: New York, 2003), p. 235.

16. Mehler, "The New Eugenics," pp. 23–23.

17. Amanda Fehd, "16-year-old testifies for autism measure," *Las Vegas Review-Journal* (April 3, 2007), p. 4B.

18. *Ibid.*

19. Sinderbrand, "A Shameful Little Secret," p. 33.

Reading 3.2

African Americans and Racial Disparities in the Criminal Justice System

Earnest N. Bracey, Ph.D.

Introduction

African Americans have been historically treated unfairly in the criminal justice system in the United States. Early on in our colonial history, for example, African Americans were slaves on various plantations, particularly in the South, and had no real access to the federal and state courts. Indeed, black people could not serve on juries (or as jurors) during the inception of our different courts, nor could some testify against white Americans, even if they were a witness to a specific crime. Moreover, after the civil war, African Americans were routinely accused of "vagrancy," which was "the offense of a person not being able to prove at a given moment that he or she [was] employed."[1] Of course, *vagrancy* was "a new and flimsy concoction dredged up from legal obscurity at the end of the nineteenth century by the state legislatures of Alabama and other southern states."[2] Political historian Douglas A. Blackmon writes that:

> It [vagrancy] was capriciously enforced by local [white] sheriffs and constables, adjudicated by mayors and public notaries, recorded haphazardly or not at all in court records, and, most tellingly in a time of massive unemployment among all southern men, [but] was reserved almost exclusively for black men.[3]

Unfortunately, many white Americans today, especially in southern states, refused to believe that African Americans can be targets of *discrimination* and *racism* in our criminal justice system. But it must be made abundantly clear that "the reason some innocent black men used to get convicted so often in the South, back before 1968, is that juries were all white, even in communities with 50 percent black populations."[4] The fact that a countless number of African Americans are denied the right to serve on juries, to be sure, is racial discrimination in its purist form. This is to say that African Americans are routinely dismissed from jury pools because of their *ethnicity*. Why? Will we ever really know? It has also been argued, mostly by conservatives that there is no impediment for African Americans to serve as jurors today. But this is not entirely true. Nonetheless, according to political journalist Joan Biskupic, "the extent of racial disparities in jury pools nationwide is difficult to determine because few courts keep statistics on the race of jurors—in part, analysts say, to protect the courts from lawsuits."[5] This disparity in jury pools, unfortunately, will not go away anytime soon.

Indeed, court battles over jury selections will continue to be an intractable problem or serious challenge for our American legal system—that is, until changes are made to ensure the method of choosing a jury is fairer and more equal.

Also, the fact that African Americans are "being overlooked for such public service is more than a fluke of a court lottery, [or] more than a personal slight."[6] In so many words, the elimination of African Americans from jury pools points out an egregious and serious weakness of the U.S. court system: African Americans and other minorities believe that white Americans are, perhaps, treated more fairly in the criminal justice system, as they have been, as mentioned, historically treated unjustly,[7] especially when it comes to capital punishment or the death penalty. This is important to understand because many American citizens still support the death penalty, at 66 percent.[8] However, capital punishment is "too random and arbitrary in its application." More importantly, "in a disturbing number of [court] cases" ... a person's skin color might make the difference in meting out punishment.[9] Unfortunately, the courts have not helped with the jury pool issue, even though they should be about providing impartial justice for *everyone*.

Moreover, the rulings made by even the highest court "do not guarantee racially representative juries only that not "systematic exclusion" of any distinct group occurs."[10] But when "systematic exclusion" *does* occur, as evidenced by unequal jury pools in mostly southern states, like Florida and Texas, it often eliminates potential black jurors—for no good reason.[11] Or so it seems. Even the Supreme Court is almost loath to do *anything* about how African Americans and other minorities are being routinely excused or eliminated from certain jury pools, throughout the country, because of race. Furthermore, as the U.S. Constitution stipulates, we should be judged by members of our peers. But what *exactly* does it mean to be judged by members of our peers? Does it mean that a defendant must be a member of the same racial or ethnic group, or socio-economic status—or something else? What it should mean is: African Americans and other minorities should be summoned to jury duty and placed on juries that match the percentage of African Americans and other minorities in their respective jurisdictions,[12] not just selecting all-white juries, which is common in many

American trials. Finally, the American "justice system is unjust," because "racism remains pernicious and entrenched" in the United States,[13] particularly in the way black men are judged and treated.

Cruel and Unusual Punishment

No matter how much we present evidence to the contrary, some white Americans believe that *racism* is a thing of the past, and that our criminal justice system is indeed fair and impartial to *everyone*. But nothing could be further from the truth. Indeed, "young black men have been put on notice that they can be executed for walking down the street in any area where they aren't personally known to every last paranoiac,"[14] as evidenced by the mostly all-white jury's acquittal of armed vigilante George Zimmerman, who killed the unarmed black juvenile Trayvon Martin in Florida.[15] As the former executive director of the National Black Police Officers Association plainly states, "Race has something to do with everything"[16] in law enforcement, especially in a white, male-dominated system. Hampton also takes his astute comments a step further by suggesting:

> When a person of color or a woman goes to work in a police institution where there is a white male culture and value system, they [too] end up carrying out racist policies and practices.[17]

Meanwhile, African Americans continue to be unfairly and unjustly targeted by white authority and law enforcement officials for punishment, even the death penalty. For example, the U.S. Bureau of Alcohol, Tobacco, Firearms and Explosives (ATF) are conducting "sting operations" to capture dangerous criminals, but they are routinely ensnaring small-time racial minorities—blacks and Hispanic crooks, who "jumped at the chance to score hundreds of thousands of dollars' worth of drugs."[18] But we must ask: Is this really unfair targeting of racial minorities since the people arrested are criminals anyway?

Moreover, does this mean that all African Americans and other minorities locked-up are victims and innocent? Absolutely not. Some law-breakers are some of the worst criminals the country has ever known, and they should be punished and imprisoned. Indeed, "extreme penalties are necessary in extreme cases."[19] But what about the *innocent* black person or other minorities, accused in capital punishment cases, who receive the death penalty, or longer, stiffer prison sentences, because they are "too poor to hire their own lawyers," or the Dream (Legal) Team, "relying instead on mostly the inadequate counsel of the court appointed attorney."[20] No doubt, African Americans are more likely to get life imprisonment, or a black person is "much more likely than a white" to receive the death penalty.[21] In point of fact, blacks and Hispanics "account for 56% of death-row inmates and 42% of executions."[22] But it also should be pointed out that "there is little evidence that capital punishment acts as an effective deterrent to violent crime."[23] So we must question the *efficacy of* even having such final and irreversible decisions/sentences.

Equally important, many African Americans are arrested at a greater rate (or extent) for actually committing some of the same type of crimes as many white Americans. For example, "African-Americans are more likely to be arrested for marijuana possession than whites, even though studies have repeatedly shown that the two groups use the drug at similar rates."[24] In the final analysis, and on a national level:

> African-Americans are nearly four times as likely to be arrested for marijuana possession as whites. The disparity is even more pronounced in some states, including Illinois, Iowa and Minnesota, where African-Americans are about eight times as likely to be arrested. And in some counties around the country, blacks are 10, 15 or even 30 times as likely to be arrested.[25]

The obvious question is why these criminal or racial discrepancies are happening in the first place? Is it because black criminals are worse than white criminals? Or is it really because they (black males in particular) are demonized by the media as animalistic, thugs, gang-bangers, crack-dealing killers, or "overpowering super human predators?"[26] The fact of the matter is, black criminals, especially *if* and *when* they commit identical crimes, should be given the same prosecution consideration and punishment as white criminals, regardless of the specific circumstances.

Additionally, certain racial stereotypes about black people shouldn't be cited or used to justify the wrong actions of law enforcement officials or police authorities. But we should consider other racial discrepancies in the criminal justice system, especially given that "black defendants continue to receive slightly longer federal sentences under a system that [is] supposed to do away with racial disparity."[27] Moreover, it should be pointed out that some white Americans automatically and wrongly assume that African Americans are predominantly crack cocaine users. This is not true, because mostly white Americans are the biggest users of crack cocaine and the affluent "power form of the illegal drug," according to a *Crisis Magazine* report in 1996, citing work done at the *Sentencing Project*.[28] But African Americans "are charged more often with crimes involving crack cocaine."[29] Furthermore, in 1998, according to government statistics, and journalist DeWayne Wickham, "74% of powder cocaine users" were white Americans, whereas only 13% were Hispanics and 12% blacks.[30] Nonetheless, "blacks were 31% of those who ended up in federal prison for selling powder cocaine, Hispanics 49% and whites only 19%."[31]

If this racial disparity isn't criminally unjust, what *exactly* is? And why do we allow this injustice to happen in a nation that prides itself on equality and justice for all? Apparently, "there is good reason to believe that the scales of justice are out of balance,"[32] in regards to cocaine penalties. Fortunately, President Obama signed a bill from Congress in 2010 that reduced "the disparity between federal mandatory sentences for convictions for crack" and the powder form of cocaine.[33] In other words, the bill altered "a 1986 law, under which a person convicted of crack cocaine possession gets the same mandatory prison term as someone with 100 times the same of powder cocaine."[34] Unfortunately, this particular law does not solve the long, inequitable sentencing of minorities who are summarily arrested for possession of the violent drug.

Furthermore, as most of the world probably knows, the United States lock-up more people (particularly minorities at a disproportionate rate) than any other nation, even more than China, which has the largest human population on the planet. According to the Justice Department, our "nation's prison and jail population in mid-2004 stood at 2.1 million, [or] a slight increase of 2.3 percent" from 2003.[35] And while some criminal records assert that "the national incarceration rate has slowed,"[36] this assumption is not entirely accurate, as we will discuss later. The question is: Who exactly are we going to incarcerate in the United States—just predominantly African Americans and Hispanics? And why are we building more prisons—to warehouse or lock up *only* minorities? A 2000 report by the Leadership Conference on Civil Rights asserts that:

> Blacks and Hispanics are disproportionately targeted by police, unfairly victimized by "racially skewed" charging and plea bargaining decisions by prosecutors, given harsher sentences by judges and deeply impacted by "get tough" crime policies enacted by lawmakers.[37]

Are such actions cruel and unusual punishment? Additionally, when did building prisons, by private firms become such big business? The reality is, these many private prisons are not being built for *nothing*, even if they are constructed by the federal or state governments, or private businesses. Clearly, if private corporations built our prisons, our governments and tax dollars will probably end up paying the bill. Although many state governments in our nation believe that "private prisons should play only a limited role," 85,000 of the millions of "prison beds nationwide [are] provided by private firms."[38] So is this the shape of things to come—that is, will private conglomerates seriously be in the future business of building more private prisons—to make a profit?

In deference to this notion, African Americans and Hispanics (or low-income people of color) are the target populations for imprisonment or incarceration in the future, as they are "likely to be in prison at some time in their lives,"[39] because of the racial disparity in the criminal justice system.

Therefore, the truth about the racial disparities in the criminal justice system must be told, which can be particularly devastating for poor minorities. It should also make us question whether private prisons are really the answer to our incarceration woes, given that we have serious overcrowding in many of our state prisons, like in California. Journalist Joan Biskupic writes that the prison population in California "at one point was 156,000, nearly double the number that buildings were designed to hold."[40] Accordingly, the U.S. Supreme Court declared that the prison overcrowding in California, unconstitutional and "upheld an order by a 5–4 vote that could force the transfer or release of more than 30,000 convicted felons."[41] This is important to point out, because "violence and disorder inside a number of institutions have raised serious questions" about the private prison's "management abilities and their profit-making approach" to operating a prison for long-term incarceration.[42] All in all, as the president and Chief Executive Officer of the National Urban League has pointed out: "Many in America just can't seem to give up the idea that a blanket, and simplistic, get tough and lock-'em-up-for-as-long-as-possible response to the problem of crime is all that's needed."[43] But this harsh attitude toward policing minorities is no solution at all, given the profound, negative consequences.

Recidivism and Rehabilitation

Unfortunately, some Americans believe that all prisoners should be treated horribly while incarcerated, maybe even fed bread and water, while being possibly abused, or left to rot in their small cells. But such "wretched living conditions will not help with rehabilitation."[44] Indeed, our broken prison system, in some states, can be deplorable. Moreover, there are those who would take away the little entertainment and personal accoutrements most prisoners already have in lock-up, like access to exercise equipment, technical training, and educational opportunities. Eliminating such prison activities, however, would be a disservice to the prisoner, because like a caged animal (to use the analogy), he or she might strike out, committing terrible crimes, or wreaking havoc on society at large, upon release from incarceration. So is this truly what Americans want? Probably not. After all, "many first-timers (convicts) are sent to over-crowded, violent prisons, [but] they leave there damaged and handicapped by the [prison] system."[45] Simply put, many prisoners will not be locked up forever, even with the high event of recidivism.

Recidivism, of course, means that some ex-convicts will relapse into criminal activity and "return to prisons after they are release," because we are not really trying "to rehabilitate prisoners and restore them as productive members of society."[46] No doubt, this is a mistake, especially as it concerns blacks and other minority groups caught up in the criminal justice system. One time boxing champion Rubin "Hurricane" Carter, an innocent black man, who "spent 20 years in a New Jersey prison for a 1996 triple murder he didn't commit" once wrote:

> The vast majority of prison inmates are going to return to society. They don't need to be brutalized, they don't need to be humiliated, they don't need to be made so low that they come out as raving maniacs. But that's what prison does to you. So people who commit crimes against other people need help, serious help. But then this whole society needs help.[47]

When it is all said and done, we must certainly denounce the habitual black or minority criminal, but we must also consider that our society essentially created many of these outlaw individuals, from my perspective, such derelicts and human monsters. Hence, this is why the concept of rehabilitation is so important. But having proactive rehabilitation in our prisons in the United States is mostly lip service. According to Carter, "there is nothing rehabilitative about prison." He goes on to state that, "Prison is the lowest level a human being can exist at without being dead."[48] But for some, prison is much more preferable than death. Therefore, "in-prison rehabilitation programs, by raising inmates' job and educational skills, [might] improve their chances of going straight once on the outside."[49] Furthermore, restoring the ex-convicts' voting rights, in every state, might also help in reforming the harden ex-convict or former prisoner. Disparities in our criminal justice system, as already mentioned, and "disenfranchising ex-convicts is [actually] counter-productive as a matter of criminal policy."[50]

Therefore, once the convict has served his or her time in prison, they should be able to vote, to participate in our political system, no matter the circumstances. To be sure, ex-convicts are human beings; and they are still American citizens too.

Put another way, the 15th Amendment to the U.S. Constitution does not say that ex-convicts should lose their right to vote because they spent time incarcerated. After all, didn't ex-convicts pay their debt to society? Americans must understand that disenfranchising ex-convicts started with white southerners, after the Civil War, to stop, *interdict* and limit the political power or clout of former black slaves. Of course, states have the responsibility of conducting all elections; but denying *any* American citizen their right to vote, especially today, says something about the current, contentious state of American politics. The question is: Why has the disenfranchisement of some ex-convicts carried over to the twenty-first century? For example, ex-convicts who had their rights restored were not even allowed to vote in the 2000 presidential election, as they were purged from the voting rolls in Florida.

Ultimately, restoring the ex-convict's right to vote would definitely say something positive about the true civility of our society. It would also make the ex-convict a part of the overall community again, restoring some of the dignity lost to them by long periods of imprisonment. Professor of law, David Cole asserts that ex-convicts "who feel connected to their communities are much less likely to commit crimes than those without community ties."[51] And voting is an essential part of this connection to *any* community. Moreover, the ex-convict shouldn't be demoralized or considered less than a human being, regardless of their race or ethnic group, because he or she might react negatively toward society, with a "devil-may-care" attitude, especially if their survival instincts kick-in. Indeed, many might feel that they have nothing else to lose, when committing a crime. In essence, ex-convicts need all of our help, not just our condemnation, ridicule or ostracism. As mentioned, if those released from prison are not given consideration, or support, many will end up incarcerated again. Toward this end, it should be noted that ex-convicts, unfortunately, "are arrested for committing another serious crime within three years; [and] 25 percent end up being sent back to prison."[52] Therefore, providing tangible support and training to ex-convicts shouldn't be a difficult proposition, or endeavor.

The Death Penalty

As briefly discussed, we should also consider the racial disparities in terms of implementation of the death penalty. Indeed, why are African Americans "far more likely than whites to receive death sentences?"[53] Or put more simply, why are more African Americans sentenced to death at the state and national levels? The obvious question is whether capital punishment is being applied fairly. Or what are the specific motives of the United States government to seek "the most severe penalty possible: the irrevocable sentence of death?"[54] In 1996, for example, "66 percent of the federal death prosecutions [were] brought against African Americans."[55] Equally important, the Justice Department seeks the federal death penalty in states that support capital punishment, where there is a higher concentration or population of African Americans.[56] Such prosecutions on the part of our federal government is deplorable, because our courts "should not be using the awesome power of the federal death penalty almost exclusively against minorities,"[57] especially African Americans.

Furthermore, what gives our governments the moral right to take anyone's life? Moreover, if the death penalty (or the ultimate punishment) is arbitrary and not an effective deterrent to serious crime, shouldn't it be abandoned? Unfortunately, the majority of Americans today favor the death penalty. However, in 1972, the U.S. Supreme Court moved forward in declaring that the death penalty had no place in civilized society. Nonetheless, the U.S. Supreme Court reversed that decision, and did an about-face in 1987 by ruling that the death penalty "was constitutional despite figures indicating that killers of whites were far more likely to be sentenced to death?"[58] Even former U.S. Supreme Court Justice Sandra Day O'Connor admitted that the death penalty can sometimes be applied unfairly, and that some innocent minority defendants are sent to *death row* because of a "lack of funds for adequate defenses and that prosecutors have inconsistent standards for seeking the death penalty."[59]

Furthermore, how can *anyone* support the death penalty, knowing something of the lawlessness and racial disparities in the American criminal justice system? We should be nonplussed in regards to this issue. Indeed, there are "public defenders who fail to perform even the most basic duties in court."[60] Moreover, there are "indifferent judges, cowardly public officials, and an absurdly rigid system which honors the letter of the rules over actual justice."[61] The American people also shouldn't take it for granted that *everything* goes on justly in our criminal justice system, nor must we ignore prosecutorial misconduct, or condone the overzealousness of some prosecutors in their pursuit to lock people up (or send people to their deaths). Sometimes prosecutors think only of their own political ambitions, while proclaiming how tough they can be in fighting crime. But there can be profound, negative consequences when prosecutors wrongly involve themselves in the conviction of *innocent* minorities. During a 2010 investigation by *USA Today*, there were:

> 201 (documented) criminal cases in which federal judges found that prosecutors had violated ethics rules or laws. Judges caught some prosecutors hiding evidence, lying to judges or breaking plea bargains. In some cases, innocent people were imprisoned. Even when defendants were released or exonerated, some lost livelihoods and reputations.[62]

Perhaps it (is or) might be easy for some prosecutors to act without thinking of the devastating consequences of their unfair actions, particularly concerning minorities, like suppressing evidence that might clear an innocent man. But the failure of prosecutors and ineffective court appointed attorney should never be accepted. As Rubin "Hurricane" Carter tells us: "There are many people in prison today who find themselves standing on the wrong side of the law, not because they went astray, but because the law, having been placed in the wrong hands, strayed from the right path."[63] Indeed, many *innocent* African Americans go through the real, frightening, humiliating and painful experience of the American Court system, which is still a bastion of racism; and made-up predominantly of white males. Consequently, in 2010 two black men, Ronald Taylor and George Gould spent 16 years in prison for a crime they didn't commit, which was the 1993 slaying of "a New Haven store owner."[64] Fortunately, their convictions were overturned when DNA evidence proved their innocence, and a star witness recanted her testimony.[65] What exactly, then, should happen to prosecutors when they are responsible for an innocent person being convicted of a crime he or she didn't commit? This question, of course, is a fundamental issue that should be seriously addressed. Unfortunately, according to journalists Brad Heath and Kevin McCoy, "one reason [prosecutorial] violations may go undetected is that only a small fraction of criminal cases ever get the scrutiny of a trial, the process most likely to identify misconduct."[66] Finally, it should be acknowledged that "prosecutors are supposed to seek justice, not merely score convictions."[67]

Conclusion

Contrary to the assertion that all African Americans are guilty of *something*, if they are arrested, is ridiculous. More importantly, "the prospect that innocent [black] people will be executed in America"[68] should never be tolerated, as it is a horrifying proposition, especially as minority citizens might view this matter. In addition, "we-the-people" should never accept the notion that mistakes will be invariably made in our criminal justice system, particularly when even one innocent person is put to death by our governments. There are even those who would strongly argue that "the federal death penalty laws are being fairly applied without regard to the racial background of the defendants and without any discriminatory intent."[69] But such notions are wrong. For example, the most important fact that supporters of the death penalty fail to mention is that many public defenders are mostly mediocre, if not incompetent,[70] which might lead to the wrongful prosecution, as earlier discussed, of innocent minority defendants.

An NAACP Legal Defense fund study found that "eighty-two percent of those executed between 1977 and 1998 had been charged with murdering a white person,"[71] so this will always be a serious racial issue. Furthermore, the appeals process should never be limited to the inmate if it is not frivolous. This is significant to note because many death row inmates have had their convictions overturned in the appeals process.[72] The reversal of many death penalty convictions has also been because of the rush to judgment by prosecutors. Indeed, it should be pointed out that in recent years, "several death penalty convictions [have been] called into question after it revealed that defense lawyers ... slept during trials."[73] More significantly, many "guilty verdicts have been based on false testimony from jailhouse snitches and misconduct by prosecutors and police [that] tainted some cases."[74] Such reckless behavior, and multiple layers of injustice, has sent the innocent to prison, while letting the guilty go free and discrediting the U.S. criminal justice system.[75] In this respect, American citizens should always be concerned about wrongfully convicting and incarcerating an innocent minority person, because our justice system can do better. It is also unforgivable that some of our courts allow such misconduct on the part of prosecutors, especially when the death penalty is involved.

And what about the expert legal help that such black defendants need? Or should we consider the *underlying* reason why a person commit a violent crime in the first place? If our criminal justice system just want to lock-up African Americans and other minorities and put them to death, we should acknowledge that the death penalty hasn't been an effective solution or deterrent to heinous crimes. Some opponents believe that the death penalty is "cruel and unusual" punishment, because "states used it in arbitrary and capricious ways,"[76] particularly when it concerns people of color. Carter reminds us finally that: "Any country that maintains the acronyms of the death penalty is, by that very fact, an uncivilized society. It's abominable that in this day and age we still kill our own citizens."[77]

The death penalty, therefore, hasn't definitively solved *any* of our social or criminal justice problems. Thus, Americans should agree "to suspend the death penalty because our governments continue to make mistakes, sending people to *death row* and ultimately their deaths."[78] This would be the *moral* and *right* thing to do if Americans believe in the principles of a free, just and civilized nation. And as a nation, we should stop locking-up minorities for non-violent offenses, or less serious crimes, or minor drug possession charges. Wade Henderson, executive director of the Leadership Conference tells us that "the biased mistreatment of racial minorities in the criminal justice system is one of the most profound civil rights crises facing America in the new century."[79] So this issue has continuing significance for the future.

Another question we should ask in regards to this issue is whether members of the dominant group are fairly prosecuted in our criminal justice system, especially in proportion to a particular community's minority population. White males, for example, commit a disproportionate number of white collar crimes, but many are not even considered criminals or ex-convicts after being released from prison, like Martha Stewart, to name just one white person and ex-convict. And as pointed out previously in this work, we must also question why African Americans are routinely locked up for certain crimes, while white criminals are most often given probation.[80] In this regard, police officers and law enforcement officials "are targeting black citizens and black neighborhoods [and] turning a comparatively blind eye to the same conduct occurring at the same rates in many white communities."[81] Historically, as professor Anne-Marie Cusac writes:

> Even as penitentiaries ... rose in the south, the southern states maintained
> legal systems that inflicted corporal pain on [black] slaves for behaviors that
> were not crimes when committed by white people.[82]

Unfortunately, such unfairness or racial disparities in the criminal justice system has been carried over into the 21st century, and still prevail today in the United States, as they did in the 1800s.[83] In order to reduce the risk of innocent minority defendants being locked-up, racially profiled, tortured and executed in our society, or even providing a fair jury pool, Americans must demand that our Congress pass a cogent bill to ensure fairness in selecting juries, as well as "improve payments to public defense lawyers in death penalty cases and to require states and the federal government to make DNA testing available to convicts, no matter the circumstances."[84] Finally, in order to correct some of the racial disparity problems in the United States—in terms of our criminal justice system—there should be more minority judges and justices, who can perhaps empathize with poor minorities and African American defendants. Unfortunately, darker-skinned people feel racial injustice by virtue of being born. And "regardless of laws in individual states," and as posited recently in the *New York Times*:

> Federal officials and local police departments need to abandon policies that evaluate officers based on numerical arrest goals, which encourage petty arrests, along with illegal stops that violate the Fourth Amendment.[85]

Notes

1. Douglas A. Blackmon, *Slavery by Another Name: The Re-Enslavement of Black Americans from the Civil War to World War II* (New York: Doubleday, 2008), 1.

2. Ibid, 1.

3. Ibid, 1. In no uncertain terms, *vagrancy* was very much like quasi-slavery, or a new kind of black slavery.

4. Vin Suprynowicz, "They're not subject to majority vote," *Las Vegas Review Journal,* July 25, 1999, 2E.

5. Joan Biskupic, "The push is on for more diverse juries," *USA Today,* August 28, 2001, 8A.

6. Ibid, 1A.

7. Ibid, 1A.

8. "Executions: Dead man walking out," *The Economist,* June 10, 2000, 21.

9. Christopher McDougall, "Death penalty, debate endure under 20-year-old judgment," *Las Vegas Review Journal,* July 2, 1996, 4E.

10. Biskupic, "The push is on," 8A.

11. Ibid, 8A.

12. Ibid, 8A.

13. "How they see us: A racist nation of vigilantes," *The Week,* July 26, 2013, 14.

14. Ibid, 14.

15. Ibid, 14.

16. "Taped beating not seen by all as race issue," *Las Vegas Review Journal,* Jul 16, 2000, 9A.

17. Ibid, 9A.

18. Brad Heath, "Do ATF stings target minorities?" *USA Today*, August 2, 2013, 3A.

19. McDougall, "Death penalty," 4E.

20. Ken Armstrong and Steve Mills, "O'Connor rethinks executions," *Las Vegas Review Journal*, July 4, 2001, 18A.

21. "Executions," 21.

22. Ibid, 21.

23. Ibid, 21.

24. "Racially Biased Arrests for Pot," *The New York Times*, June 16, 2013, 10.

25. Ibid, 10.

26. "Taped beating," 9A.

27. Mary Pat Flaherty and William Casey, "Blacks receive more time for same crimes," *Las Vegas Review Journal*, October 9, 1996, 1A.

28. Malaika Home, "Race and the Criminal Justice System," *Crisis*, January 1996, 12 and 14. Home tells us that there was a 90% conviction rate for blacks arrested for crack cocaine, but only 3.5 white convictions for being busted for crack cocaine.

29. "Obama signs off on cocaine-disparity law," *USA Today*, August 4, 2010, 5A.

30. DeWayne Wickham, "Gore view falls short on cocaine disparity," *USA Today*, November 23, 1999, 19A.

31. Ibid, 19A.

32. Ibid, 19A.

33. "Obama Signs off."

34. "Congress closes gap in cocaine penalties," from The Associated Press in *USA Today*, July 29, 2010, 5A.

35. Marc H. Morial, "America's misguided response to crime," *Las Vegas Review Journal*, April 29, 2005, 11b. See Nicholas Kristof, "Help thy neighbor and go to prison," *Las Vegas Sun*, August 18, 2013, 6. According to *New York Times* columnist Nicholas Kristof, "With less than 5 percent of the world's population, the United States has almost one-quarter of the world's prisoners." Therefore, "we have invested in mass incarceration in ways that are crushingly expensive, break up families and are often simply cruel."

36. Ibid, 11b.

37. "Report eyes racial disparities," *Las Vegas Review Journal*, May 4, 2000, 2A.

38. Peter Slevin, "The Missing Profits in Private Prisons," *The Washington Post*, National Weekly Edition, February 26–March 4, 2001, 29.

39. Morial, "America's misguided," 11b.

40. Joan Biskupic, "Prison crowding is unconstitutional," *USA Today*, May 24, 2011, 3A.

41. Ibid, 3A.

42. Slevin, "The Missing Profits," 29.

43. Morial, "America's misguided," 11b.

44. "Jail broken: 5 ways to fix USA's prisons," *USA Today*, July 14, 2011, 7A.

45. Ibid, 7A.

46. Ibid, 7A.

47. Samuel Hine, "Talking with the Hurricane," *The Plough Reader,* April–May 2000, 6–7.

48. Ibid, 6.

49. Morial, "America's misguided," 11b.

50. David Cole, "Denying felons vote hurts them, society," *USA Today,* February 3, 2000, 17A.

51. Ibid, 17A. Cole also tells us that "crime is so much higher in anonymous inner-city setting than in equally impoverished rural communities."

52. Morial, "America's misguided," 11b.

53. Richard Willing, "Support for the death penalty might be declining," *USA Today,* December 14–16, 2001.

54. William D. Matthewman, "Congress must investigate death penalty abuses," *Las Vegas Review Journal,* March 19, 1996, 5B.

55. Ibid, 5B.

56. Richard Willing, "Death penalty policies examined," *USA Today,* September 5, 2000, 3A.

57. Matthewman, "Congress must investigate," 5B.

58. Andrew Welsh-Huggins, "Race found to play role in Ohio capital cases," *Las Vegas Review Journal,* May 8, 2005, 18A.

59. Warren Cohen, "Putting a hold on executions," *U.S. News & World Report,* May 31, 1999, 29. See also Ken Armstrong and Steve Mills, "O'Connor rethinks executions," 18A.

60. "The death penalty: Theirs but to do and die," *The Economist,* May 1, 2010, 85.

61. Ibid, 85.

62. "When prosecutors go astray, justice takes a beating," *USA Today,* October 8, 2010, 8A. See also Brad Heath, "Locked up but Innocent?" *USA Today,* June 14, 2012, 1A and 5A.

63. Hine, "Talking with the Hurricane," 4–5.

64. Stephanie Reitz, "Two released after witness recants," *Las Vegas Review Journal,* April 2, 2010, 13A.

65. Ibid, 13A.

66. Brad Heath and Kevin McCoy, "Prosecutors' conduct can tip the scales," *USA Today,* September 23, 2010, 10A.

67. Ibid, 10A. Heath and McCoy go on to write that "prosecutors, at worst, [make mistakes], even when judges who presided over the trials ruled that there was serious misconduct," 11A.

68. Alan Berlow, "The Wrong Man," *The Atlantic Monthly,* November 1999, 66.

69. Mattewman, "Congress must investigate," 5b.

70. Berlow, "The Wrong Man," 66.

71. Cohen, "Putting a hold on executions," 25.

72. Fox Butterfied, "Death Sentences Being Over-turned in 2 of 3 Appeals," *The New York Times,* June 12, 2000, Al.

73. Toni Locy, "Push to reform death penalty growing," *USA Today,* February 20, 2001, 5A. Because of the incompetence of prosecutors, Walter McMillian, a black man was wrongly convicted and sentenced to death in Alabama for the death of a white, eighteen-year-old college student. Fortunately, McMillian was later exonerated and released, because of DNA evidence. See Arlene Levinson, "Not guilty death row inmates the system's worst nightmare," *Las Vegas Review Journal,* November 8, 1998, 26A and 27A.

74. Ibid, 26A and 27A.

75. Heath and McCoy, "Prosecutors' conduct," 1A.

76. Arlene Levinson, "Not guilty death row inmates the system's worst nightmare," *Las Vegas Review Journal,* November 8, 1998, 27A.

77. Hine, "Talking with the Hurricane," 5.

78. Richard Willing, "Death penalty advocates join call for moratorium," *USA Today,* May 16, 2000, 12A.

79. "Report eyes racial disparities," 2A.

80. Horne, "Race and the Criminal Justice System," 11.

81. "Racially Biased Arrests," 10.

82. Anne-Marie Cusac, *Cruel and Unusual: The Culture of Punishment in America* (New Haven & London: Yale University Press, 2009), 75.

83. Ibid, 75.

84. Willing "Death penalty advocates," 12A.

85. "Racially Biased Arrests," 10.

References

Armstrong, Ken, and Steve Mills. "O'Connor rethinks executions." *Las Vegas Review Journal,* July 4, 2001.

Berlow, Alan. "The Wrong Man." *The Atlantic Monthly,* November 1999.

Biskupic, Joan. "Prison crowding is unconstitutional." *USA Today,* May 24, 2011.

Biskupic, Joan. "The push is on for more diverse juries." *USA Today,* August 28, 2001.

Blackmon, Douglas A. *Slavery by Another Name: The Re-Enslavement of Black Americans from the Civil War to World War II.* New York: Doubleday, 2008.

Butterfied, Fox. "Death Sentences Being Over-turned in 2 of 3 Appeals." *The New York Times,* June 12, 2000.

Cohen, Warren. "Putting a hold on executions." *U.S. News & World Report,* May 31, 1999.

Cole, David. "Denying felons vote hurts them, society." *USA Today,* February 3, 2000.

"Congress closes gap in cocaine penalties." The Associated Press in *USA Today,* July 29, 2010.

Cusac, Anne-Marie. *Cruel and Unusual: The Culture of Punishment in America.* New Haven & London: Yale University Press, 2009.

"Executions: Dead man walking out." *The Economist,* June 10, 2000.

Flaherty, Mary Pat, and William Casey. "Blacks receive more time for same crimes." *Las Vegas Review Journal,* October 9, 1996.

Heath, Brad. "Do ATF stings target minorities?" *USA Today,* August 2, 2013.

Heath, Brad. "Locked up but innocent?" *USA Today,* June 14, 2012.

Heath, Brad, and Kevin McCoy. "Prosecutors' conduct can tip the scales." *USA Today,* September 23, 2010.

Hine, Samuel. "Talking with the Hurricane." *The Plough Reader,* April–May 2000.

Horne, Malaika. "Race and the Criminal Justice System." *Crisis,* January 1996.

"How they see us: A racist nation of vigilantes." *The Week,* July 26, 2013.

"Jail broken: 5 ways to fix USA's prisons." *USA Today,* July 14, 2011.

Levinson, Arlene. "Not guilty death row inmates the system's worst nightmare." *Las Vegas Review Journal,* November 8, 1998.

Locy, Toni. "Push to reform death penalty growing." *USA Today,* February 20, 2001.

Matthewman, William D. "Congress must investigate death penalty abuses." *Las Vegas Review Journal,* March 19, 1996.

McDougall, Christopher. "Death penalty debate endure under 20-year-old judgment." *Las Vegas Review Journal,* July 2, 1996.

Morial, Marc H. "America's misguided response to crime." *Las Vegas Review Journal,* April 29, 2005.

"Obama signs off on cocaine-disparity law." *USA Today,* August 4, 2010.

"Racially Biased Arrests for Pot." *The New York Times,* June 16, 2013.

Reitz, Stephanie. "Two released after witness recants." *Las Vegas Review Journal,* April 2, 2010.

"Report eyes racial disparities." *Las Vegas Review Journal,* May 4, 2000.

Slevin, Peter. "The Missing Profits in Private Prisons." *The Washington Post,* National Weekly Edition, February 26–March 4, 2001.

Suprynowicz, Vin. "They're not subject to majority vote." *Las Vegas Review Journal,* July 25, 1999.

"Taped beating not seen by all as race issue." *Las Vegas Review Journal,* Jul 16, 2000.

"The death penalty: Theirs but to do and die." *The Economist,* May 1, 2010.

Welsh-Huggins, Andrew. "Race found to play role in Ohio capital cases." *Las Vegas Review Journal,* May 8, 2005.

"When prosecutors go astray, justice takes a beating." *USA Today,* October 8, 2010.

Wickham, DeWayne. "Gore view falls short on cocaine disparity." *USA Today,* November 23, 1999.

Willing, Richard. "Death penalty advocates join call for moratorium." *USA Today,* May 16, 2000.

Willing, Richard. "Death penalty policies examined." *USA Today,* September 5, 2000.

Willing, Richard. "Support for the death penalty might be declining." *USA Today,* December 14–16, 2001.

Reading 3.3

Thomas Jefferson, Sally Hemings and the Question of Equality in the United States

Earnest N. Bracey, Ph.D.

Introduction: Notes on the Issue of Racial Equality

Imagine if we were transported back in time to the beginning or founding of our nation, and you had the opportunity to ask Thomas Jefferson exactly what he meant by *equality* and the specific words that he wrote in the *Declaration of Independence*—that all men were created equal—given that Jefferson was a slave owner, and reportedly "had six children by his mulatto mistress, Sally Hemings, who was his wife's half-sister."[1] Indeed, it turns out that, for many years while he lived, the third president of the United States, Thomas Jefferson carried on an illicit affair with his black slave, Sally Hemings, as recent genetic DNA tests were consistent with descendants of Eston Hemings, their son, who was born on May 21, 1808. The relationship between Jefferson and Hemings affirms what legal scholar and political historian and Harvard Professor Annette Gordon-Reed has so insightfully written about in her ground-breaking book, *Thomas Jefferson and Sally Hemings: An American Controversy*. For example, Gordon-Reed cogently writes:

> Significantly, biographies and articles that purport to debunk the Jefferson-Hemings liaison do not even tell readers the essential facts of the lives of Sally Hemings and her children that give rise to evidence that the story might be true. In some instances, when the writers do try to recount the facts, they make major errors. Thus, the normal and necessary process of accumulating and weighing evidence largely has been circumvented. The evidence must [therefore] be considered as a whole before a realistic and fair assessment of the possible truth of this story can be made.[2]

Earnest N. Bracey, "Thomas Jefferson, Sally Hemings and the Question of Equality in the United States," *American International Journal of Humanities and Social Science*, vol. 5, no. 2, pp. 11–21. Copyright © 2019 by Center for Global Research Development. Reprinted with permission.

Infuriated, perhaps, by the interracial liaison and even the knowledge, some of Jefferson's white descendants have tried to vehemently deny this relationship, even with the conclusive DNA evidence. But according to Gordon-Reed, "this is a rescue mission, not a search for historical truth, and they [some white descendants] don't care whose reputation gets hurt in the process—as long as it's not Thomas Jefferson's."[3] Even more important, Afrocentric scholars have verbally attacked Jefferson for his hypocrisy, as he owned many black slaves. Professor of history Brenda E. Stevenson tells us that "Thomas Jefferson, the principal author of the Declaration of Independence, owned more than 100 slaves at the time of the Revolution and more than 200 at his death in 1826, most of whom were sold [at auction] to pay his debts."[4] So what does this say about Jefferson and his notion of *equality*? No one should be proud of Jefferson's position on *chattel slavery*, as he often talked about the inviolable dignity of human beings, save blacks in bondage. Jefferson, of course, felt that black people were inferior, even as he advocated and persuasively wrote about liberty, justice, freedom and the equality of *all* men. Further, there was no excuse for Jefferson's deeply-seated, staunch racialist beliefs, as he carried on with his black mistress or slave, Sally Hemings, "mother to his [mulatto] children," and "lover of more than thirty years."[5] Historian Jon Meacham, in his Pulitzer Prize winning biography, *Thomas Jefferson: the Art of Power*, put it this way:

> The emotional content of the Jefferson-Hemings relationship is a mystery. He may have loved her, and she him. It could have been, as some have argued, coercive, institutionalized rape. She might have just been doing what she had to do to survive an evil [slave] system, accepting sexual duty as an element of her enslavement and using what leverage she had to improve the lot of her children. Or each of these things may have been true at different times.[6]

So was Jefferson aware even of the truth and concept of *equality*? Indeed, his inability to do the right thing for his slaves showed that he was not necessarily supportive of justice and *equality* for black people in the culture at large at that time. And what about the terrible injustices he reaped upon black men and women at his Monticello plantation? To be sure, Jefferson was perhaps clueless about the irreparable harm he caused his black slaves. In essence, Jefferson's "behavior [was] shaped in accordance with practical circumstances and [personal] goals rather than ideological objectives."[7] In a nutshell, Jefferson's equivocal position on slavery and *equality* seemed to reflect his abject hypocrisy on both the issues of *slavery* and *equality*. Moreover, did Jefferson even care about the human rights and dignity of black people? Probably not. Human rights, of course, are those "rights that belong to an individual as a consequence of being human."[8] No doubt, white supremacists (at that time) believed that black people were sub-human, who deserved to be enslaved and exploited. Therefore, we must ask: Was Sally Hemings exploited by Jefferson? Or was she treated equally? Perhaps not. After all, she had to deal with Jefferson's demands as a slave master. Presumably, Sally Hemings' quiet protestations were barely acknowledged by Thomas Jefferson.

This is important to understand because as professors Eric S. Lander and Joseph J. Ellis have written:

> Nothing in the vast historical literature, sheds any light on the character of the relationship between Jefferson and Sally Hemings. Was it, as his contemporary critics charged, a tale of lust and rape? Was it, as several twentieth-century scholars and novelists have suggested, a love story rooted in mutual affection? Or was it something in between? These questions are open to endless interpretation, but in a broader sense, the findings give blacks and whites alike an opportunity to confront a largely secret, shared history.[9]

What is significant is the fact that despite sometimes espousing a free, aspirational world, where men (and later women) could be treated with respect in terms of the brotherhood of mankind, *black slaves* were not included in this so-called enlightened discussion—that is, in terms of all people beings truly (created) equal. Additionally, Jefferson never spoke out against social injustices and *racial inequality* against black people, so it became obvious that he was selling the notion that *everything* he did toward his slaves was proper and righteous. But nothing could have been further from the truth. Jefferson mostly deflected questions about Sally Hemings; but he was obsessed with her and particularly agitated when she refused to return with him to Monticello when he served as U.S. minister or ambassador to France. So Jefferson missed cues that Sally Hemings was pregnant with his child, and extremely unhappy, particularly with all the strange political nuances and talk about freedom she heard in Paris, France. Indeed, Hemings grew bolder in expressing her displeasure with being his (Jefferson's) slave. After all, she tried to leave him and stay in France as a free woman. According to Meacham, "Jefferson was unaccustomed to encountering resistance to his absolute will at all, much less from a slave."[10] Clearly, Jefferson was more concerned with how he could *cajole* and *manipulate* Sally Hemings. But Meacham tells us that:

> She [Hemings], not he [Jefferson], was in control. It must have seemed surreal, unthinkable, even absurd. For the first time in his life, perhaps, Jefferson was truly in a position of weakness at a moment that mattered to him. So he began making concessions to convince Sally Hemings to come home to Virginia.[11]

To be sure, Sally Hemings was emotionally connected to the man (Jefferson). But for Hemings, it was also a matter of dignity. Nevertheless, she eventually acceded to Jefferson's wishes, because she was promised her freedom, along with the children she would bear with Jefferson: "Beverly, Harriet, Madison ... and Eston—three sons and one daughter,"[12] and two others who died in childbirth. Still it is unfathomable that Hemings would return to Monticello, to be Jefferson's slave again, even with "extraordinary privileges" solemnly "pledged to her;"[13] but she did. Was it because she suffered from some kind of *Stockholm Syndrome*? Or was there sincere love and passion between Jefferson and Hemings? Of course, Sally Hemings was "bound by love for her suffering [black] people—and Jefferson—but [she was] denied acceptance by Jefferson's family."[14] More importantly, how exactly can *anyone* get used to being a slave? It is not enough to just point at the time and circumstances—that is, to think that human bondage (of any kind) was/is acceptable. Perhaps Jefferson didn't give it a second thought. But there is a larger issue at hand in regards to *equality*. Further, the "Jefferson-Hemings affair casts new light on the president's tortured position on [black] slavery and his public stand against racial mixing—echoing the country's unresolved issues of race relations and racial identity,"[15] particularly as it concerned the *equality* of his black slaves. It is worth noting that black slavery has always been a touchy and controversial issue in American culture as it has polarized our country along racial lines. So was it easy for Jefferson to ignore the pain and suffering of his own slaves?

If *anyone* should have repudiated slavery and manumitted all of his slaves, it should have been Thomas Jefferson. But this was not to be. According to historian Willard Sterne Randall, Thomas Jefferson "evidently had decided that the time was not ripe to openly defy the slave system all around him and reopen the debate over emancipation at a time when the new government was so unstable."[16] But this assumption on the part of Randall is only an excuse. And why didn't he acknowledge his relationship with Sally Hemings? Jefferson could have escaped from *politics* entirely—to be exclusively with Hemings. But he had presidential aspirations. And he wouldn't let *anyone* stand in his way from becoming President of the United States, as he struggled to keep things together at Monticello—and his hold on Sally Hemings, which was (perhaps) at times cringe worthy. And even before he died in 1826, Jefferson was hesitant to put "the name Sally Hemings in his will," as "it would have exposed a truth for which, as far as he knew, white America would never forgive him."[17] Nevertheless, it should have been clear to Jefferson that serious changes needed to be made at Monticello in regards to the enslavement of other human beings. After all, Jefferson was supposedly "a slave-holder who opposed slavery."[18]

This nagging inconsistency and concern about Jefferson was perhaps infuriating for Sally Hemings and exasperating for others. Beyond that, Thomas Jefferson, the revered third American President, and architect of our national creed, and some of his fellow Founding

Fathers believed in the ideas and principles of freedom, citizenship, and equality. But *equality* for whom? According to Professor Kathleen DuVal of North Carolina at Chapel Hill, Americans came to define *equality* during the 1790s and earlier 1800s, and even "citizenship as the right of all white men, non-white men and [later] all women [who initially] were explicitly excluded."[19] Unfortunately, *equality* and *citizenship* meant different things to different people during Thomas Jefferson's life time.

The Inception of American Equality and Equal Rights

Jefferson was also all about securing "the rights of life, liberty and the pursuit of happiness,"[20] but not when it came to giving particular human rights and freedom rights to black slaves. For Jefferson, *equality* and other "such ambiguities and unacknowledged truths were part of life."[21] Or so he (Jefferson) thought. So what then is *equality*? Generally, *equality* is "an ideal of uniformity in treatment or status by those in a position to affect either."[22] So in a diverse democracy, this sentiment is always a good thing. Professor Barry R. Gross also tells us that "there are two ways to write about *equality*. One may think long and hard about the many different often incompatible meanings of equality, the desirability of achieving human equalities in one form or other, and the impediments to that achievement. Or one may simply not think about it at all."[23] Indeed, should we even mention the latter of these two ways of addressing *equality*? And why is *equality* really necessary? Furthermore, *equality* might be interpreted to mean the absolute state of treating human beings the same and equal in all aspects of life in a respective society; however, it must be stated again that the *equality* Jefferson and other American Framers referred to was not initially considered for *everyone*. Afrocentrist Professor Molefi Kete Asante of Temple University writes in his provocative book, *Malcolm X as Cultural Hero*: "George Washington and Thomas Jefferson were slave owners, *inter alia*, who did not believe in the equality of African [Americans];"[24] and this fact cannot be ignored or omitted from history. In other words, Jefferson was a *racialist* and *non-egalitarian*, who dismissed or ignored the issue of *equality* entirely. Of course, this is a descriptive fact about Thomas Jefferson. So can acknowledging the truth about Jefferson be excused (by us today) on the grounds of misinterpretation, or different values and moral standards? Professor Asante goes on to point out that, "one can claim ignorance, one can argue that their good points outweigh their bad points, and so on; but the fact is that [our Founding Fathers] believed in the inferiority of African [Americans]."[25]

Therefore, we must ask the question: Should all American citizens today "be introduced to this factual information in order to make proper assessment and judgments" about the past?[26] Indeed, should we not mention, in discussing *equality*, the "racist heritage of the founding fathers?"[27] According to noted documentary filmmaker, Ken Burns, "we-the-people" must come to terms (if we are to be true to ourselves) with the human frailties and ambiguities of our past and elected leaders and representatives. That is, we should not hide the truth from Americans, or try to *sugar-coat* the hypocrisy of our founding heroes.[28] Burns goes on to note that: "We, as Americans, want-need-an honest, complicated past that is unafraid of controversy and tragedy, but are equally drawn to those stories that suggest an abiding faith in the human spirit and especially the unique role this extraordinary country seems to have in the positive progress of mankind."[29] We must also be cognizant that black "slavery, not only induced Americans to embrace liberty ardently but also nourished the American notion of democracy, while *racism* [my emphasis] encouraged equality among whites."[30] Toward this end, Journalist Benjamin Schwarz states that "the equality and unity of white Americans of different ethnic and religious backgrounds, [cultures] and classes were built largely on a common hatred and fear of black Americans."[31]

Essentially, this means that black slaves were thought of as less than human, barbarous, and savages to earlier whites in America, so they were summarily denied those constitutional rights guaranteed and enjoyed by most whites. Even the idea that black people are human beings today is a relatively recent phenomenon. Furthermore, "under [black American] slavery, African-Americans had no power to hold their white [slave] masters accountable. [And] although [black] slaves were usually treated as valuable property, some [white] slave masters abused their power,"[32] by having their slaves severely beaten, if they would run away. Thomas Jefferson was even guilty of this terrible transgression, especially with his black slaves that tried to escape to freedom by running away.

Jefferson's biographer, William Cohen, in a titillating and scathing 1969 article, entitled *"Thomas Jefferson and the Problem of Slavery,"* writes:

> In early September 1805, James Hubbard, a stout Negro [black man] who worked in the [Monticello] plantation nail factory, ran away, but was soon apprehended and returned. About five years later he escaped again. A year passed before Jefferson learned that Hubbard was living in the area of Lexington and dispatched Isham Chisolm to retrieve the bondsman. It was too late, however; Hubbard had departed only a few days earlier for parts unknown. When Chisolm returned empty-handed, Jefferson offered him a bonus of twenty five dollars to go after the man a second time. This time Hubbard was caught and brought back in irons, and Jefferson reported: "I had him *severely* flogged in the presence of his old companions. ..." He then added that he was convinced that Hubbard "will never again serve any man as a slave, the moment he is out of jail and his irons off he will be off himself." Before Jefferson could implement plans to have him sold out of the state, Hubbard disappeared again.[33]

This extended quote in Cohen's article is important and necessary, because contrary to popular beliefs, African Americans or black people were not particularly happy, or grateful to be slaves—that is, to be in miserable bondage—even in forced servitude for our third President, Thomas Jefferson. In fact, such a notion is absolutely absurd, because the historical record does not support this inconceivable view. Therefore, we must ask this question: Should Jefferson be vilified in the pantheon of American heroes for his role as a slave owner, or viewed as a hypocrite for being a particularly aggressive racist?[34] As mentioned, Jefferson is known for writing eloquently about justice, liberty and the equality of men, but such glorious words were reserved, as mentioned, for *only* white, male citizens at that time. Even more important, Jefferson's ideas and words today, especially about the so-called inferiority of black people, in his book, *Notes on the State of Virginia* should be considered "blatant, scientific racism."[35] Moreover, Jefferson proposed at the 1776 Virginia legislature "new restrictions and penalties applying to free Negroes and to 'miscegenation' involving white women."[36] Yet, he never mentions his illicit affair with Sally Hemings in his writings. Jefferson, of course, was full of terrible contradictions, because he was proposing such harsh penalties and measures for black people, but not for himself. To say the least, it is sad and ironic, because "the entire body of Jefferson's writings show that he never seriously considered the possibility of any form of racial coexistence on the basis of equality, and that, from at least 1778 until his death, he saw colonization as the only alternative to slavery."[37] Moreover, the many alternatives to slavery suggested by Thomas Jefferson never materialized. The bottom line is: Jefferson and most of his contemporaries "talked the talk, [but] most of them never got around to walking the walk."[38] Although the Founding Fathers aspired to the highest ideals and principles of *equality* and freedom in forming a national creed for our country, they failed—in many ways—to live up to those standards. As Burns has written:

> Most other societies have seen themselves as an end unto themselves. We Americans still quest, relentlessly. We see our growth as a country central to its survival. We are saying to all who would listen that we are willing to learn. And we have taken the narrow phrase of Jefferson's that all men were created equal—that is to say, all white men of property—and [expanded] it to include blacks and other minorities, women, handicapped people, gays, etc. Our genius as a people has been in continually enlarging the ideas we have inherited from those giants who went before us.[39]

Equally important, in such a thoroughly diverse culture and ethnic society such as ours, the ideal of *equality* is no longer an *elusive* concept. Which is to say that all Americans should be able to equally benefit from the riches of our democratic society—not just a privileged few.

This notion, of course, supports a *real* "majoritarian model" of democracy. Furthermore, we must recognize that the U.S. Constitution is a work in progress, because we can change it through the amendment process. Essentially, "the Constitution as it now stands is the work not just of Founding Fathers but of many kinds of people, over many generations. Both abolitionists and feminists—overlapping categories in the nineteenth century—[which] played their part in bringing the Constitution into the shape in which we have it today."[40] Keep in mind that if the Constitution was not a *dynamic* political document that we can adapt for the times, perhaps black people would still be in some type of slavery, like during the times of Jefferson and Reconstruction. Fortunately, the Thirteenth Amendment (after the Civil War) finally abolished black American slavery. Sadly, this is a part of our *ugly* history that we should *never* be proud of; but nor should we forget (through some kind of *mutability*) that such a past did indeed existed in our country—the United States of America.

Nor should we dismiss the fact that our Constitution as originally written, considered or counted blacks as only three-fifths (a person) of the free population, solely for White Southerners could gain more representation in the new Congress or the New Government. To be sure, white male landowners were also thinking about their bottom lines in terms of spending money on taxes. In other words, they wanted to save on taxes by reporting their slaves as less than a whole person. Professor of history Jack N. Rakove put it this way:

> The three-fifths clause, then was neither a co-efficient of racial hierarchy nor a portent of the racialist thinking of the next century. It was rather the closest approximation in the constitution to the principle of one person, one vote—even if in its origins it was only a formula for apportioning representation *among*, as opposed to *within*, states, and even if it violated the principle of equality by over-valuing the suffrage of the free male population of the slave states.[41]

For Thomas Jefferson, the three fifths clause was a *prosaic* issue, because he believed that the human traits of whites were superior. Indeed, Jefferson's racialist thinking proved *intractable* and unyielding. According to journalist Britni Danielle, "Despite fathering Hemings' children, Jefferson argued against race mixing because black people were "inferior to the whites in the endowments both of body and mind."[42] This attitude raises concerns that Jefferson was nothing but a white supremacist. Or was he? More important, perhaps, is the fact as far as his slaves were concerned, Jefferson had a "plantation mentality," as he orchestrated what was happening at Monticello—good or bad. Invariably, "for four decades, Jefferson kept meticulous records of every dollar he spent and the activities of the [black] people he held as slaves—the fee for hiring a midwife to birth an enslaved woman's child, the cost of sending someone on an errand. But Jefferson rarely wrote of Hemings, possibly in an attempt to cloak her role in his life."[43] In this respect, historians and scholars have been more than a little mystified about Jefferson's position about *racial equality*, given that he argued against the idea of slavery, in principle. But in reality, Jefferson was fallible, and no different from the other white slave masters of the time. Never mind that he didn't even want to give the appearance of *fairness* to all of his slaves. Not surprisingly, Jefferson was more concerned about his own self-worth more than *anything* else, as can be ascertain from what has already been written. Having said all this, we must ask if Jefferson was totally accepting and tolerant of black people. Probably not. Moreover, was Sally Hemings an embarrassment to him?

Racism and Discrimination after Jefferson

It should be pointed out here that "the Thirteenth Amendment" as mentioned [which prohibited or barred slavery], "like the Fourteenth Amendment's guarantee of the *Equal Protection of the Law*, [which laid] dormant, [offered] no effective protection against racial discrimination,"[44] as was the case even during the times of Jefferson. Hence, the whole concept of *inequality* took hold in the minds, perhaps, of white male land-owners, and white supremacists, particularly in their misguided and racist beliefs about black people. Indeed, these white Americans didn't care even about the impact of *racism*. So we can perceive that the intractable problem of providing racial equality has always existed in America, because of white supremacy and racial discrimination. Later, unfortunately, and even more important, the formulation of certain ingrained "political principles have not been able to make black and white Americans truly one people [as we] cannot wash away the color-line which remains the fundamental and most obdurate problem of American life."[45]

Therefore, the very foundation of our history and nation was founded upon the ideologies of racism, prejudice, inequality, and discrimination. Or in essence, white supremacy. Black people lived under the worst of circumstances, because Jefferson and those of his *ilk* had the upper-hand with a force of arms. Further, Thomas Jefferson, and others with a racialist philosophy, built on the ideas of racial "separateness," allowed them to justify their poor treatment of black people, or their slaves, despite words to the contrary. Indeed, why didn't Jefferson and other slave-owners move forward with something like the 13th amendment, which only happened in 1865 after the Civil War? To his credit, Jefferson's subconscious mind, perhaps, never stopped churning in regards to the *racial equality* issue and superficial notions about what he should have done about his black slaves. Again, freeing his slaves immediately would have been the logical and right thing to do. Manumission, however, was not necessarily on Jefferson's mind; but this was no excuse. Furthermore, Jefferson didn't have a clear idea about *equality* for black people, nor was he committed to making things more equitable going forward for his slaves. Therefore, the slaves at Monticello didn't have an eye toward a promising future. But the indefatigable spirit of his black slaves, in general, couldn't be defeated, as they found a way to survive. Furthermore, it is not an understatement to say that Jefferson's disingenuous approach to *racial equality* amounted to a *lie*.

According to Joseph Ellis, in his "stirring and *elegiac* biography," *American Sphinx: The Character of Thomas Jefferson*, "he [Jefferson] was living a lie."[46] Perhaps Jefferson lost all perspective when he tried to assert dominance over Sally Hemings and all of his black slaves at Monticello. And maintaining his slaves was unbecoming for a man of his stature. More than anything, black slaves only wanted to live a better life; but it was a nightmare for many of them, a sort of *purgatory* on earth. Of course, there were very specific restrictions for people of color; and the political voices of his black slaves at Monticello were mostly silent. This kind of unfair treatment was unacceptable under *any* circumstances. And Jefferson never enjoyed the high ground on the issues of *slavery* and *equality*. Finally, the bloodshed and human misery of black slaves wasn't something to laugh at, or dismiss. Eventually, and when it was all said and done, "Prohibiting racial discrimination became the principal strategy of the American legal system for achieving *equality* for blacks ... and yet, for purely historical reasons, the development of those laws would be unimaginable apart from the struggle of blacks for equality in America."[47] As O'Brien reminds us:

> Modern America is, and has been for more than a quarter of a century, a post-racist society, juridically and institutionally, and in the ethos of all its establishment: political, social, financial, academic, [and scientifically]. ...[48]

Conclusions

There is no denying that the relationship between Thomas Jefferson and Sally Hemings occurred. It was not an *aberration*, or some idle speculation. As far as Sally Hemings was concerned, the opportunistic Jefferson kept secrets from her, and withheld personal information about their relationship to the nation that might have negatively affected his reputation, especially if their affair got out to the wider public at that time. Jefferson, nonetheless, got more than he bargained for with Sally Hemings. She remained defiant even as she was vulnerable and succumbed to Jefferson's desires. Of course, it is probably hard to process the intensity of feelings Hemings had for the great man. Was she then, flattered by Jefferson's attention? Perhaps. Hemings' itinerant childhood in Paris, where she learned how to read and write both French and English, and where she served Thomas Jefferson as the United States ambassador (or U.S. minister from 1785–1789) to France, perhaps, made her an easy sexual target, because of her budding young womanhood. And Hemings was understandably wary of Jefferson's eventual sexual entreaties, particularly during those trying times for her.

But Hemings always tried to make the best of things, resigning herself to such a new, frustrating life and the circumstances that she found herself in. From her mother, Sally Hemings had learned that she was the half-sister of Jefferson's dead wife Martha Wayles; so she was a distant relative, and closely interlinked with Thomas Jefferson's family. Therefore, was Sally Hemings submissive in their relationship? Was she even flirtatious around Ambassador Jefferson, or a willing participate in her sexual seduction? Probably not. In the end, Hemings learned how to adapt to Jefferson's overtures and promises, even as she learned about his racialist beliefs about black people. So was she treated the way she wanted to be treated—as an equal? Probably not.

In a probing movie about the relationship between Jefferson (played by Sam Neill) and Hemings (played by Carmen Ejogo), called *Sally Hemings: An American Scandal*, later entitled *Sally Hemings: An American Love Story*, the idea that Jefferson supported *equality*, even for Sally Hemings was totally missing, or glossed over from this controversial film. Indeed, how can *anyone* understand Jefferson's apprehensive racialist thinking and trepidations toward Sally Hemings? Journalist Britni Danielle put it this way:

> Romanticizing Hemings and Jefferson's so-called relationship minimizes the deadly imbalance of power that black people suffered under before the Civil War. It also obscures our collective history as a nation that moved from being built on the blood, bones and backs of enslaved African Americans and indigenous people, to being the imperfect, hopeful and yet still unequal country we are today.[49]

When it is all said and done, the controversy of Jefferson and Hemings' relationship isn't going away, despite what others think to the contrary; and scholars and historians will continue to dissect and keep this issue in front of the public. Finally, Thomas Jefferson did not take a stand or fight against his "slave-master" mentality. This is to say that Jefferson had an obligation to rid America of slavery; but he never took *any* definitive actions to do so. In this regard, Jefferson failed miserably. But whether he did *anything* toward real *equality* is still debatable today. Unfortunately, the *erstwhile* life of Thomas Jefferson was also about the so-called inherited deficiencies he thought about black people, which was farcical in itself. And for some reason, Jefferson did not have the skills to intuitively make the right decision toward the humans he enslaved.

In essence, Jefferson did not believe in *racial equality*, because he thought that people of color (or black slaves, who were human beings like himself) were only suited for *servitude*. Most regrettably, and during Jefferson's lifetime, black slaves were never on an equal footing with white Americans. Hence, it should come as little surprise about how Jefferson felt about *equality*. In so many words, we cannot ignore Thomas Jefferson's blatant hypocrisy, because he wanted his cake, and to eat it too—so to speak—that is, he wanted two separate American people with white Americans always on top, and blacks subservient. This raises concerns that Jefferson didn't really care about the rights of black slaves, as he probably thought that it was a non-issue for him. So was Jefferson correct in his understanding of what was really going on with his own black slaves, like with Sally Hemings? Jefferson made huge contributions in forming our great nation; however, he certainly had different, *separatist* ideas about *race*. He also valued consistency, control, and order more than anything else in his life, even if it meant downplaying *equality*.

Although much has changed since the days of Jefferson and Hemings, our nation is still struggling with the issues of *inequality* and *equality* for black people. Even today, in the twenty-first century, the issue of *racial equality* is hard to achieve, mostly because white supremacists don't want people to believe that it is actually a *real* problem. Jefferson, unfortunately, preferred to avoid the pertinent facts about the humanity of his slaves, rather than face the truth; whereas Sally Hemings was particularly unrelenting in standing for something in terms of fighting for *racial equality* and against black slavery. And according to Harvard Professor Annette Gordon-Reed, "Sally Hemings helped shape her [own] life and the lives of her children, who got an almost 50-year head start on emancipation, escaping the system that had engulfed their ancestors and millions of others. [And] whatever we may feel about it today, this was important to her."[50] In the final analysis, *equality* is "the founding creed of U.S. society, but equality among all the races and between [ethnic groups] has proved easier to legislate than to achieve in practice."[51] Unfortunately, we are still living in a society that tolerates *inequality* and discrimination against black people, and others. And the degradation and marginalization continues (today) throughout the United States. But the real issue is whether we can truly come together as a nation. Or will we be mired in racial conflict over *equality* forever? Or perhaps this question will remain unanswered? All the same, we haven't resolved the issue of *racial equality* in the United States, and our past—that is, American Slavery—the *black holocaust*.

Notes

1. Kathleen T. Hill and Gerald N. Hill. *Real Life Dictionary of American Politics: What They're Saying and What It Really Means* (Los Angeles: General Publishing Group, 1994), p. 356. For whatever reasons, Jefferson gave Sally Hemings his keen attention, and she became a big part of his life, much to the chagrin of some of his family members.

2. Annette Gordon-Reed. *Thomas Jefferson and Sally Hemings: An American Controversy* (Charlottesville: The University Press of Virginia, 1997), p. xv. Historian Willard Sterne Randall, for example, desperately tries to

exonerate Jefferson and debunk the relationship between Jefferson and Sally Hemings, without providing any evidence to support his assumptions. What Randall writes is pure speculation, which is not history. See Willard Sterne Randall. *Thomas Jefferson: A Life* (New York: Henry Holt and Company, 1993), pp. 476–477.

3. Dennis Cauchon, "Group Flags Younger Jefferson as Father: Says DNA Test Results Have Been Misinterpreted," *USA Today* (January 7, 1999), p 3A.

4. Brenda E. Stevenson. *What is Slavery?* (Cambridge: Polity Press, 2015), p. 97. Unfortunately, Jefferson was in a bad position when it came to managing his monetary affairs and finances, even though, according to Britni, "he owned 607 men, women and children at Monticello to do his bidding." See Britni Danielle, "Sally Hemings Wasn't Thomas Jefferson's mistress. She was his property," *op.cit.*, p. 2.

5. Liner Notes to DVD Movie, *Sally Hemings: An American Love Story* (Echo Bridge Home Entertainment, 2009). In other words, Jefferson wasn't ready to commit or provide his slaves with the means to obtain their freedom or emancipation; because for him, this action wasn't a big thing.

6. Jon Meacham. *Thomas Jefferson: The Art of Power* (New York: Random House Trade Paperbacks, 2013), p. 217. Hemings was cautiously optimistic about getting her freedom, along with her four children, who lived. Jefferson, however, didn't inspire confidence that he would do *anything* to free his black slaves while he lived.

7. Andrew Heywood. *Political Ideologies: An Introduction* (New York: Worth Publishers, 1998), p. 336. Jefferson was unrepentant about the management of his slaves, because he sold them, as mentioned in this article, to pay off his debts. If he truly struggled with the notion of *equality*, he would have freed his slaves, like founding father Benjamin Franklin did.

8. Mark A. Stevens, editor, "Equality" *Merriam-Webster's Collegiate Encyclopedia* (Massachusetts: Merriam-Webster, Inc., 2000), p. 777. While it may seem appalling that Jefferson professed superiority based on race, given his relationship with Sally Hemings, he grappled with the thorny issue of *racial equality* all his life. But Jefferson did not have a sense of urgency in regards to providing *racial equality* for his black slaves.

9. Eric Lander and Joseph J. Elis, "Founding Father," *Nature*, Vol. 396 (November 5, 1998), pp. 13–14. According to Journalist Britni Danielle, Sally Hemings "wasn't Jefferson's mistress. She was his property. And he raped her." See Britni Danielle, "Sally Hemings wasn't Thomas Jefferson's mistress. She was his property," *op.cit.*, p. 1.

10. Meacham, "Thomas Jefferson: The Art of Power," *op.cit.*, p. 218. Ultimately, Jefferson was able to cajole Sally Hemings into going back to the plantation in Virginia at Monticello—that is, to leave and return from France. Make no mistake, Hemings was in a really bad spot in Paris.

11. *Ibid.* So was Sally Hemings a *marionette* or mindless automaton, who danced or acquiesced to *any* of Jefferson's demands or wishes? Or did she have to mimic acceptable human behavior—to get along with Jefferson; no doubt her lover.

12. *Ibid.* Of course, Sally Hemings "knew that she could stay in Paris, where she would be free; slavery was illegal in France"—Or was she just following her heart? See Jill Lepore, "President Tom's Cabin," *The New Yorker* (September 22, 2008), p. 11. https://www.newyorker.com/magazine/2008/09/22/president-toms-cabin (10/17/2017), p. 1–14.

13. *Ibid*. It certainly caught Jefferson by surprise when she decided initially to stay in Paris, France, but she returned, because Sally Hemings "implicitly relied" on Jefferson's promises. See Annette Gordon-Reed, "Sally Hemings, Thomas Jefferson and the Ways We Talk About Our Past" *The New York Times* (August 24, 2017), p. 4. https://www.nytimes.com/2017/08/24/books/review/sally-hemings-thomas-jefferson-annette-gor ... (10/17/2017), pp. 1–5.

14. Liner Notes to DVD Movie, *Sally Hemings: An American Love Story, op.cit*. Keep in mind that "some argue that he [Jefferson] "loved" Hemings," but he *never* granted her freedom. See Britni Danielle, "Sally Hemings wasn't Thomas Jefferson's mistress. She was his property," *op.cit.*, p. 2. Jefferson, after all, was a fallible human being, not perfect. People continue to try to *extrapolate* about how Jefferson felt by the way he treated his black slaves.

15. Leef Smith, "Tests Link Jefferson, Slave's Son," *Washington Post* (November 1, 1998), p. A1. http://www.washingtonpost.com/wp/srv/digest/nat001, pp. 1–4. It should be pointed out that Jefferson "freed only five people in his will. Beverley and Harriet Hemings simply left Monticello as white people with no formal emancipation." See Annette Gordon-Reed. *The Hemingses of Monticello: An American Family* (New York: W. W. Norton & Company, 2008), p. 657.

16. Willard Sterne Randall. *Thomas Jefferson: A Life* (New York: Henry Holt and Company, 1993), p. 494.

17. Annette Gordon-Reed. *The Hemingses of Monticello: An American Family* (New York: W. W. Norton & Company, 2008), p. 657. Jefferson was aware that the issues of *equality* and *slavery* were dangerous for him politically; and he wasn't willing to risk his political career and the presidency for the sake of his love for Sally Hemings and feelings for his black slaves. And unfortunately, "racial equality" was not at the center of the American conversation in the late 1700s and early 1800s. And probably there would have been widespread shock and condemnation by the white community had he admitted his affair with Sally Hemings.

18. Mark Stevens, editor, "Jefferson Thomas," *Merriam-Webster's Collegiate Encyclopedia* (Massachusetts: Merriam Webster, Inc., 2000), p. 841. Jefferson supposedly fought against slavery; but he achieved no results in this regards, even when he was elected President in 1801. As President of the United States, he had the opportunity to thoroughly abolish or eliminate slavery, but he did not.

19. Kathleen DuVal, "A Nation Forged In Discord," *The Wall Street Journal* (June 1, 2017), p. A15. Jefferson always had his reservations about the humanity of black people, so he was an *ineffective* representative for them.

20. *Ibid*. There was always a racial undercurrent with almost all his political and social actions, mostly because Jefferson really didn't have a grand vision about *racial equality* and other racial matters. He certainly didn't make positive changes for all his black slaves, as they lived a precarious existence.

21. Meacham, "Thomas Jefferson: The Art of Power," *op.cit.*, p. 455.

22. Stevens, editor, "Equality," *op.cit.*, p. 537.

23. Barry R. Gross, "Equality and Partiality and Racism and Justice: The Case for Affirmative Action," *Society*, Vol. 30, No. 2 (January/February, 1993), p. 94.

24. Molefi K. Asante. *Malcom X as Cultural Hero and Other Afrocentric Essays* (New Jersey: Africa World Press, Inc., 1993), p. 87.

25. *Ibid*. Worse, however, was the fact that such racist stereotypes were common in the United States at the founding of the United States, and drafting our Constitution.

26. *Ibid*. We must also consider the political ramifications made by our founding fathers, in terms of slavery, which negatively affected black people.

27. *Ibid*. It should be noted here that, "Acknowledgment of the right to equality often must be coerced from the advantaged by the disadvantaged." It is also improbable that slave-owning founders would have taken issue with keeping their own slaves, as their reasoning, perhaps, especially about *equality*, was essentially morally impoverished. See Mark Stevens, editor, "Equality," *Merriam-Webster's Collegiate Encyclopedia* (Massachusetts: Merriam Webster, Inc., 2000), p. 537.

28. Ken Burns, "What Thomas Jefferson Means Today," *USA Weekend* (February 14–16, 1997), p. 5.

29. *Ibid*. The truth of the matter is that blacks, as humans, have gone through terrible suffering in the Americas; but as steadfast human beings, they have been able to survive with heart and might—and common decency.

30. Benjamin Schwarz, "What Jefferson Helps to Explain," *Atlantic Monthly*, Vol. 279, No. 3 (March 1997), p. 66.

31. *Ibid*. Unfortunately, some white Americans still see black people as backward, and frighteningly savage, especially those white supremacists who are culturally ignorant about racial politics and policy, and not ready for *freedom* and *equality*.

32. Larry Tomlinson and Alan Balboni. *A Critical Inquiry Into American Politics*, 3rd edition (Iowa: Kendall Hunt Publishing Company, 1993), p. 192.

33. William Cohen, quote by Conor C. O'Brien in "Thomas Jefferson: Radical and Racist," *The Atlantic Monthly*, Vol. 278, No. 4 (October 1996), p. 66. With Jefferson's slave Hubbard, it was a life decision, or an escape, tit-for-tat game of cat-and-mouse; because short of death, Hubbard would continue to run away, again and again; and even if he was beaten relentlessly and savagely by Thomas Jefferson's overseer.

34. Cohen, "Thomas Jefferson: Radical and Racist," *op.cit*., p. 68. In this regard, we must question Jefferson's notion of human rights, and his feelings about black people, in general. To be sure, Jefferson didn't have a "noble-calling" to erase *inequality* when he had a chance as President. And for white males in power, who owned slaves, it was how black people could be exploited for their personal gain.

35. Burns, "What Thomas Jefferson Means Today," *op.cit*., p. 7. *Racism* is something that is irksomely wrong with humans, and may never be eliminated. Further, *equality* wasn't an important concept to Jefferson, all things considered. Indeed, Jefferson's ideas for equality were never clearly spelled out.

36. Cohen, "Thomas Jefferson: Radical and Racist," *op.cit*., p. 64. Bear in mind that Jefferson didn't believe in the *mixing* of so-called races, as he thought it was an *abomination*; but he made an exception with his own affair with Sally Hemings. Jefferson even argued against assimilating with blacks in white society.

37. Cohen, "Thomas Jefferson: Radical and Racist," *op.cit*., p. 66. Jefferson's argument of "black colonization" was certainly a weak effort, because they (black slaves), or many of them were born in the United States, but not granted citizenship at that time. Further, the idea of relocating black people, born in the U.S., was a preposterous proposition.

38. Burns, "What Thomas Jefferson Means Today," *op.cit.*, p. 6. Jefferson certainly wasn't waiting for the legacy of his life and Presidency to be written; nor was he sitting around deciding on how many of his black slaves he was going to manumit; or that Jefferson saw them even as human beings.

39. *Ibid*. In this regard, it should be noted that it would be decades later before the end of black slavery took place in the United States. So were white colonists—later American citizens—ready to fight to the death for the freedom of black slaves? Probably not.

40. Cohen, "Thomas Jefferson: Radical and Racist," *op.cit.*, p. 72.

41. Jack N. Rakove. *Original Meanings: Politics and Ideas in the Making of the Constitution* (New York: Alfred A Knoph, 1996), p.74.

42. Britni Danielle, "Sally Hemings wasn't Thomas Jefferson's mistress. She was his property," *The Washington Post*, Outlook (July 7, 2017), p. 2. https://www.washingtonpost.com/outlook/sally-hemings-wasn't-thomas-jeffersons-mistress ... (10/17/2017), pp. 1–3. Make no mistake, humans have always been "mixed" genetically, but *white supremacists* have refused to believe this evolutionary fact.

43. Krissah Thompson, "For decades they hid Jefferson's relationship with her. Now Monticello is making room for Sally Hemings," *The Washington Post*, Life Style (Feb 19, 2017). https://www.washingtonpost.com/lifestyle/for-decades-they-hid-jeffersons ... (10/17/2017), pp. 1–6. As President, Thomas Jefferson was juggling the demands of his office and as master of Monticello; and he was unequivocal about what he wanted. Sally Hemings didn't demand any time from the man, however.

44. Leonard W. Levy, Kenneth L. Karst, and Dennis J. Mahoney. Selections from the *Encyclopedia of the American Constitution, Civil Rights and Equality* (New York: Macmillan Publishing Company, 1989), p. 107.

45. Benjamin Schwarz, "What Jefferson Helps to Explain," *op.cit.*, p. 72. It was unfortunate that the controversial issue of *equality* was dismissed by most of the slave-holding founders, as many *never* took constructive and necessary steps to assiduously move forward on *equality*, and manumission, or ending slavery.

46. Jill Lepore, "President Tom's Cabin: Jefferson, Hemings, and a disclaimed lineage," *The New Yorker* (September 22, 2008), p. 6. https://www.newyorker.com/magazine/2008/09/22/president-toms-cabin ... (10/17/2017), pp. 1–14. More than anything else in the world, Jefferson's reasons for enslaving human beings was unfathomable, as there was no constitutional freedom for black slaves. Therefore, Thomas Jefferson's actions did not match his words.

47. Kenneth L. Karst, "Brown v. Board of Education," in *Civil Rights and Equality* (New York: Macmillan Publishing Company, 1989), p. 17. Despite words to the contrary, Jefferson's slaves at Monticello were regimentally controlled, and didn't have free reign of the plantation, with the possible exception of Sally Hemings and her family.

48. Conor C. O'Brien, quoted in "Thomas Jefferson: Radical and Racist," *The Atlantic Monthly*, Vol. 278, No. 4 (October 1996), p. 68. It has always been evident that a separate-but-equal policy or doctrine doesn't work in a diverse Democracy such as the United States.

49. Danielle, "Sally Hemings wasn't Thomas Jefferson's mistress. She was his property," op.cit., p. 3. Jefferson's relationship with Sally Hemings, as presented in this aforementioned movie presents more than complications

about family and feelings for her and his black (or mulatto) children; or his reluctantly beloved offspring? Some of the scenes in this movie seem contrived and perfunctory, however, even the bedroom scene in Paris when Jefferson invited himself to Sally Hemings bedroom. Was it all about lust or love?

50. Annette Gordon-Reed, "Sally Hemings, Thomas Jefferson and the Ways We Talk About Our Past," *The New York Times* (August 24, 2017), p. 5. https://www.nytimes.com/2017/08/24/books/review/sally-hemings-thomas-jefferson ... (10/17/2017), pp. 1–5. Perhaps, in the end, Jefferson had little time to regret his contradictory writings and notions about race. More importantly, could Sally Hemings really interject her personal opinions and feelings about Jefferson, her lover?

51. Stevens, editor, "Equality," *op.cit.*, p. 537. The question is whether "preferential treatment" should be given to "those historically treated unequally." See same reference source. Even in hindsight, Jefferson did not usher in a new era in race relations.

Bibliography

Asante, Molefi K. *Malcom X as Cultural Hero and Other Afrocentric Essays.* New Jersey: Africa World Press, Inc., 1993.

Burns, Ken. "What Thomas Jefferson Means Today." *USA Weekend,* February 14–16, 1997.

Cauchon, Dennis. "Group Flags Younger Jefferson as Father: Says DNA Test Results Have Been Misinterpreted." *USA Today,* January 7, 1999.

Cohen, William, quote by Conor C. O'Brien in "Thomas Jefferson: Radical and Racist." *The Atlantic Monthly*, Vol. 278, No. 4, October 1996.

Danielle, Britni. "Sally Hemings wasn't Thomas Jefferson's mistress. She was his property." *The Washington Post*, Outlook, July 7, 2017.

DuVal, Kathleen. "A Nation Forged In Discord." *The Wall Street Journal,* June 1, 2017.

Gordon-Reed, Annette. "Sally Hemings, Thomas Jefferson and the Ways We Talk About Our Past." *The New York Times,* August 24, 2017.

Gordon-Reed, Annette. *The Hemingses of Monticello: An American Family.* New York: W. W. Norton & Company, 2008.

Gordon-Reed, Annette. *Thomas Jefferson and Sally Hemings: An American Controversy.* Charlottesville: The University Press of Virginia, 1997.

Gross, Barry R. "Equality and Partiality and Racism and Justice: The Case for Affirmative Action." *Society*, Vol. 30, No. 2, January/February, 1993.

Heywood, Andrew. *Political Ideologies: An Introduction.* New York: Worth Publishers, 1998.

Hill, Kathleen T., and Gerald N. Hill. *Real Life Dictionary of American Politics: What They're Saying and What It Really Means.* Los Angeles: General Publishing Group, 1994.

Karst, Kenneth L. "Brown v. Board of Education." in *Civil Rights and Equality.* New York: Macmillan Publishing Company, 1989.

Lander, Eric, and Joseph J. Elis. "Founding Father." *Nature*, Vol. 396, November 5, 1998.

Lepore, Jill. "President Tom's Cabin: Jefferson, Hemings, and a disclaimed lineage." *The New Yorker,* September 22, 2008.

Levy, Leonard W., Kenneth L. Karst, and Dennis J. Mahoney. Selections from the *Encyclopedia of the American Constitution, Civil Rights and Equality.* New York: Macmillan Publishing Company, 1989.

Liner Notes to DVD Movie. *Sally Hemings: An American Love Story.* Echo Bridge Home Entertainment, 2009.

Meacham, Jon. *Thomas Jefferson: The Art of Power.* New York: Random House Trade Paperbacks, 2013.

Rakove, Jack N. *Original Meanings: Politics and Ideas in the Making of the Constitution.* New York: Alfred A Knoph, 1996.

Randall, Willard Sterne. *Thomas Jefferson: A Life.* New York: Henry Holt and Company, 1993.

Schwarz, Benjamin. "What Jefferson Helps to Explain." *Atlantic Monthly*, Vol. 279, No. 3, March 1997.

Smith, Leef. "Tests Link Jefferson, Slave's Son." *Washington Post*, November 1, 1998.

Stevens, Mark A., editor. "Equality." *Merriam-Webster's Collegiate Encyclopedia.* Massachusetts: Merriam-Webster, Inc., 2000.

Stevens, Mark A., editor. "Jefferson Thomas." *Merriam-Webster's Collegiate Encyclopedia.* Massachusetts: Merriam Webster, Inc., 2000.

Stevenson, Brenda E. *What is Slavery?* Cambridge: Polity Press, 2015.

Thompson, Krissah. "For decades they hid Jefferson's relationship with her. Now Monticello is making room for Sally Hemings." *The Washington Post*, Life Style, February 19, 2017.

Tomlinson, Larry, and Alan Balboni. *A Critical Inquiry Into American Politics*, 3rd edition. Iowa: Kendall Hunt Publishing Company, 1993.

Reading 3.4

The Politics and Impact of Environmental Racism

Earnest N. Bracey, Ph.D.

Introduction

From the outset, it should be pointed out that industrial wastes and contamination in areas where African Americans, Hispanic Americans, Asian Americans, Pacific Islanders and Native Americans live is a serious environmental issue that must be continuously addressed and brought to the attention of the mass public, without equivocation. This dangerous trend, which is called *environmental racism* refers "to the specific targeting of a minority community with industrial operations that use unsafe environmental procedures resulting in an unsafe environment for that community."[1] It should also be made abundantly clear that polluting industries and corporations profit mightily from building and erecting chemical plants or coal-fired power plants, and waste treatment facilities, as well as establishing contaminant landfills in these predominantly low-income, ethnic minority communities.

Of course, selective industrial pollution should trouble us all; especially as mostly poor people are being exposed to hazardous wastes and carcinogenic chemicals on almost a daily basis. Indeed, many toxic substances detected in many minority neighborhoods includes deadly and noxious "chemicals that can potentially cause birth defects; neurological, renal, and liver impairment; and disorders of other bodily systems."[2] In this regard, Americans must understand and know the unimaginable dangers of lethal and toxic waste, which could have disastrous consequences for the health of all humans, as we (humankind) are not impervious to various man-made toxins and pollutions.

Beyond all measure, some American communities are becoming saturated (to a great extent) with certain pollutants. According to Professor Michael K. Heiman, "residents of poor communities and in communities of color in the United States bear a "disproportionate" burden of toxic

Earnest N. Bracey, "The Politics and Impact of Environmental Racism," *American International Journal of Humanities and Social Science*, vol. 3, no. 3, pp. 19–28. Copyright © 2017 by Center for Global Research Development. Reprinted with permission.

contamination, both through the generation and release of hazardous chemicals in their neighborhoods, and via the location of waste management facilities."[3] To be sure, industrial operations have been a disruptive force in many of these minority neighborhoods, with their economic growth and entrepreneurial endeavors.

Unfortunately, some minority populations, like the two-hundred African-American families in Augusta, Georgia's *Hyde Park*, who have been fighting for over twelve years for environmental justice and compensation from the polluting industries in the area, are frustrated over their inability to stop respective, corporate polluters.[4] No doubt, the people in such minority communities, living next door to such polluting, *behemoth* industries and toxic sites are in danger. However, some polluting industries don't seem especially bothered by the damage they are causing to minority communities.[5] Or so it seems. Question: How can "we-the-people" hold polluting industries accountable for their pollution activities? This question for some minority community members, can be terribly frustrating and irritating, to say the least. It is sure no accident or coincidence that polluting waste materials and/or different polluting industries are being deliberately established in these poor minority neighborhoods.

For example, "three out of five Americans in the United States live in communities with uncontrolled toxic waste sites."[6] Moreover, in Michigan, "8.3 percent of the people living in high-risk areas are Hispanic, though Hispanics make up [only] 3.3 percent of state-wide population."[7] As things stand, some polluting industrialists simply do not respect the dignity of the people in these particular minority neighborhoods. Is it because dark-skinned individuals and certain other minorities are expendable people? Or is this a subtle way by those who are in power, to commit some sort of *genocide* on people of color?

According to Heiman, "race is the central determining factor with toxic exposure."[8] Similarly, the 1987 breakthrough environmental report, "Toxic Wastes and Race in the United States," tells us that there is "a serious relationship between the treatment, storage and disposal of hazardous wastes and the issue of race" in America.[9] Unfortunately, the surging demand for scarce and/or precious resources, like natural oil and gas and coal energy has produced excessively greedy industries and polluting corporations that actually hurt the health and well-being of countless human beings.

Indeed, according to Professor James Lee Ray, "perhaps the most notorious pollution *results* from the world's reliance on fossil fuels (coal, oil, and natural gas) to generate most of [our] industrial energy."[10] Unfortunately, the production of this energy is accomplished and accompanied by entrenched racial barriers and pollution of certain minority communities. Indeed, such facts raise troubling allegations about the *real* reasons why industrial polluters are not that concerned about the long-term consequences of their business/

pollution activities. Some polluters, perhaps, don't even believe that there should be environmental regulations to govern them, like government control of the polluting emissions from power plants.

Of course, Robert Bullard, the former Director of the Environmental Justice Resource Center at Clark Atlanta University states that "People of Color across the United States have learned the hard way that waiting for government to respond to toxic contamination can be hazardous to their health and health of their communities."[11]

Some industrial leaders, moreover, don't see the problem with selective waste dumping; nor do many see it as being a good or bad thing; but, perhaps, they see it as somewhere in between. Or sometimes it seems that the captains of industry and private industrial businesses don't necessarily care about the legal or ethical dilemma inherent in their callous, environmental decisions, especially about the placement of polluting enterprises. About polluting industrialists, environmentalist Herman E. Daly tells us that, in the end, "an efficient servant will become an unjust and unsustainable master,"[12] especially if they are not checked by the political forces that be. In the final analysis, "environmental racism and justice has become a pressing issue in many neighborhoods, especially poor minority areas where housing has knowingly been built on contaminated land."[13]

Environmental Equilibrium

Although many polluting industries and misbegotten businesses believe that science and scientific methods support their positions on the environment and should *trump* anyone's fears about waste storage or toxic spills, and dictate the necessity for dumping hazardous materials, the political and health issues are more complicated than what some of these polluting companies make them out to be.[14] In fact, never before has indigenous people and other minority communities been threatened and under assault as much as now. Which is to say that "inequities in the distribution of toxic waste sites in minority communities remain common place in America."[15]

Therefore, all of us should be concerned with the survival of indigenous people and other minorities in industrial polluted locations. Or we must be certainly concerned about the massive suffering and ecological damage being done to specific polluted communities today. In fact, such places should be considered ill-conceived urban planning, or environmental disaster areas.

According to sociologists Ralph W. Conant and Daniel J. Myers, "Inadequate local arrangements [about pollution and trash-disposal facilities] can be costly and [indeed] hazardous to human life and urban communities."[16] Consequently, "prevention of [environmental] perturbations [in minority neighborhoods should be] a major goal of ecosystem management."[17] This is important to understand, because according to Bullard, "hazardous waste and toxic products pose some important health, environmental, legal, political, and ethical dilemmas."[18] Additionally, it should be noted that many of the toxins released into our environment and atmosphere never entirely break down, because of the very nature of some deadly chemicals.[19] Hence, we must be engaged with these environmental issues for the long haul, and on an ongoing basis, particularly in regards to how we cope with a shortage of scarce or energy resources—and the fact that polluting corporations illogically dump man-made waste and other pollutants, which will create more environmental problems, such as a chemically altered environment.[20]

Knowing this, people should *never* be fraught with such dangers and self-destructiveness; but we are, nonetheless, faced with escalating environmental lawlessness (by some industrial polluters), which will negatively affect all humankind in the future. Furthermore, many industries that pollute seem to resent the fact that environmentalists and others question their "goodwill" and ability to make a profit from their corporate activities or businesses.[21] However, if "approximately 75 percent of all landfills are located in close proximity to African American communities,"[22] these industries and our various governments (no doubt) should be definitely concerned about the health and welfare of those who reside in these particular areas. Indeed, the American people should be given the opportunity to see and understand *exactly* what is happening in these sometimes decimated, ethnic minority communities.

Unfortunately, as Deans writes, "Some of the industries that produce pollution as a byproduct of their operations expect the public to pay for that pollution, through dirty water, for example, poisoned air, loss of arable lands, health problems, missed work days, mental impairment, or premature deaths."[23] In this regard, "African American children and adults are disproportionally affected" by environmental pollutants, and "are known to have higher rates of certain types of cancer, like leukemia and neurological malignancies,"[24] which have increased tremendously in recent years because of environmental pollution by corporations. Toward this end, and generally speaking, Professor Benjamin Cardozo suggests that a new Civil Rights Movement be instituted that would focus on "the segregation of minorities concerning environmental hazards."[25]

Of course, adopting such a civil rights approach is especially necessary today because many minorities affected by pollution are besieged by various health problems, and might likely die or suffer health complications—in the future—from being exposed to waste landfills, carcinogenic chemicals and other contaminants.[26] In fact, Native Americans are put at even greater risk for certain pollution related illnesses—like neurological and metabolic disorders or certain mental diseases and death—who live within a one mile radius of many of these big-time polluting operations.[27] Consider, for example, the Native American-Moapa

Paiute community in southern Nevada, which is being negatively affected by toxic dust blown from an affiliated NV Energy Plant's "coal-ash waste landfill." This polluting subsidiary business has contaminated the surrounding environment and irreparably harmed some nearby Moapa residents.[28] Indeed, members of this Native American Paiute Tribe blame the severe pollution from NV Energy's *Reid Gardner Generating Station* "for a host of medical problems, including respiratory ailments, heart disease, headaches and strokes."[29]

Furthermore, nothing has been really done to completely remedy these pollution issues and horde of health symptoms that make this Native American Paiute Tribe sick. Unfortunately, "across the country, a disproportionate number of power plants operate near or on tribal lands."[30] In this respect, is it true that many industrial businesses have personal and commercial interests in mind, and are only concerned about profits, instead of their pollution? Or is their goal really to make money at the expense of unfortunate people? In the early 1990s, for example, the Shintech Corporation wanted to build a $700 million polyvinyl chloride plant in the predominantly poor African American community of Romeville, Louisiana; but Shintech abandoned this plan after the Environmental Protection Agency (EPA), in 1997, ordered the delay of the proposed plant, deciding that "blacks would suffer disproportionately from allegedly cancer-causing emissions from the plant."[31]

But to avoid any further EPA delays and opposition, the Shintech Corporation decided "to locate its plant in a nearby community that was largely white."[32] As we can perhaps ascertain from the aforementioned case, some pollution producing companies can be so unprincipled that they will quickly switch focus, or change their corporate plans, to sell their ideas to establish even more polluting power plants—sometimes stating that it would be in the best interest to the respective minority community—supposedly because of the jobs they (industrial power plants) would provide. But jobs created from polluting industries are usually elusive and not guaranteed in the long term. The problem for polluting industries, of course, has always been to figure out expedient ways to dispose of the dangerous waste they produce, in an effort to provide energy (in some cases), and the ultimate monetary payoff.

Suffice it to say, some environmental technologies are worrisome for industrial polluters, because of government regulations, and the enormous cost involved, as well as any delay in new, factory-building. But establishing such polluting industries can be disingenuous if there is a *cover-up* about the possible waste produced by the facilities. At the very least, polluting industries should inform individuals about the potential dangers of their businesses/operations. Indeed, CEOs and top executives at such industries should be more concerned about people, in general, and certain fragile eco-systems. Many industrial polluters, however, are not particularly enthusiastic about telling people of color (in minority neighborhoods) the truth about the devastating effect of their pollution. Moreover, it is just unimaginable or inconceivable that some polluting industries just won't admit to what they are doing, in terms of destroying our different environments, and lives of minority people and their communities.

The Polluted Environment

Corporate pollution remains a reality and a serious problem in regards to environmental racism. This is to say that energy-plant pollution on minority lands is not some abstract or hypothetical thing. Hence, polluting corporations often think about their *bottom line* in terms of profits, as mentioned, and the cost-benefit analysis of their sometimes deliberate, polluting activities. But polluting industries must also consider the *human equation*, especially as their pollution and/or other dangerous particulate matters will cause harm or unnecessary harm to people. No doubt, it might be too expensive for some polluting industries to consider alternatives to dumping terrible toxins in minority neighborhoods; but they shouldn't have *carte blanche* to do whatever they want. This is to say that pollution and "toxic dumping" *anywhere* comes at a high price when it comes to the personal, causative, health-risk factors on humans. More importantly, exposure to airborne pollution, including carbon pollution, as well as water and land pollution, and a wide variety of toxic chemicals can be deadly.

In essence, we must control industrial waste and other pollution at all cost. The key is to penalize industrial polluters—that is, make them pay fines for creating pollution at the federal and state levels. Furthermore, industrial polluters should be made, by our governments, to consider *where* they build power plants, most especially if such operations are in someone's backyard, so to speak. Unfortunately, some industrial polluters may see some toxic dumping in local minority communities as their only alternative. Indeed, they may believe that "the dumping and recycling have to take place somewhere. [But] many of the recycling plants and trash dumps are located in areas where poor people and minorities live." [33] Therefore, it is important to understand the nature of the various industries that pollute, for the stakes are certainly high for minorities living in these affected communities.

Moreover, the leaders of these polluting operations must realize that storing man-made waste *anywhere* will have an economic and detrimental effect on many people in the long run. Consequently, the idea of trying to reverse or fix affected, polluted areas, especially in minority neighborhoods, might prove to be insurmountable. However, it is unimaginably important to expose the pretense, greed, and treachery taking pace in some minority communities by polluting corporations. Furthermore, it is crucial that polluting industries even with state and local government involvement, shouldn't ignore the real problems of their pollution, and despite clean emission technologies. The question for all polluting industries should be: How *exactly* can affected minority environments be restored and protected? Professor Tony Arnold suggests that minorities, affected by industrial pollution, should continue to rely on the environmental justice movement, which "has used political activism, civil rights and constitutional law, environmental law, and new policies at all levels of government to seek fairness in environmental and land used decisions."[34]

Moreover, can minority people on polluted lands depend on the government at all levels to help protect them? Perhaps. These concerns present the heart of this matter: Do corporate polluters, in general, really care about the health and well-being of affected minorities? Perhaps not. Equally important, as Bullard writes:

> Why do some communities get dumped on while others escape? Why are environmental regulations vigorously enforced in some communities and not in other communities? Why are some workers protected from environmental and health threats while other workers (such as migrant farm workers) are allowed to be poisoned? How can environmental justice be incorporated into environmental protection? What institutional changes are needed in order to achieve a just and sustainable society? [Finally], what community organizing strategies and public policies are effective tools against environmental racism?[35]

Ultimately, we must figure out the factual impact of corporate studies and economies of scales and basic outlooks (when it comes to ecological/environmental disasters); which to say the least, should be the immediate concern about this controversial issue. Unfortunately, it is a regrettable fact that many polluting industries are not necessarily concerned, as already mentioned, about the negative impact of their businesses on certain fragile environments; nor is toxic dumping in the backyards of poor minority neighborhoods a serious concern with them either. To be sure, certain polluting industries disrupt the lives of some minority communities, creating environmental sprawl and danger, while psychologically affecting the people who reside in such places. Take for example the intrepid city of Chester, Pennsylvania, which should confirm our worst suspicion about corporate pollution.

This small city of 60 percent African Americans, ten miles south of Philadelphia, is under siege as the place has been essentially bombarded by "a profusion of waste treatment facilities."[36] Unfortunately, the city of Chester, Pennsylvania is "governed by a Republican political machine that's been in near-continuous control of the city for more than 130 years."[37] Many of these conservative politicians are not going to change things or challenge the polluters in the foreseeable future, or *opt* for a possible relocation of some of these waste treatment facilities, especially if it means that certain monies or private funds will no longer go into the financial coffers of the local city government. Furthermore, the risks of contamination to the black inhabitants of Chester, Pennsylvania are *real*, not imagined, as evidenced by the high mercury content in some fresh water fish from the location.[38]

Therefore, the African Americans in Chester, Pennsylvania should continuously *agitate* and voice their considerable concerns about removing some of these waste treatment facilities through the environmental justice movement.

After all, many of the African Americans living in these "toxic hot spots" are not blind to this monumental, environmental problem, as they know that these waste treatment facilities are a threat to their very existence.

We should also be cognizant that many of the black people in such polluted locations do not have the economic wherewithal, or simply can't afford to pick-up and move out of affected areas; nor can they protect themselves against certain diseases and cancers caused by pollutants, and other toxic substances found in waste landfills and groundwater.

Thus, can the city government of Chester, Pennsylvania do what's right by its minority citizens in this case? These are just a few of the questions that need to be seriously addressed and answered, as some polluting industries establish their contaminating networks in former *pristine* environments. To that end, also, it should be understood that some contaminating former factories in the United States, which "operated from the 1930s to the 1960s" are still leaching contaminants like "dangerous levels of lead" where unsuspecting people live nearby.[39] Again, the sad truth is that industrialists and owners of these lumbering waste sites could care less about the lives, welfare and possible health concerns of the people living near such locations. Or so it seems. Is this because the residents are a disposable people?

Journalist Alison Young, for example, points out that the lead contamination at former polluting foundry sites, which has left toxic dust in the soil in places like Newport, Kentucky and Portland, Oregon, put our children "at risk of lost intelligence and other health problems if they put dust-covered hands or toys in their mouths."[40] In many ways, this should be cause for concern and alarm. Finally, the conservative city fathers of Chester, Pennsylvania should seriously look at the negative impact that the waste treatment facilities are having on the inner and outlying black communities. But will they? Probably not. Of course, closing down such waste treatment facilities would be an incredibly bold and correct thing to do, if it ever happens.

More importantly, how exactly can black members of such minority communities engage in a positive dialogue that would divert waste treatment facilities and prevent their neighborhoods from being targeted for toxic dumping? If city officials in Chester, Pennsylvania are unwilling to do *something*, to stem the tide of toxic dumping, it is possible that such polluting industries will get away with what they have done in the past, and are continuing to do. Interestingly, this entire issue is not an inconsequential matter. There is certainly a need to tackle this controversial issue and towering environmental problem. But it remains to be seen if politicians throughout our nation will legislate industries into doing the right thing in cleaning up our polluted, ethnic minority communities, where power plants, mining operations, and hazardous waste disposal facilities are located. Julian Agyeman and Tom Evans offer us the following novel solution to the issue of environmental racism. Essentially, any decision about establishing a polluting industry must be made by the residents of a particular area in what Agyeman and Evans call "community-based decision making."[41] In the long term, this residential decision-making will allow for clean, livable communities for all people in order to reduce all forms of pollution.[42]

Conclusions

Mass publicity and a national debate about the industrial pollution of ethnic minority communities are crucial if *anything* is going to be done about polluting companies. Moreover, "direct action" should be used against corporations that pollute, where minorities who are affected by pollution can demand to be heard and voice their complaints. Of course, such a tactic will be an uphill battle, as these polluting industries might hide behind (the cloak of) conservative support for deregulation. Our politicians, however, on both sides of the ideological spectrum shouldn't politicize the lives of humans for the sake of obtaining natural resources, or campaign contributions from polluting corporations. In this regard, many environmentalists claim that industrial development on the part of polluting companies is often the result of thoughtless environmental exploitation. [43] If this is true, our politicians should not feel ambivalent about environmental protection when it comes to protecting the lives of people.

This is why it is critical for us to have a federal regulatory agency, like the Environmental Protection Agency (EPA). Indeed, the U.S. Environmental Protection Agency is ultimately responsible for regulating pollution and carbon emissions from related businesses, which is a tough job in itself. Nevertheless, our government can and should do more to protect the lives of all American citizens from unscrupulous, polluting industries by creating more stringent regulations and policies to control them. Additionally, there must be an urgent need to make sure that toxic waste and other harmful by-products are removed or carried away from affected minority neighborhoods.

Unfortunately, some dumping in many ethnic minority communities has already set a dangerous precedent. Still, our federal and state governments must be willing to "foot-the-bill" to relocate American citizens in harm's way from polluting industries. Furthermore, appropriate compensation must be given to those sick and dying individuals—and minority community members who are displaced by the pollution.

Equally important, "we-the-people" cannot be indifferent to the negative effects of pollution on the mentioned communities. The question that remains is whether our federal government is willing to limit the number of polluting industries in the United States? Moreover, an empowerment plan, perhaps under the auspices of the United Nations, could be instituted for ethnic minorities living in affected areas. This plan would "empower low-income communities of color to shape the environments in which they live and work."[44] Although this measure might not seem like much of a solution on the surface, it has the potential to develop into something more substantial down the line, where affected minorities could take unilateral action to dispel polluting corporations from their neighborhoods.

In this context, ethnic minorities must never *tough* it out, so to speak, or take a "wait-and-see" attitude while being paid to keep quiet about what corporate polluters are actually doing. More importantly, the alarm must be sounded about the dangers of allowing such polluting ventures. Clearly, it is a very difficult thing to be optimistic about allowing for polluting companies and toxic dumping for *anyone*, anywhere. Which is to say that our whole society should be extremely upset about the contamination of our minority environments; meanwhile, we must make an extraordinary effort to dismiss certain corporate polluters outright, and enforce their accountability. Furthermore, corporations must spend the necessary funds for other technologies and alternatives to deal with pollution in specific depressed neighborhoods. African Americans and other minorities must also be included in the greater discussions about our nation's energy and waste storage facilities, especially if the development of polluting businesses pollute areas with a wide variety of dangerous chemicals, or aggravates; and specifically, if the operation creates health problems for minorities in the places where they live.

In addition, minorities living in affected areas must recognize that they don't have to tolerate certain pollution inconveniences, if their specific health is being compromised. In the end, many industries that pollute actually miss this crucial point. This is to say that polluting corporations often argue constantly about missed business opportunities without really considering the negative, *long-term* effect of their operations on the environment; perhaps this is because such industries are afraid of the truth or the revelation that their polluting organizations can cause serious harm to people. In the short run, we must also recognize why environmental issues, like building landfills, or dumping toxic waste and other hazardous materials, which wreak havoc in predominantly minority neighborhoods, "are often linked to wider demands for sociopolitical change and/or economic reform from groups lacking [political] power,"[45] like with the Moapa Paiute Tribe in Southern Nevada, who refuse to move or relocate from their tribal/ancestral lands, to appease or accommodate a polluting industry. It behooves the corporate bosses of industry, then, to stop trying to come up with extravagant ways to pollute, without anyone noticing; or devising new, ingenuous methods to hide their pollution.

Furthermore, polluting corporations must clean up their contaminated sites and communities, no matter the cost; or they might risk converging environmental catastrophes. Indeed, it should be pointed out that not cleaning up massive waste treatment areas will become a major problem in the future; therefore, any delay in addressing such environmental issues might be, as discussed earlier, to our detriment as humans. Also, in this regard, our federal government must continue to create proactive legislation that will combat environmental pollution everywhere in the future. The idea of doing nothing about such matters is breathtakingly wrong, as it will definitely affect the long term survival of mankind, or all living beings around the world. The fact that some corporate polluting giants complain mightily about the necessity for government regulations, which are used to police these businesses environmentally, should be ignored. And if such corporations do things, needlessly, to harm people, it should be pointed out to the public immediately, or the whistle should be blown, especially if their actions create unnecessary risks for certain ethnic minority groups.

Corporate polluters must also know that we are all part of a greater whole, as humans, even if this environmental issue is about the "conflict between haves and have nots."[46] Question: Is the trade-off in human lives worth the profits made by polluting corporations? There is really only one answer to this question, and that is—No. Hence, industrial polluters must clean up their act, as mentioned, and put their respective houses in order, while doing penance by cleaning up the environmental areas they helped to pollute and inundate with contamination sources.

Establishing new government policies could possibly help them along the way. In the final analysis, the American public should also support the idea of cleaning up these contaminated areas for the good of *everyone*.

All in all, the public outcry about this serious environmental matter (in terms of negatively affecting minorities) should be deafening. Environmentalist Ervin Laszlo argues that "if humanity does not respond in time, we face an irreversible collapse that may spell the end of civilization."[47] Finally, the people must illuminate the truth and try to drive home the message that there is something profoundly wrong with the devastation of some ethnic minority communities by corporate pollution/polluters, which will have far-reaching, negative consequences in the future. Let us hope that we are not at a point of no return.

Notes

1. "Environmental Racism Continues in U.S," *The Media Freedom Foundation*, http://www.mediafreedominternational.org/2010/02/21/environmental-racism-continues-in-u-s (4/18/2013), 1–3. See also Deborah M. Robinson, "Environmental Racism: Old Wine in a New Bottle," *Echoes*, May 27, 2007.

2. Jewel Crawford, Wade W. Nobles, and Joy De Gruy Leary, "Reparations and Health Care for African Americans: Repairing the Damage from the Legacy of Slavery," in *Should America Pay? Slavery and the Raging Debate on Reparations*, ed. Raymond A. Winbush (New York: Amistad, 2003), 272.

3. Michael K. Heiman, "Race, Waste, and Class: New Perspectives on Environmental Justice," Editor's Introduction for a Special Edition of Antipode, *Antipode*, April 1996, 28.

4. Melissa Checker, *Polluted Promises: Environmental Racism and the Search for Justice in a Southern Town* (New York: NYU Press, 2005), 6–150.

5. Steve Coll, *Private Empire: Exxon Mobil and American Power* (New York: Penguin Books, 2012), 177–193.

6. "Environmental Racism Continues in U.S," 1–3.

7. Dave Pace, "More Blacks Live With Pollution," The Associated Press, 2006, in Paula S. Rothenberg and Kelly S. Mayhew, *Race, Class, and Gender in the United States: An Integrated Study* (New York: Worth Publishers, 2014), 35.

8. Heiman, "Race, Waste, and Class," 28.

9. "Toxic Wastes and Race in the United States: A National Report on the Racial and Socio-Economic Characteristics of Communities with Hazardous Waste Sites," *Commission for Racial Justice: United Church of Christ* (New York: New York, 1987), ix.

10. James Lee Ray, *Global Politics*, 7th edition (New York: Houghton Mifflin Company, 1998), 551.

11. "Toxic waste and race: Report confirms no progress made in 20 years," (/new/releases/3253-toxic-waste-and-race-report-confirms-no-progress-made-in-20-years), http://ns.umich.edu/new/releases/3253 (7/14/2013), 1.

12. Herman E. Daly, "Free-Market Environmentalism: Turning a Good Servant into a Bad Master," *Critical Review* 6 (1992), 182. It should be pointed out that some polluting corporations are good at secretly defying government regulations, while publicly denying any wrong doings when it comes to their conscious pollution of the respective environments. Many polluting businesses also are not strong enough to take criticism about what they are doing to poor people, in terms of polluting their communities.

13. Jeanne H. Ballantine and Keith A. Roberts, *Our Social World: Introduction to Sociology* (Thousand Oaks: Pine Forge Press, 2012), 523.

14. Bob Deans, *Reckless: The Political Assault on the American Environment* (Lanham, Maryland: Rowman & Littlefield Publishers, 2012), 52–53.

15. Benjamin N. Cardozo, "Environmental Justice: A New Chapter in the Civil Rights Debate," unpublished paper (2005), 1. When it comes to the issue of pollution in poor neighborhoods, it is time for a new environmental paradigm, to change things for the better. See also Julian Agyeman and Kee Warner, "Putting 'Just Sustainability' into Place: From Paradigm to Practice," *Policy and Management Review*, volume 2, issue 1 (2002), 8–40.

16. Ralph W. Conant and Daniel J. Myers, *Toward a More Perfect Union: The Governance of Metropolitan America* (Novato: Chandler & Sharp Publishers, 2006), 235. Unfortunately, black people and other minorities are sometimes considered nonentities; but corporations must respect the rights of minorities in the ongoing political and environmental debate.

17. Marten Scheiffer, et.al, "Catastrophic Shifts in Ecosystems," *Nature* 413 (2001), 596.

18. Robert D. Bullard, "Poverty, Pollution and Environmental Racism: Strategies for Building Healthy and Sustainable Communities," http://www.ejrc.cau.edu/povpolej.html (3/18/2013), 1.

19. Donella H. Meadows, Dennis L. Meadows, Jorgen Randers, and William W. Behrens III, *The Limits to Growth: A Report for the Club of Rome's Project on the Predicament of Mankind* (New York: Universe Books, 1981), 45–87.

20. Benjamin Ross and Steven Amter, *The Polluters: The Making of Our Chemically Altered Environment* (New York: Oxford University Press, 2010), 1–171.

21. Deans, "Reckless," 53.

22. Crawford, Nobles and Leary, "Reparations and Health Care," 273.

23. Deans, "Reckless," 52.

24. Crawford, Nobles and Leary, "Reparations and Health Care," 273. To ameliorate such environmental health problems, corporations that pollute must judiciously focus on resolving this matter, not dismiss these affected minorities as irrelevant or superfluous.

25. Cardozo, "Environmental Justice," 1. Creating potentially larger environmental risks, there is apparently no hand-wringing by corporate polluters about some of the adverse environmental decisions they make in regards to their polluting industries/businesses.

26. Ibid. See also "Emerging Links between Chronic Disease and Environmental Exposure: Parkinson's Disease," (Washington, D.C.: Physicians for Social Responsibility, 2003), 4.

27. Frankie Sue Del Papa and Timothy Hay, "Out with the Old," *Las Vegas Review Journal*, May 13, 2012.

28. Ibid. Clearly, there will come a point in time when poor Native Americans, affected by pollution, will say enough is enough, as some industrial polluters cannot credibly justify their actions, no matter how they try to *spin* things about their environment damage in minority communities.

29. Henry Brean, "Paiutes Relate Pollution's toll," *Las Vegas Review Journal*, May 4, 2012.

30. Cristina Silva, "Many on Indian Reservations situated close to power plants," *Las Vegas Review Journal*, July 5, 2012.

31. Steffen W. Schmidt, Mack C. Shelley, and Barbara A. Bardes, *American Government and Politics Today*, 2001–2002 edition (Belmont, California: Wadsworth/Thomson Learning, 2001), 467.

32. Ibid.

33. Ballantine and Roberts, "Our Social World," 440.

34. Tony Arnold, "Planning for Environmental Justice," *Planning & Environmental Law*, volume 59, issue 3 (March 2007), 3.

35. Robert D. Bullard, "Poverty, Pollution and Environmental Racism: Strategies for Building Healthy and Sustainable Communities," A Discussion Paper prepared for the National Black Environmental Justice Network (NBEJN) Environmental Racism Forum World Summit on Sustainable Development (WSSD) Global Forum Johannesburg, South Africa, July 2, 2001, http://www.ejrc.cau.edu/povpolej.html (3/18/2013), 1.

36. Jim Motavall, "Toxic Targets: Polluters that Dump on Communities of Color are Finally Being Brought to Justice," *emagazine*, October 25, 2005, http://www.emagazine.com/view/?250.

37. Ibid. Occurring at an alarming rate, the waste treatment facilities in Chester, Pennsylvania, has negatively changed the landscape of the place. Indeed, the actions of the white city fathers have actually hurt the black community, especially psychologically.

38. Ibid.

39. Alison Young, "Senator Calls on Ohio EPA for Answers on Lead Risk," *USA Today*, May 21, 2012. The waste from pollution in certain areas is a major problem; it has also been psychologically damaging to the people who live in polluted communities.

40. Alison Young, "2 States Follow Up on Testing Soil for Lead," *USA Today*, May 25, 2012. For some reason, corporate bosses feign concern for the people living in polluted areas, when clearly they have other business agendas. And they purposely speak out publicly to defend themselves against any criticism about their polluting businesses/activities.

41. Julian Agyeman and Tom Evans, "Toward Just Sustainability in Urban Communities: Building Equity Rights with Sustainable Solutions," *Annals of the American Academy of Political and Social Science* 590 (November 2003), 36. See also Julian Agyeman, *Sustainable Communities and the Challenge of Environmental Justice* (New York University Press: New York, 2005), 14–112.

42. Ibid. See also Robert D. Bullard, ed, *Growing Smarter: Achieving Livable Communities, Environmental Justice, and Regional Equity* (Cambridge, Massachusetts: The MIT Press, 2007), 1–8, 50–69, 103–121, 345–363.

43. Jeff Haynes, *Politics in Developing Worlds: A Concise Introduction* (Malden: Blackwell Publishers, 2002), 216. As a result of corporate pollution, drastic changes have been made in some areas, where some neighborhoods have been fundamentally altered for the worst, as short-sighted executives don't really care about the viability of the polluted communities for the future.

44. Tony Arnold, "Planning for Environmental Justice," 3–12.

45. Haynes, "Politics in Developing Worlds," 215. Polluting corporations should have some kind of social responsibility for their actions. Indeed, they should not indecorously laugh in the face of people, as they cannot finesse this environmental issue away.

46. Ballantine and Roberts, "Our Social World," 523.

47. Ervin Laszlo, *The Chaos Point: The World at the Crossroads* (Charlottesville: Hampton Roads Publishing Company), 85.

Bibliography

Agyeman, Julian, and Kee Warner. "Putting 'Just Sustainability' into Place: From Paradigm to Practice. *Policy and Management Review*, volume 2, issue 1 (2002): 8–40.

Agyeman, Julian. *Sustainable Communities and the Challenge of Environmental Justice*. New York: New York University Press (2005): 14–112.

Agyeman, Julian, and Tom Evans. "Toward Just Sustainability in Urban Communities: Building Equity Rights with Sustainable Solutions." *Annals of the American Academy of Political and Social Science* 590 (2003): 36.

Arnold, Tony. "Planning for Environmental Justice." *Planning & Environmental Law*, volume 59, issue 3 (2007): 3.

Ballantine, Jeanne H., and Keith A. Roberts. *Our Social World: Introduction to Sociology*. Thousand Oaks: Pine Forge Press (2012): 523.

Brean, Henry. "Paiutes Relate Pollution's Toll." *Las Vegas Review Journal*, May 4, 2012.

Bullard, Robert D, ed, *Growing Smarter: Achieving Livable Communities, Environmental Justice and Regional Equity*. Cambridge, Massachusetts: The MIT Press (2007): 1–8, 50–69, 103–121, 345–363.

Bullard, Robert D. "Poverty, Pollution and Environmental Racism: Strategies for Building Healthy and Sustainable Communities." http://www.ejrc.cau.edu/povpolej.html (3/18/2013): 1.

Cardozo, Benjamin N. "Environmental Justice: A New Chapter in the Civil Rights Debate." unpublished paper (2005): 1.

Checker, Melissa. *Polluted Promises: Environmental Racism and the Search for Justice in a Southern Town*. New York: NYU Press, 2005.

Coll, Steve. *Private Empire: Exxon Mobil and American Power*. New York: Penguin Books, 2012.

Conant, Ralph W., and Daniel J. Myers. *Toward a More Perfect Union: The Governance of Metropolitan America*. Novato: Chandler & Sharp Publishers (2006): 235.

Crawford, Jewel, Wade W. Nobles, and Joy De Gruy Leary. "Reparations and Health Care for African Americans: Repairing the Damage from the Legacy of Slavery." in *Should America Pay? Slavery and the Raging Debate on Reparations*, ed. Raymond A. Winbush. New York: Amistad (2003): 272.

Daly, Herman E. "Free-Market Environmentalism: Turning a Good Servant into a Bad Master." *Critical Review* 6 (1992): 182.

Deans, Bob. *Reckless: The Political Assault on the American Environment*. Lanham, Maryland: Rowman & Littlefield Publishers (2012): 52–53.

Del Papa, Frankie Sue, and Timothy Hay. "Out with the Old." *Las Vegas Review Journal*, May 13, 2012.

"Environmental Racism Continues in U.S." *The Media Freedom Foundation*. http://www.mediafreedominternational.org/2010/02/21/environmental-racism-continues-in-u-s (4/18/2013): 1–3.

Haynes, Jeff. *Politics in Developing Worlds: A Concise Introduction*. Malden: Blackwell Publishers (2002): 216.

Heiman, Michael K. "Race, Waste, and Class: New Perspectives on Environmental Justice." Editor's Introduction for a Special Edition of Antipode. *Antipode* (1996): 28.

Meadows, Donella H., Dennis L. Meadows, Jorgen Randers, and William W. Behrens III. *The Limits to Growth: A Report for the Club of Rome's Project on the Predicament of Mankind*. New York: Universe Books (1981): 45–87.

Motavall, Jim. "Toxic Targets: Polluters that Dump on Communities of Color are Finally Being Brought to Justice." emagazine, October 25, 2005. http://www.emagazine.com/view/?250.

Pace, Dave. "More Blacks Live With Pollution." The Associated Press, 2006, in Rothenberg, Paula S., and Kelly S. Mayhew. *Race, Class, and Gender in the United States: An Integrated Study*. New York: Worth Publishers (2014): 35.

Ray, James Lee. *Global Politics*. 7th edition. New York: Houghton Mifflin Company (1998): 551.

Ross, Benjamin, and Steven Amter. *The Polluters: The Making of Our Chemically Altered Environment*. New York: Oxford University Press, 2010.

Scheiffer, Marten, et.al. "Catastrophic Shifts in Ecosystems." *Nature* 413 (2001): 596.

Schmidt, Steffen W., Mack C. Shelley, and Barbara A. Bardes. *American Government and Politics Today*. 2001–2002 edition. Belmont, California: Wadsworth/Thomson Learning (2001): 467.

Silva, Cristina. "Many on Indian Reservations situated close to power plants." *Las Vegas Review Journal*, July 5, 2012.

"Toxic Wastes and Race in the United States: A National Report on the Racial and Socio-Economic Characteristics of Communities with Hazardous Waste Sites." *Commission for Racial Justice: United Church of Christ*. New York: New York, 1987.

"Toxic waste and race: Report confirms no progress made in 20 years." (/new/releases/3253-toxic-waste-and-race-report-confirms-no-progress-made-in-20-years). http://ns.umich.edu/new/releases/3253 (7/14/2013): 1.

Young, Alison. "Senator Calls on Ohio EPA for Answers on Lead Risk." *USA Today*, May 21, 2012.

Young, Alison. "2 States Follow Up on Testing Soil for Lead." *USA Today*, May 25, 2012.